THE WORLD'S BLOODIEST HISTORY

TO JOSEPH S. CUMMINS, SR.,
A TRUE SURVIVOR

This edition published in 2013 by
CRESTLINE
a division of BOOK SALES, INC.
276 Fifth Avenue Suite 206
New York, New York 10001
USA

This edition published by arrangement with Fair Winds Press.

Text © 2010 by Joseph Cummins

First published in the USA in 2010 by
Fair Winds Press, a member of
Quayside Publishing Group
100 Cummings Center
Suite 406-L
Beverly, MA 01915-6101
www.fairwindspress.com

10 9 8 7 6 5 4 3 2 1

Library of Congress Cataloging-in-Publication Data
Cummins, Joseph.
  The world's bloodiest history : massacre, genocide, and the scars they left on
civilization / Joseph Cummins.
    p. cm.
  Includes bibliographical references and index.
  ISBN: 978-0-7858-3056-6
  1. Massacres—History. 2. Massacres—Social aspects—History. 3. War and society—History. 4.
History—Anecdotes. 5. Military history—Anecdotes. I. Title.
  D24.C86 2010
  303.6'6—dc22

                                                            2009026715

Cover design: Peter Long
Book design: Peter Long
Book layout: Megan Jones Design
Cover image: Holly Wilmeth/ Getty Images

Printed and bound in Singapore

THE WORLD'S BLOODIEST HISTORY

MASSACRE, GENOCIDE, AND THE SCARS THEY LEFT ON CIVILIZATION

JOSEPH CUMMINS

CRESTLINE

CONTENTS

INTRODUCTION

W HAT DO THE WORLD'S MOST ENLIGHTENED DEMOCRACIES HAVE IN common with the most oppressive totalitarian states?

The massacre of the innocent.

The history of humankind has been constructed, not with bricks, mortar, and steel, but with gore, gristle, and blood—buckets of it.

An overly bleak view? Perhaps. There is the matter of degree and intent. No one can say that Adolf Hitler's murdered millions match up with the United States' paltry few dead in the Indian Wars of the nineteenth century, no matter how horribly butchered. Certainly Rome's devastation of Carthage—sometimes called "the first genocide"—outnumbered those who died at Sharpeville by the thousands, yet the glory that would become Rome far outshone the narrow-minded, repressive, and short-lived South African regime. But one fact is indisputable: there is not a single great country or political movement in the history of the world that has not resorted to large-scale killing to achieve its ends.

The World's Bloodiest History contains stories of massacre and genocide ranging from the destruction of Carthage in the second century BCE to the murderous spring and summer of 1995 in Rwanda, where 800,000 Tutsi men, women, and children were slaughtered by their Hutu neighbors. The killings included have been chosen for their impact on world history and human societies. For example, the Spanish massacre of the Mexica and subsequent usurpation of Mexica riches financed its rise to power in Europe as well as the New World, while the Nazi extermination campaign against the Jews, as represented by the chapter here on the killings at Babi Yar, simply wiped out almost an entire class of people and a long-standing way of life, especially in Eastern Europe.

Not all the incidents in the book describe killing on such an epic scale. Only 500 people died in 1968 when U.S. GIs slaughtered innocent civilians in the Vietnamese village of My Lai—small change in the larger currency of genocide and manslaughter. But the deaths of these innocents became a rallying point that tipped the scale of U.S. public opinion against the war.

Whether perpetrated by Pol Pot's robotic minions or fanatical Mormons, all massacres share certain elements. One is propaganda. Propagandists on the side of both the victims and perpetrators incvitably distort massacres to further political ends. There was a Black Hole of Calcutta and people died horribly in it, but nowhere near as many people as the British claimed when they used it as an excuse to conquer India. The Nazis and the Russians fought an epic public relations battle over the Polish officers murdered at Katyń Forest.

Another invariable feature of massacre is that perpetrators blame the victims. The Huguenots were about to attack the Catholics in Paris, the students who died in Tiananmen Square were attempting to overthrow the Chinese government, the murdered hundreds of thousands of Armenians sided with the Russians against the Young Turks during the First World War. Ad nauseum. Hence, all must be killed to protect the state. Holocaust deniers go further and say the killings never happened, or happened on a very small scale, or happened not because the state ordered it, but because rogue elements—regrettably but perhaps understandably driven to murderous rage by the perfidy of the victims—simply lost control. Perhaps the only thing worse than the atrocity of mass killing is listening to those responsible try to explain it away.

Yet another constant of massacre is the horrific treatment of women. Men have perpetrated every mass killing in history, but women make up far more than their share of victims. Women are usually not targeted solely because of their sex—they are often simply part of the ethnic, religious, or political group that happens to be chosen for slaughter at the moment, or they are unlucky enough to be home while their men are away. But once the killing is underway, they are singled out for the most brutal treatment, including rape and dreadful mutilation, the victims of a truly frightening, astounding, and primal rage.

In 1944, Raphael Lemkin, a Polish-born scholar working for the U.S. War Ministry, became more and more disturbed by the reports of the mass killings of Jews and other minorities by Nazi Germany, and felt that a new word was needed to describe the organized, state-sponsored slaughter of innocents because of their race, ethnicity, or religion. "New conceptions require new terminology,"

Lemkin wrote in his book *Axis Rule in Occupied Europe*. He therefore grafted the Greek *genos*, meaning "race" or "tribe" onto the Latin suffix *cide*, "to kill." And *genocide* therefore entered our vocabulary. In 1948, the United Nations adopted the Genocide Convention, making genocide an international crime. Interestingly and ironically, the United States was instrumental in drafting the Genocide Convention, but did not sign it until 1988 because of fears that Native Americans or African Americans might use these very conventions to accuse the U.S. government of genocide.

UNFORTUNATELY, THE ODDS APPEAR TO BE THAT IF ANOTHER GENOCIDE OCCURS TOMORROW, IT WILL GO UNCHECKED BY THE WORLD COMMUNITY AND YET ANOTHER CHAPTER WILL BE ADDED TO THE BLOODIEST HISTORY OF THE WORLD.

This inconsistency, taking the moral high ground but treading cautiously when it comes to aiding those who are victims of genocide, is still very much with us today. Unfortunately, genocide remains largely a crime without punishment. The United Nations has failed to intervene in genocides in Cambodia, Bosnia, and Rwanda. The United States has refused even to condemn them as they occurred or to use the word "genocide" (which Bill Clinton famously disavowed when it came to the murder of hundreds of thousands of Tutsis in Rwanda). Despite the fact that polls consistently show the support of the U.S. people for military intervention in case of genocide, U.S. leaders have steadfastly refused to commit troops, possibly fearing that such support will erode as U.S. casualties mount, but most likely making the calculation that intervention in the affairs of a sovereign state, unless there is a material gain to the United States (as George Bush perceived there might be in Iraq) is simply politically unwise.

Without courageous and principled stances on the part of world community, genocides will continue. There is a vehicle for such support, a doctrine known as Responsibility to Protect, most commonly called by its shorthand name R2P. International thinkers and scholars formulated R2P in 2001, in response to a debate in the United Nations and elsewhere as to when it was permissible to

intervene in a country's internal affairs. R2P posits that "each international state has the primary responsibility to protect its populations from genocide . . . [but] when a state manifestly fails in its protection responsibilities, and peaceful means are inadequate, the international community must take stronger measures, including use of force."

At the 2005 World Summit, attending countries agreed in principle to R2P, and since then the United Nations has announced the appointment of a Special Advisor to the Secretary-General, to focus on genocide, ethnic cleansing, and war crimes. Yet resistance to R2P remains within the United Nations and as yet there has been no significant international response to developing situations in Darfur, Sudan, Somalia, Burma, or the Democratic Republic of Congo. Unfortunately, the odds appear to be that if another genocide occurs tomorrow, it will go unchecked by the world community and yet another chapter will be added to the bloodiest history of the world.

GRAFFITI MARKS ONE OF THE WALLS OF THE FORMER TUOL SLENG PRISON IN CAMBODIA, NOW THE MUSEUM OF GENOCIDE. THE KHMER ROUGE SENT MORE THAN 20,000 MEN, WOMEN, AND CHILDREN TO THE INFAMOUS PRISON, WHERE THEY WERE TORTURED AND KILLED, DURING THE 1970S.

CHAPTER I

"CARTHAGE MUST BE DESTROYED!"

THE FIRST GENOCIDE, 146 BCE

IN WHAT HAS BEEN CALLED "THE FIRST GENOCIDE," THE ROMANS
DESTROYED THE CARTHAGINIANS, THEIR LONG-TIME ENEMIES,
AND BUILT THE ROMAN EMPIRE OVER THEIR BONES

THE PEOPLE OF THE ANCIENT CITY OF CARTHAGE WERE BRILLIANT, sophisticated, convinced of the superiority of their civilization—one founded by Phoenician seafarers plying their way along the North African coast in the eighth century BCE—, and fiercely dedicated to the expansion of their way of life.

They were deeply pagan, worshipping ancient gods whose roots went all the way back to the Assyrians, Babylonians, and Egyptians—the all-powerful lord Baal Hammon, sometimes known simply as El; Tanit, the goddess who protected the city of Carthage itself; Astarte, goddess of beauty, to whom a cult of ritual prostitution was devoted. Child sacrifice, most archeologists now believe, was widespread (see "The Roasting Place," page 14) and superstition governed almost every aspect of Carthaginian life. Omens and foreshadowings were seen or claimed in the slightest misstep or unusual natural occurrence.

With the exception of child sacrifice, the above description could apply to the Romans, the people who ruthlessly destroyed the Carthaginians and in doing so perpetuated what genocide historian Ben Kiernan has termed "the first genocide." Rome, founded at the confluence of several trade

THE ROMANS ADVANCE. DURING THE ATTACK ON CARTHAGE, ROME USED FIRE, BATTERING RAMS, SWORDS, SPEARS, AND ARROWS— EVERY WEAPON AT THEIR EMPLOY—TO UTTERLY DESTROY THEIR ENEMY.

routes along the Tiber River in 750 BCE, also harbored a superstitious people with a pantheon of gods and a powerful expansionistic impulse. By the end of the fourth century BCE, Rome had conquered much of Italy. Indeed, Rome and Carthage first clashed over territory, as Carthage attempted to spread its sphere of influence to include the Iberian Peninsula and Sicily.

THESE ROMANS HATED WHAT THEY TERMED "CARTHAGINIAN TREACHERY" WITH THE SAME PHOBIC INTENSITY THAT MANY PEOPLE RESERVE FOR SNAKES OR SPIDERS.

But imperialistic ambitions alone did not explain the unreasoning hatred that many powerful Romans had for Carthage, the kind of intense emotion that is the main ingredient—one could even say requirement—of massacre and genocide. These Romans hated what they termed "Carthaginian treachery" with the same phobic intensity that many people reserve for snakes or spiders. Thus, in an explosion of violence in 146 BCE, the Romans wiped the Carthaginian civilization of roughly half a million people off the face of the Earth. The massacre was then concealed from history by Roman distortions, only to be rediscovered again in ancient texts found in fifteenth-century Europe. But by that time Rome had its thousand-year rise and fall, influencing western civilization forever—and all of it stained with the blood of the once-mighty Carthaginians.

"ADVANCED GREATLY IN POPULATION AND POWER"

The wars between Rome and Carthage—known as the Punic Wars, from the Latin *Punicus*, which means "Phoenicians," the Roman name for the Carthaginians—lasted from 264 to 164 BCE. Fought over a vast area of the Mediterranean basin, they were the longest running conflicts in ancient history, as well as the largest in scale, involving armies of hundreds of thousands of men. The Punic Wars began in 264 when Carthaginians captured Messana (modern-day Messina) in Sicily, which the Romans considered a move that placed the Carthaginians in a strong strategic position to invade Italy. The First Punic War was a mainly naval affair, and ended in Roman victory and full control of Sicily in 241.

The Second Punic War was a different matter entirely. Objecting to the spread of Carthaginian influence in Spain, the Romans sought an excuse to destroy what they considered to be an inferior Carthaginian army; but they had not bargained on the leadership of young Hannibal Barca, one of the most brilliant commandeering generals of all time. In 218, Hannibal famously crossed the Alps to lead a polyglot army of mercenaries down the Italian Peninsula, defeating the Romans in battle after battle and striking fear in the hearts of the citizens of Italy. In a culminating battle in 216, Hannibal encircled and destroyed a Roman army at Cannae (see "The Bloodiest Day," page 17) killing nearly 50,000 Roman soldiers, including the cream of the Roman officer class, in a display of butchery that was not equaled until the first day of the Battle of the Somme in 1916. It was the worst defeat Rome would ever suffer, and the stories that drifted back to the city—how the Carthaginians casually sliced the hamstrings of the Roman soldiers who lay helpless on the field, so that they could return to kill them at their leisure the next day—were never forgotten.

However, without real support from a vacillating Carthaginian Senate, Hannibal was unable to win in Italy. He was finally forced to retreat to North Africa, where Scipio Africanus, the famed Roman general, defeated him decisively in the battle of Zama in 202. Carthage sued for peace and Rome accepted but offered them harsh terms: Carthage was forced to pay heavy war indemnities over a period of fifty years and also to give up all her foreign colonies.

Yet, surprisingly, Carthage actually managed to thrive during this period, perhaps because the country was no longer supporting a large standing army and navy. The second-century-CE historian Appian wrote:

THE ROMAN GENERAL PUBLIUS SCIPIO AFRICANUS, KNOWN AS SCIPIO AFRICANUS MAJOR, WAS INSTRUMENTAL IN DEFEATING THE FEARED HANNIBAL AND FORCING CARTHAGE TO SUE FOR A PEACE THAT WAS GENUINE, IF SHORT-LIVED.
GETTY IMAGES

THE ROASTING PLACE

Ancient writers, from Polybius to Virgil, mention that the Carthaginians engaged in child sacrifice, but for a long time relatively few historians believed this. There were a number of reasons why, chief among them the fact that Carthaginian history was now being written by the Romans, who might have wanted to demonize Carthaginians to excuse their eradication of an entire people. Also, while the Romans engaged in the occasional human sacrifice during the Punic Wars, most Mediterranean civilizations had given up the practice, resorting instead to offerings of dead animals.

However, in the 1920s, archeologists began excavating a grassy area near where the harbor once existed in Carthage and found that it was a cemetery—or, to be more exact, a place where thousands of large urns full of ashes and tiny bone fragments were buried. This place was known to the ancient Carthaginians as the *tophet* (the roasting place). Forensic scientists who analyzed the remains in hundreds of these jars concluded that they contain the ashes of children from infancy to the age of two or three. The dedications on the *stelae,* or markers, above the urns are from all sorts of Carthaginians—doctors, teachers, lawyers, jewelry makers, sailors, incense sellers, and the like. Apparently, as their society became more democratic, sacrifices were opened to all.

A vow was usually made to sacrifice a child in return for a favor from Tanit or Baal Hammon. Written evidence from ancient historians, plus the thousands of children's ashes buried in this tophet (as well as other tophets in Carthaginian territory) irrefutably makes the case for child sacrifice.

One would take one's infant (or bought one from a poor person, or used the child of a slave) and bring it in front of a large statue of Baal; the deity's arms were outstretched and beneath these blackened stone arms was a brazier full of flaming coals. The child almost certainly had its throat cut first, and then was placed in the arms of the statue. The flames would cause the infant's limbs to contract and then it would tumble into the flames and be consumed.

THIS HAND-COLORED WOODCUT OF A NINETEENTH CENTURY
ILLUSTRATION CAPTURES SOME OF THE TERROR ASSOCIATED
WITH THE ANCIENT PHOENICIAN GOD BAAL HAMMON, ONE OF
THE DEITIES TO WHOM THE CARTHAGINIANS SACRIFICED
THEIR INFANTS.

NORTH WIND PICTURE ARCHIVES/ALAMY

"Carthage, blessed with unbroken peace, advanced greatly in population and power" at this time—a little like the rise of Japan in the period following World War II. The city, previously ruled by a corrupt oligarchy, was even becoming more democratic, with a more representative assembly.

And there were those in Rome—especially Marcus Porcius Cato, the aging and powerful Senator—who did not like this at all.

"DELENDA EST CARTHARGO!"

By 153 BCE, Carthage had paid off its entire war debt to Rome and was well on its way to establishing itself again as a well-off trading nation, but found itself being threatened by a Numidian king named Masinissa, who was gradually gobbling up Carthaginian territory to the west of the city. Masinissa was a Roman ally, and this left Carthage in a quandary—should it allow Masinissa to take over its land with impunity? But if Carthage fought him, it would be in violation of the peace treaty against Rome. As Masinissa approached closer to Carthage, the Carthaginians implored the Romans to intercede on their behalf. A Roman delegation arrived in Carthage, headed by Marcus Porcius Cato. Cato was the eighty-one-year-old hero of the Second Punic War, the vicious orator who had hounded Scipio Africanus to an early death after claiming he had committed financial improprieties.

Cato, seeing the peace and prosperity of Carthage, was incensed. The city, as the ancient historian Plutarch wrote, "was overflowing with wealth . . . and full of confidence at this revival of its strength." When he returned home to Rome, he appeared in the Senate, where he showed his colleagues the luscious figs he had bought from Carthage, only three days' sail away. This close neighbor was both rich and malevolent, Cato said. Thereafter, every time he made a speech, no matter what the topic, he would end it with the words: *Delenda Est Carthago!* "Carthage must be destroyed." While not all Roman senators felt this way, Cato managed to inflame the Roman masses by calling on them "to crush the city which had always borne them an undying hatred."

Thus, gripped by what one historian calls "a military hysteria," Rome invaded North Africa in 149, taking over the Punic port of Utica, some twelve miles from Carthage. Carthage surrendered immediately and agreed to draconian Roman terms, which included giving up all of its arms—every sword, spear, and siege machine—and sending 300 of its noble children to Rome to be held as hostages. But Rome was not satisfied and called for one final measure: The citizens of Carthage were to evacuate their beloved ancient city on the coast and move inland ten miles (16 km) away from the sea. The Carthaginians must cease being traders and seafarers—the lifeblood of these former Phoenicians—and become farmers. In the meantime, the Romans would raze the city, leaving only its tombs and temples intact.

These humiliating terms were not meant to be accepted and they were not. The Carthaginians named a military commander, Hasdrubal, and prepared themselves for war. Because all their arms had been turned over to the Romans, there was a frantic search for metal to make new ones—lead was found on rooftops, iron in walls. Temples and public buildings were turned into workshops, where ordinary citizens labored day and night to produce swords, shields, and javelins. Women cut off their long hair and plaited it into thick strands to use for slings. And all the slaves in the city were set free, to aid the war effort.

THE SIEGE

Carthage, in present-day Tunisia, was built on a promontory that jutted out into the Mediterranean and was connected to it by a narrow isthmus. The city had an elaborate outer and inner harbor system, covered an area of seven square miles (11.3 km²), and was protected by more than twenty miles (32.2 km) of walls. The walls on its western side, considered the most vulnerable by the Carthaginians, were some 45 feet (13.7 m) high. For two years, the Romans besieged the ancient city with 40,000 to 50,000 troops led by two Roman consuls who confidently expected that the Carthaginians would capitulate.

Their confidence turned out to be misplaced. The Carthaginians fought off every attempt to scale their walls and sortied out numerous times with cavalry to harass the Romans in vicious short skirmishes that left hundreds of Romans dead, and only served to heighten the tensions between the two enemies. The Carthaginians had only about 20,000 fighting men and were trapped in their city, so there was little doubt how this Third Punic War would end, but the siege dragged on for two years and the Roman public was becoming impatient.

THE BLOODIEST DAY

In 216 BCE, on a sweltering hot day at an undetermined site probably near the modern-day Italian town of Monte di Canne, one of the bloodiest battles of all time was fought, a battle that would harden Roman hatred of the Carthaginians, and help lead to the massacre that occurred in 146.

The Battle of Cannae was the crowning battle of Hannibal Barca's career, the bloodletting that would ensure his place in history and cause generals all the way through to the twenty-first century to seek to emulate his feat. After fighting his way down the Italian Peninsula following his epic crossing of the Alps, Hannibal defeated Roman forces in several battles, but was longing for a knockout punch against a major Roman army. He finally had his chance when a Roman force numbering 80,000 (twice the number of Hannibal's men) came out to meet him near the little Italian village of Cannae. The overconfident Romans attacked, certain that they would destroy Hannibal. At first, things seemed to be going their way. The center of Hannibal's line kept retreating from the sword-wielding legionaries—soon, the Roman officers were certain, they would break through and put Hannibal to flight.

But it all turned out to be a trap. Hannibal had deliberately weakened his center to draw the Roman forces in. The Carthaginian left and right wings—where Hannibal had stationed his strongest troops—slowly closed in on the Roman flanks in what became known as the most famous double-envelopment in history. Soon the Romans were completely surrounded, and the slaughter began. Fifty thousand Romans were killed on this day, a figure not equaled in a single day of battle until the twentieth century. And it must be remembered that these Romans were killed mainly by hand—by sword and spear thrust. The terror was such in the Roman center that many soldiers were found with their heads literally buried in the dirt, smothered to death in small holes they had dug to commit suicide rather than face the horror of what happened.

IN ONE OF THE BLOODIEST DAYS OF WARFARE IN HUMAN HISTORY, HANNIBAL AND HIS POLYGLOT ARMY DESTROYED THE ROMANS IN SOUTHERN ITALY AT THE BATTLE OF CANNAE. HERE, THEY LOOT THE DEAD AND DISPATCH THE WOUNDED IN THE AFTERMATH OF THE BATTLE.
TIME & LIFE PICTURES/GETTY IMAGES

THE BEAUTIFUL CITY OF
CARTHAGE. BEFORE ITS
DESTRUCTION, CARTHAGE, THE
JEWEL OF THE NORTH AFRICAN
SHORE, HAD A MARVELOUS
CIRCULAR HARBOR WITH A
CAPACITY FOR MORE THAN
TWO HUNDRED WARSHIPS,
APARTMENT BUILDINGS TALLER
THAN SIX STORIES HIGH, AND
NUMEROUS RICH PRIVATE
HOMES BUILT AROUND LUSH
CENTRAL COURTYARDS.

Finally, in 147, Scipio Aemilianus, adopted grandson of the famous Scipio Africanus, was elevated to leadership of the Roman forces besieging Carthage. This Scipio was young and aggressive, and under his command, Roman forces closed in on the walls. Carthage's defenses had a weak point on the south-west side of the city; a 300-foot (91.4 m) -wide sandbar in the harbor that the Carthaginians felt protected them from the Romans getting too close, and thus they had built only a single wall there.

But, under Scipio Aemilianus, the Romans repeatedly assaulted this area, little by little making headway into the city in small attacks. At first, these were driven back by the desperate Carthaginians in bloody counterattacks; Hasdrubal ordered any Roman prisoners they captured to be taken atop the walls of the city and tortured to death by having their limbs hacked off so that the Romans (and any faint-hearted Carthaginians) might see that Carthage had no intention of surrendering.

Finally, in an assault led by Tiberius Sempronius Gracchus, Scipio's sixteen-year-old cousin, the walls on the southwest part of the city were breached for good, and a flood of Roman soldiers poured in. The destruction of Carthage was about to begin.

"VENGEFUL GODS"

The Romans poured into the agora, or marketplace, that was next to Carthage's inner harbor just as the retreating Carthaginians set it on fire. It was an apocalyptic scene—Roman soldiers racing through flaming stalls while Carthaginians ran uphill, through the city's streets, toward the sanctuary of the Byrsa, the walled citadel high on the hill above the harbor. The pent-up fury of the Romans was now unleashed—when they caught up with any Carthaginian, man, woman, or child, they skewered or decapitated them. Babies were thrown into the flames, women were dragged aside and raped before being eviscerated.

Although it was common practice in ancient times to show little mercy to a city that had put up a fight during a siege, the violence of the Romans was virulent even by these standards. They seem to have considered the Carthaginians to be animals, ripe for the killing, and to have objectified them in order to cast aside any doubts they may have felt about so ruthlessly taking human lives. One Roman soldier, dripping with blood as he worked his way uphill, seemed to an ancient chronicler to be a devil incarnate, a "vengeful god."

And the Romans felt that this was the way it should be. After all, they were merely doing away with a people so savage that they were willing to sacrifice their own children to the gods, a people whose highest god was commerce, and whose hallmark was double-dealings. This view has been handed down through history. The modern historian Brian Caven has written: "The Carthaginians were hardly an attractive people. They did not have it in them to be the standard-bearers of a higher civilization. [They were] selfish, parasitic, money-grubbing, corrupt, and, when it cost them nothing, oppressive. . . ."

Perhaps. But in this, their last stand, they were also brave. After the Romans slaughtered their way through the marketplace (and then stopped to strip the magnificent Temple of Apollo of its gold treasures, a breach of discipline that infuriated Scipio), they were faced with a daunting task. Directly uphill, three streets led to the Byrsa, where a huge portion of Carthage's terrified population, as well Hasdrubal and his family and a large group of Roman deserters, had taken refuge. These streets were lined with the equivalent of modern apartment buildings, each as high as six stories. The apartments had central courtyards and were crisscrossed by narrow alleys. The main streets were only about seven yards (6.4 m) wide, and thus Romans were unable to assault the Carthaginians in force.

PAVING THE STREETS WITH BONES

The minute the Romans approached these buildings, they were met by a hail of stones and spears—it was evident that the Carthaginians had prepared well for the onslaught. The legionaries did not dare venture into the narrow streets, which were immediate killing zones. Instead, they engaged in vicious house-to-house fighting, described in detail by the historian Polybius, who was Scipio Aemilianus' tutor and an eyewitness.

THE STONE STAIRWAYS OF THE HOUSES RAN RED AND SLIPPERY WITH BLOOD.

The Romans fought their way into the first buildings through windows and doors, and then slaughtered their way up to the rooftops. Modern soldiers equipped with guns and hand grenades can attest to how vicious street fighting within a city can be, and it was even more so for people who were fighting with swords, stones, and spears. The stone stairways of the houses ran red and slippery with blood. The Romans made no distinction between the soldiers or civilians they found in these homes—all were killed, first hacked to the ground with a downward stroke of the Roman *gladius*, or short sword, and then gutted. When the Romans got to the roof, they threw wooden planks across to the next building and then repeated the process there, working their way down through the stairs in an orgy of slaughter.

Those in the Bysra could now hear another sound added to the cracking and burning of the city—the shrieks and shouts of citizens being murdered. This horrible cacophony went on for seven days as the Romans worked their way up the hill. Because the narrow streets did not allow room for the siege engines he would need to assault the Bysra, Scipio ordered that the apartment buildings be burnt to the ground. Once they had been turned into rubble, Roman crews set to work with a vengeance, leveling the rubble to create wide streets. The historian Appian (who apparently gained much of his material from manuscripts written by Polybius, which are now lost to us) describes what happened:

> A number of old men and women and children had concealed themselves only too skillfully in the cupboards or the cellars of the houses in which the fighting had been going on, and these were now burned alive, or fell with the falling buildings; while others, half-roasted or half-suffocated, flung themselves headlong from the windows into the streets. There they lay, and thence they were shoveled, dead and dying alike, amidst charred beams and crumbling masonry, into any hollows which required filling up. Heads or legs might be seen protruding from the reeking and smouldering mass til they were trampled into nothing by the oncoming cavalry.

Lest anyone think this description is an ancient exaggeration, archeologists have found human bones crushed into paving material in this area. When this grotesque project was finally finished, Scipio made ready to move, at last, against the mighty Bysra.

"WHEN SACRED TROY SHALL FALL"

Just as this final attack was about to begin, however, the gates of the citadel opened up, and a small group of citizens waving olive branches advanced toward the Roman lines. They were surrendering, begging for the lives, and this Scipio allowed them—but nothing more beyond the clothes on their back. From all over the city, Carthaginians appeared, long lines of bedraggled and starving men, women, and children. The victorious Romans took them to holding areas near the harbor or outside the city. Eventually, there would be 50,000 in all, and the Romans sold every last one of them into slavery, flooding the markets of the known world and providing homes throughout Italy with free labor.

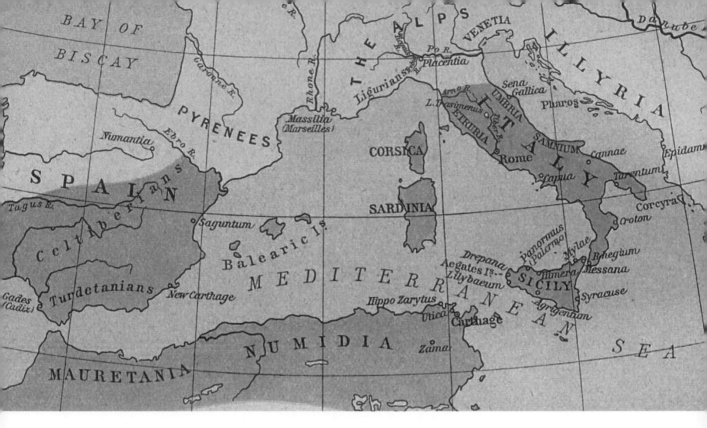

A MAP OF ROME AND CARTHAGE AT THE BEGINNING OF THE SECOND PUNIC WAR—TERRITORIES BELONGING TO ROME ARE IN PINK, CARTHAGE BROWN. AS THIS MAP SHOWS, IT WAS INEVITABLE THAT THESE TWO POWERS WOULD FIGHT TO THE DEATH FOR CONTROL OF THE MEDITERRANEAN BASIN.

This left only Hasdrubal, his wife and children, and about 900 Roman deserters barricaded now in the Temple of Aesculapius, in the highest point of the Bysra. The deserters, knowing they were facing certain crucifixion, set fire to the temple and committed suicide by falling on their swords. Hasdrubal, who had previously vowed never to give in, abandoned his wife and family and, running down the hill waving an olive branch, fell at Scipio's feet and begged for mercy. This Scipio scornfully allowed him.

Then, in a scene that was permanently engraved in the minds of all who watched—especially Polybius, who captured it for history—Hasdrubal's wife, dressed in her finest clothes, appeared atop the walls of the Temple. She shouted down to Hasdrubal that he was a coward and a traitor and then threw her two children, and herself, into the flames, where they perished.

And with this dramatic moment, the massacre of the Carthaginians ended—Scipio was now conqueror of the city, which was mostly rubble and charred timber. To the surprise of Scipio's friend Polybius, the great commander broke into tears and quoted Homer: "The day will come when sacred Troy shall fall, and Priam and Priam's people, too." By which he meant that, as Rome had done to Carthage, someone, someday, would do to Rome.

Although Rome would fall because of internal corruption and external pressures in the fifth century CE, its civilization would not be entirely wiped out, and its influence lasts until this day. But the Romans moved to make the Carthaginians extinct. After stripping the city of all its finery, its gold and silver ornaments and treasures, Scipio ordered the remaining buildings of the once-great city demolished (although it is a latter invention that he cursed the city and sowed its fields with salt to keep crops from growing). There was wild rejoicing in Rome when the first ship carrying Carthaginian booty arrived, and those who had been heroes of the war were lionized.

Rome's destruction of Carthage was at odds with its usual practice of co-opting captured peoples and allowing them to become Roman citizens. The relentless Roman destruction of this ancient civilization and its people was a way of ridding itself, in a single stroke, of its chief rival for empire and its only equal in the Mediterranean world. Carthage was swept away, obliterated—its laws, sciences, literature, and religion left for future generations of archeologists to piece together.

After the initial rejoicing in Rome, a different reaction would set in, a realization of what the Romans of the second century BCE had done. When Virgil wrote his *Aeneid*, he used as his model of the destruction of Troy the fall of Carthage; when Aeneas meets Dido (the Phoenician princess who was the mythical founder of Carthage) she eventually kills herself in the way that Hasdrubal's wife did, destroyed by Aeneas' willingness to abandon her.

It would not be until much later, when lost works of Polybius and Livy were discovered, that the destruction of Carthage would be remembered. But by that time, Rome itself was gone.

CHAPTER 2

"WE HAVE TORN OUR HAIR WITH GRIEF"

THE MASSACRE OF THE MEXICA 1521

THE CONQUERING SPANISH MURDERED A CIVILIZATION ALONG WITH A PEOPLE WHEN THEY STORMED TENOCHTITLÁN, THE ANCIENT CITY OF THE MEXICA

THE FOLLOWING ACCOUNT OF THE MASSACRE OF THE AZTECS—or Mexica (pronounced Me-shee-ca) as they call themselves and should more accurately be known—comes from *The Broken Spears: The Aztec Account of the Conquest of Mexico*:

> At this moment in the fiesta, when the dance was loveliest and when song was linked to song, the Spaniards were seized with an urge to kill the celebrants . . . They ran in among the dancers, forcing their way to the place where the drums were played. They attacked the man who was drumming and cut off his arms. Then they cut off his head, and it rolled across the floor.
>
> They attacked all the celebrants, stabbing them, spearing them, striking them with their swords. They attacked some of them from behind, and these fell instantly to the ground with their entrails hanging out. Others they beheaded; they cut off their heads or split their heads to pieces . . .
>
> The blood of the warriors flowed like water and gathered into pools. The pools widened and the stench of blood and entrails filled the air.

THIS SIXTEENTH CENTURY ENGRAVING, WHILE FANCIFULLY RENDERED, CAPTURES SOME OF THE SAVAGERY OF PEDRO DE ALVARADO'S SUDDEN ATTACK ON THE MEXICA DURING THEIR FESTIVAL.

PEDRO DE ALVARADO AND HIS SOLDIERS MASSACRING THE AZTECS, C.1520 (ENGRAVING), BRY, THEODORE DE (1528-98) / JOHN JUDKYN MEMORIAL, BATH, AVON, UK / THE BRIDGEMAN ART LIBRARY INTERNATIONAL

The Broken Spears, published by Miguel Leon-Portilla in 1962, is a remarkable book. It contains the testimony of the Mexica priests, warriors, and ordinary people who survived the bloody conquest of Hernán Cortés from 1519 to 1521 and were able to tell their story as early as 1530, once Spanish mendicant friars were able to transcribe their Nahuatl language into the Latin alphabet.

Their story is a desperate one, the tale of a once-mighty people in the fabulous island city of Tenochtitlán brought low by strange invaders whom they at first took to be gods, but who turned out to be opportunistic conquerors thirsty for blood. The Mexica weren't adverse to blood—with their penchant for constant warfare and the thousands of human sacrifices they made every year, they shed rivers of it—but they had never met a people who, armed with such fantastic weapons, could wreak bloody havoc the way the Spaniards did.

THE GLORY OF TENOCHTITLÁN

When the Mexica and Spanish clashed in 1519, they were two young empires on the move. The Mexica arose during the first millennium CE as a wandering tribe from what is now northern Mexico. After the mysterious civilization of the Toltecs collapsed at the beginning of the thirteenth century, the Mexica migrated south into the Valley of Mexico. In the early fifteenth century, led by their founding figure, King Izcóatl, they conquered a territory stretching from the Gulf of Mexico to the Pacific Ocean, encompassing some 80,000 square miles (128,748 km²).

By the early sixteenth century, the Mexica, under their leader Montezuma, ruled eight million people divided into some fifty small nations from the capital city of Tenochtitlán. Bigger than Paris, Constantinople, or Naples, Tenochtitlán was built on an island near the western shore of Lake Texcoco. The Mexica had enlarged the island with landfill made of rocks and mud, and the city held some 250,000 inhabitants. It contained thirty palaces made of red volcanic rock, where the nobility lived, and was dominated by the massive Great Temple and its central plaza. It was a bustling city, with three huge causeways that connected it to the mainland. Aqueducts carried stream water down from the mountains around the city—for their time, the Mexica were a remarkably clean people who washed daily and whose streets were swept by a veritable army of street cleaners.

THE "HORRID AND ABOMINABLE CUSTOM"

One of the most debated aspects of Mexica civilization is human sacrifice. After Hernán Cortés' barbarous conquest of the Mexica, he provided a lengthy account of what he called this "most horrid and abominable custom," in part to justify his own slaughter of the Mexica. Some later commentators felt that this was racist propaganda made up by the Spanish and that the Mexica did not engage in human sacrifice, but archeology and contemporary records—including those of the Mexica themselves—does not bear this out.

The Mexica practiced human sacrifice on a daily basis—perhaps 3,000 to 4,000 victims perished per year. This is amply depicted in Mexica writing and art. The victims were sacrificed to the war god Huitzilopochtli, who would in turn take the offering to the sun, to save the Mexica from famine—perhaps the same kind of famine that destroyed the Toltecs.

The victims were usually captives from the wars that were fought expressly for this purpose. At dawn each day, a captive, often drugged on hallucinogens like peyote, or at least semi-drunk on "obsidian wine" (or pulque, a type of fermented beer made from the maguey plant), was dragged up the steps of one of the main temples of Tenochtitlán, perhaps even the Pyramid of the Sun, some 200 feet (61 m) high. Four priests held the person over a stone block, while another priest ripped out the victim's still-beating heart with a stone or obsidian blade. The heart would then be lifted to the sun, while the priest chanted a prayer about how this "little cactus flower" would keep darkness away for another day. After this, the heart was ritually burned, the body was decapitated, and the torso fed to dogs while the arms and legs were ritually eaten with maize and chili. The blood of the victim was sprinkled around the city to ward off evil spirits—and the next day, a new cycle would begin all over again.

A GORY SIXTEENTH-CENTURY RENDERING OF A MEXICA SACRIFICE. THE MEXICA PRACTICE OF HUMAN SACRIFICE TERRIFIED AND DISGUSTED THE SPANIARDS AND WAS THE FIRST MEXICA RELIGIOUS RITE THAT THEY CRACKED DOWN UPON.

FOL. 70V HUMAN SACRIFICE, 1579 (VELLUM), DURAN, DIEGO (SIXTEENTH CENTURY) / BIBLIOTECA NACIONAL, MADRID, SPAIN / GIRAUDON / THE BRIDGEMAN ART LIBRARY INTERNATIONAL

They were the most powerful people in the Americas, with the possible exception of the Inca of Peru; but despite their glory, the Mexica had a flaw. They—and in particular Montezuma, who took power in 1502—were superstitious and believed their fates to be powerfully ruled by their myths and legends.

At around the same time, the Spanish, united under the rule of King Ferdinand and Queen Isabella, having finally won their 700-year war to drive the Moors from the Iberian Peninsula, were looking westward. In 1492, Christopher Columbus sailed across the Atlantic to discover a New World; soon, Spanish adventurers explored farther west, landed along the Yucatan Peninsula. There they heard and reported back stories of the rich civilization of the Mexica, although none actually saw it.

THE COMING OF CORTÉS

Born in Spain in 1485, Hernán Cortés sailed for the Americas to seek his fortune, like many other ambitious young Spaniards of his era. In 1511, he joined Diego Velazquez de Cuéllar on his successful expedition to conquer Cuba. Upon hearing rumors about the great empire of the Mexica, he convinced Velazquez to let him lead an eleven-ship, 500-man expedition to explore the western shores of the Gulf of Mexico.

As Cortés was about to disembark in 1519, Velazquez grew concerned about his lieutenant's overweening ambition, and ordered him to relinquish the leadership of the expedition to a Velazquez crony. Cortés refused and sailed anyway, a move that showed his extraordinary determination to have his own way, but which also paved the way for the first massacre of the Mexica.

In April 1519, Cortés and his fleet arrived on the Mexican coast at what is now Veracruz and, coming ashore on Good Friday, thanked God for their safe voyage. He was met by emissaries sent by Montezuma, who was concerned about these strange visitors. The year 1519 was the Mexica year 1-Reed, the year that the god Quetzalcóatl was supposed, by legend, to return. Quetzalcóatl literally meant "feather serpent," but was a difficult god to define. Sometimes he was indeed a serpent, other times a god with white skin who had sailed off to the east from Mexico on a raft made of serpents, foretelling his return.

Montezuma had decided, judging from the reports of Cortés' skin color, his fabulous armament, the snorting stags his men rode—their horses—, and his terrifying and thunderous weapons, that Cortés was Quetzalcóatl returned to claim his throne. Thus, as Cortés began to progress inexorably from the coast toward Tenochtitlán—after ruthlessly burning his own ships to show his men there would be no retreat—Montezuma began a strange courting dance with him, sending emissaries with gold, silver, monkeys, beautiful feather headdresses, yet telling Cortés that he should come no farther.

Cortés could not have fully understood Montezuma's responses to him, but he could smell weakness. Although belittling Montezuma's gifts—"Is this all?" he demanded of the emissaries. "Is this your gift of welcome? Is this how you greet people?"— he sent messages to Montezuma, telling him that he wanted to visit the great lord in his fabulous city. As Cortés headed toward the mountains that separated Tenochtitlán from the eastern shore, he fought battles with several tribes whose territory he went through, most notably the Tlaxcala, who were rivals of the Mexica and whose thousands of warriors, once defeated, became great allies of Cortés.

Despite Montezuma's pleadings and excuses—he was sick, the roads were too rough for Cortés to travel, the Mexica people, regrettably, did not want Cortés there—Cortés kept on coming, showing the almost superhuman determination that marked all his dealings with the Mexica during the conquest. On November 8, 1519, he entered Tenochtitlán.

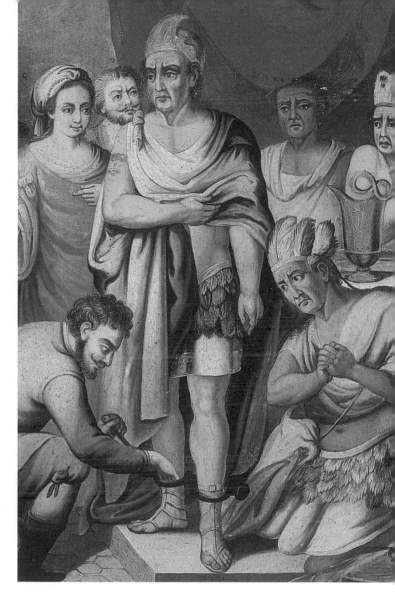

MONTEZUMA BEING TAKEN INTO CAPTIVITY. THE WOMAN AT LEFT IS NO DOUBT SUPPOSED TO REPRESENT THE INDIAN WOMAN WHOSE BIRTH NAME WAS MALINTZIN, BUT IS OFTEN KNOWN AS MALINCHE, CORTÉS' TRANSLATOR AND LOVER.

"KILL THEM!"

The conquistador Bernal Díaz del Castillo who accompanied Cortés later wrote that, upon entering Tenochtitlán, "some of the soldiers even asked whether the things they saw were not a dream." The city had fine masonry buildings, its temples towered as high as the great cathedrals of Seville; hundreds of commercial canoes filled the lake, coming and going; and so many people crowded the marketplaces "that the murmur and hum of their voices and words they used could be heard more than a league off."

Mexica nobles met the conquistadors as they entered the city on the southern causeway of Iztapalapa, wearing jaguar skins with the heads still attached. They bowed low, placing their hands to the Earth and kissing their fingers in a sign of deference. Then Montezuma himself showed up, carried on a litter and wearing a green-feathered headdress and gold sandals decorated with precious stones. He also wore gold lip and ear plugs, something the Spanish noted greedily.

Montezuma said to Cortés: "Our lord, you are weary. The journey has tired you, but now you have arrived on Earth. You have come to your city, Mexico. You have come to sit on your throne."

The Mexica ruler addressed Cortés as if he were Quetzalcóatl, but he would soon realize Cortés was not. Within a week, by November 14, Cortés had audaciously seized Montezuma and, despite his protests—"My person is not such as can be made a prisoner of"—imprisoned him. Cortés ruled Mexico through Montezuma until the spring of 1520, gathering gold and silver plunder from all over the city, when he learned that Governor Velázquez was sending a force of Spanish conquistadors to bring Cortés back to Cuba for disobeying orders. Cortés immediately marched east to meet and defeat this group, leaving matters in Tenochtitlán in the hands of a chief lieutenant, Pedro de Alvarado, who had with him about 100 soldiers.

During this time, the Mexica traditionally held the important festival of Toxcatl, a celebrated of the warrior god Huitzilopochtli, which culminated with the ritual sacrifice of a beautiful Mexica youth representing the god from the top of the Great Temple. Before he left, Cortés had given permission for this festival to occur, without the human sacrifice, but during his absence Alvarado lost his nerve. He saw in the preparations for the festival—the stockpiling of food, the building of a grotesque effigy of Huitzilopochtli, the gathering of the Mexica nobility (who participated in the festival's initial ritual dancing)—a secret rebellion being fomented.

During the festival, as the Mexica began to dance and sing in the precincts around the Great Temple, Alvarado and his men, as well as their Indian allies, quickly sealed off the streets and then ran into the central plaza. The plaza probably held 400 noble warriors dancing and singing, as well as several thousand clapping and chanting onlookers. All of a sudden, a shout in Spanish arose above the noise of the crowd. It was Alvarado giving the order: *¡Mueran!* meaning, "Kill them!"

MEXICAN NOBLES MET THE CONQUISTADORS AS THEY ENTERED THE CITY ON THE SOUTHERN CAUSEWAY OF IZTAPALAPA, WEARING JAGUAR SKINS, HEADS STILL ATTACHED.

Suddenly the plaza was flooded with conquistadors. "They came on foot," the Mexica survivors recalled, "carrying their swords and their wooden or metal shields." The dancers were unarmed. The carnage was immediate. They attacked and killed the drummers (who were priests, recognizably painted in black), the noble young man who led the dancers, and all the other celebrants, and then they turned their attention on the trapped and panicked spectators, men, women, and children. From *The Broken Spears*:

> They wounded some in the thigh and some in the calf. They slashed others in the abdomen, and their entrails spilled to the ground. Some attempted to run away, but their intestines dragged as they ran, they seemed to tangle their feet in their own entrails. No matter how they tried to save themselves, they could find no escape.

These Mexicans, having not yet fought the Spanish, had not seen the razor-sharp Castilian swords doing their bloody work, and were horrified at the ease with which limbs and heads were hacked off—the Mexica sword at the time was a wooden club stubbed with pieces of sharpened obsidian. The Mexica usually fought to wound and capture, not to kill, and were shocked by these monstrous white men who were all too obviously intent on the total destruction of their enemy. Frenzied conquistadors tracked the Mexica down, running into the houses in the area and killing those who cowered in rooms and closets. "They invaded every room, hunting and killing." Some Mexica played dead and survived, but if anyone breathed the Spanish would run them through.

NIGHT OF SORROWS

This first massacre of the Mexica took place on May 16. Cortés returned a little over a month later, having successfully defeated the Spanish army sent to depose him, only to find that the careful balance he had wrought in the city, with Montezuma as hostage, had been completely undone by Alvarado's rash actions. The Spanish were trapped in their quarters while the Mexica prepared for war outside. Cortés's dreams of winning this wonderful city intact for the King of Spain were now in ruins. With a force of about 1,000 conquistadors, his numbers swelled by men from Veláquez's army who had gone over to his side, Cortés realized he was no match in city fighting for a maddened Mexica army.

To make matters worse, on June 30, Montezuma died, probably as a result of having been stoned by his own people after trying to make a conciliatory speech from the roof of the palace where he was held captive. Without his hostage, Cortés was even more convinced that he needed to leave. He decided to make his escape at night, since the Mexica traditionally did not like to fight in the dark. At midnight on July 1, 1520, he began to lead his men out of the city during a light rainfall. He was heading for the western causeway. The Spanish carried a portable wooden bridge with them that they used to span the canals that twined through the city. They were on the causeway and heading out across the lake when a Mexica woman, out to get water, saw them and raised the alarm. Priests began shouting: "Mexican chiefs, our enemies are leaving, run to your canoes of war!" and a drum atop the Great Temple began to pound.

The warriors of Tenochtitlán ran for their large canoes and paddled to the causeway, firing showers of arrows at Cortés's men, who were trapped there. Others charged on foot down the causeway, in their rage forgetting to try to capture the Castilians, and clubbing them to death where they stood. Many of the Spanish had gold with them and these were the ones caught and killed, or who drowned after falling into the lake. Cortés himself fell in the water and was nearly captured before he was saved by his men. Finally, he made his way across the lake to safety on the other side, but the escape attempt—thereafter forever dubbed *Noche Triste*, or "Night of Sorrows"—had been a disaster.

The Mexica captured or killed 600 Spanish soldiers. Those unfortunate enough to be made prisoner were dragged moaning up the steps of the Great Temple where they had their hearts cut out by obsidian knives, after which they were beheaded and their bodies thrown down the steps to be eaten by the priests. The heads, along with the severed heads of captured horses, were placed on a huge skull rack.

THE ATTACK

For most men, this kind of setback would have been enough and they would have returned to Cuba chastened. But Cortés, spurred on by greed for Mexica gold and his own lust for power and glory, was preternaturally determined to bring down the Mexica. Reaching the capital city of the Tlaxcala with the people who were now his allies, he rested his men throughout August. In September, a smallpox epidemic—probably brought by the men sent by Velazquez—broke out in Tenochtitlán with disastrous effect. Thousands upon thousands of Mexica died, "covered with agonizing sores from head to foot," as one survivor wrote. With the city's population depleted, Cortés decided that the time would be ripe for attack. In December 1520, he set off again for Tenochtitlán, with about 550 Spanish and 20,000 of his Tlaxcala allies.

Cortés's goal was not, immediately, to attack the city, but to cut it off and starve it a little first. So from January through May he moved around the shores of Lake Texcoco with his forces conquering cities loyal to the Mexica, and adding captured warriors to his swelling fighting force. This also had the effect of shutting down food supplies to the Mexica. He also had his men destroy the main aqueduct that brought fresh water into the isolated city, so that the Mexica were forced to drink the polluted and unhealthy lake water close to their shores, bringing further disease into the city.

CONQVISTA DE MEXICO POR CORTES. 7

In late April 1581, Cortés launched his offensive, a combined amphibious–land operation. He sent 200 conquistadors and 25,000 Indian allies down the three causeways that linked the mainland to the city. The rest of the attack was made across the water by brigantines Cortés had his shipbuilders make, each carrying harquebusiers, cannon, and crossbowmen; these formidable vessels were more than a match for the war canoes of the Mexica, pounding them into splinters and keeping the Mexica from attacking the Spanish crossing on the causeways.

Once the Spanish and their allies entered the city, the slaughter truly began.

"THE DEEP THROBBING OF THE DRUMS"

In Tenochtitlán, the fighting was fierce. The Spaniards made their way through the city by filling in the canals with roof beams and adobe bricks from nearby houses. The Mexica fought desperately. Some later told of cornering a Spanish horseman who had wounded a friend with his lance. The Mexica "ran to the aide of their friend and twisted [the lance] from the Spaniard's hands. They knocked the horseman from his saddle, beat and kicked him as he lay on his back on the ground, and then cut off his head."

The Spaniards fought their way through the city toward the Great Temple. "The priests began to beat their great ritual drums from the top of the pyramid," one account in *The Broken Spears* relates. "The deep throbbing of the drums resounded over the city, calling the warriors to defend the shrine of their god. But two Spanish soldiers climbed the stairway of the temple platform, cut the priests down with their swords, and pitched them headlong over the brink."

The Spanish were unable to break through the lines of the Mexica warriors, led by their new king, Cuauhtémoc, despite repeated attempts, and so for several months the fight for Tenochtitlán settled into bloody street raids and house-to-house combat. Whenever the Mexica caught a Spaniard alive he was dragged up the steps of the main temple and immediately sacrificed in front of his fellows. "Some of the captives were weeping," as they were dragged up the steps of the temple, "some were keening, others were beating their palms against their mouths." More than sixty conquistadors and hundreds of their Indian allies met their deaths in such a horrible fashion.

Watching, Bernal Díaz del Castillo, the conquistador who would later write *A True History of the Conquest of New Spain*, and his fellow Spaniards were horrified and enraged at the way "the Indian butchers who were waiting below [the temple] cut off the arms and legs and feet [of the Spaniards] and flayed the skin off their faces and prepared it afterwards like glove leather with the beards on." As the Mexica pressed home their counterattacks, they threw the legs and arms of the sacrificed victims at the Spanish and their allies, telling them they had already eaten enough—"we are already glutted with this [human flesh], you can glut yourself with it."

THE FINAL MASSACRE

All of this enraged the Spanish and made them thirst for revenge. Despite the fact that Cortés himself wanted the Mexica to stop fighting so that he might salvage something of their great city as a prize, they resisted the Spanish for three

full months. Finally, however, worn down by hunger and thirst, they were forced to retreat and made a last stand in Tlatelolco, the market district of the city.

Cornered by Pedro Alvarado and his ruthless horsemen, as well as thousands of their Indian allies, the Mexica were slaughtered. The ferocity of the Tlaxacalans—who were using the Spanish in an attempt to overthrow their hated enemy—was so barbaric that Cortés later wrote "no race has ever practiced such fierce and unnatural cruelty." The Indians swept into the homes of the Mexica, killing women and children, shattering their bones with clubs, throwing their limp bodies out into the streets. They climbed to the roofs of the houses and smashed infants against the low roof edges and then hurled their limp bodies out across the smoldering city. Whenever the Spanish saw a crowd of Mexica together—and by this time these people were exhausted, starving, dressed in rags—they would run them down with their horses, spearing unlucky ones who could not get away fast enough and tossing their bodies over their shoulders.

The first major historian of the conquest, William H. Prescott, wrote of the scene in his great 1843 work *History of the Conquest of Mexico*:

> Hemmed in like deer surrounded by hunters, the besieged were cut down on all sides. The ground was piled with slain bodies, until the maddened combatants were obliged to climb over human mounds to get at [their victims]. The miry soil was saturated with blood, which ran off like water and colored the canals a bright red. All was uproar and terrible confusion. The hideous yells of the [Mexica], the invectives and curses of the Spaniards, the cries of the wounded, the shrieks of women and children, the heavy blows of the conquerors, the death-struggles of their victims, the reverberating echoes of musketry, the hissing of the missiles, the blazing buildings crushing hundreds in their ruins, the blinding dust and sulphurous smoke—all made a scene appalling even to Cortés' soldiers.

And Cortés himself was appalled as well. Soon the streets were so filled with corpses that, as the conquistador Bernal Díaz wrote, "even Cortés was sick from the stink in the nostrils." He went back to his camp. It was August 13, 1521. Tenochtitlán lay smoking and in ruins, but the Spanish had conquered it.

WHENEVER THE SPANISH SAW A CROWD OF MEXICA TOGETHER, THEY WOULD RUN THEM DOWN WITH THEIR HORSES, SPEARING UNLUCKY ONES WHO COULD NOT GET AWAY FAST ENOUGH AND TOSSING THEIR BODIES OVER THEIR SHOULDERS.

THE FINAL TOLL

Perhaps 40,000 Mexica in all were slaughtered in the final days of the siege of their capital city, although 200,000—four-fifths of the population—had died of wounds and disease since January. The Mexica ruler Cuauhtémoc was captured. Cortés promised him his life, but would later hang him after torturing him to

A MAP OF MEXICO AT THE TIME OF THE CONQUEST. THE RED LINE SHOWS A PORTION OF THE ROUTE THAT CORTÉS TOOK OVER THE MOUNTAINS TO TENOCHTITLÁN.

find out the location of any gold. From Cortés's often-repeated point of view, the Mexica had brought the massacre of their population upon themselves—if only they hadn't resisted so fiercely, if only they had taken advantage of the opportunities he had offered them to surrender to him.

But Cortés had proved his untrustworthiness from the very beginning, when he seized Montezuma. He wanted to make the Mexica and their country vassals and keep their city as a prize. They only thing they had left was their valor, and they used it against him until they were so worn down they could no longer fight. The massacre of the Mexica worked to the advantage of Cortés and Spain—for they had little worries about resistance from the pitiful remnants of the population who remained, and they were thus able to begin flowing the treasures of the country into Spain, which in turn became a powerful force in European war and politics.

The great Mexica civilization was no longer in existence. By the time the Spanish friars came along to talk to them, all they had, living in their huts, were memories of their greatness, and poems of mourning, such as this one from *The Broken Spears*:

Broken spears lie in the roads;
we have torn our hair in our grief.
The houses are roofless now, and their walls
are red with blood.

Worms are swarming in the streets and plazas,
and the walls are splattered with gore.
The water has turned red, as if it were dyed,
and when we drink it,
it has the taste of brine.

THE QUETZAL-OWL WARRIOR

Civilizations in their final throes will try anything to salvage a victory, and the Mexica pulled out all the stops against the Spanish toward the end of the siege of Tenochtitlán by sending out a quetzal-owl warrior, a heroic warrior dressed in a ceremonial feather costume that had been worn by Ahuitzotl, who was Montezuma's predecessor as emperor of the Mexica. Such a quetzal-owl figure had been employed at previous dire times in the Mexica's history and had always brought them success.

Armed with special darts sacred to the warrior god Huitzilopochtli, the warrior sallied forth against the Spanish and their allies, and apparently astonished the conquistadors. The warrior himself was hidden completely beneath the multicolored feathers, which had been glued to a frame around him. "The Castilians fought as if they had seen something inhuman," one of the chronicles reports, and even seemed to withdraw in fear. The quetzal-owl managed to capture three of the Spaniards' Indian allies, who were immediately sacrificed to the gods. However, despite his bravery, this warrior in his traditional finery could not turn back the Spanish tide. His comrades watched him from a distance as he engaged in battle; but then the figure of the quetzal-owl fell over the side of a terrace and was seen no more.

CHAPTER 3

BLOOD IN THE NAME OF GOD

THE ST. BARTHOLOMEW'S DAY MASSACRE, AUGUST 24, 1572

THOUSANDS OF HUGUENOTS WERE MURDERED BY THEIR CATHOLIC NEIGHBORS IN A SLAUGHTER THAT WOULD SEPARATE THE CATHOLIC AND PROTESTANT CHURCH IN EUROPE FOR CENTURIES TO COME

STARING OUT OVER HIS AUDIENCE, THE POPE SPOKE CAREFULLY: "On the eve of 24 August we cannot forget the "sad Massacre" of St. Bartholomew's Day, an event of very obscure causes in the political and religious history of France. Christians did things which the Gospel condemns . . . I am convinced that only forgiveness, offered and received, leads little by little to a fruitful dialogue, which will in turn ensure a fully Christian reconciliation."

The Pope was John Paul II, the year was 1997, and the place was Paris. The "sad Massacre of St Bartholomew's Day" to which he referred began in this city exactly 425 years earlier and yet even after four centuries, the head of the Catholic Church still needed to address the unresolved resentments and unhealed wounds of this shocking slaughter of Huguenots, or French Protestants, by Catholics. The massacre is by no means the worst religious killing on record—modern estimates on the number of deaths vary wildly, from five thousand to thirty thousand, with the lower number being generally accepted—but the savagery of it continues to shock even to this day.

"The streets were covered with dead bodies; the river tinted with blood; and the doors and gates to the king's palace painted the same color," was

THE MASSACRE OF THE HUGUENOTS. IN RENDITION OF A PAINTING BY THE NINETEENTH CENTURY AMERICAN ARTIST ALONZO CHAPPEL, HUGUENOT WOMEN AND CHILDREN LIE PILED DEAD ON THE STREETS OF PARIS WHILE FRENCH SOLDIERS MASSACRE STILL OTHERS.

the way one contemporary account described the end of the day in Paris on August 24, 1572. The massacre was terrible not just because "it epitomized the horrors of fanaticism and unexamined belief," as the historian Barbara Diefendorf writes, but because differences in worship ran so high that neighbors slaughtered their neighbors. This was no mere government-ordered killing of political enemies—although it was that, too—but a spontaneous and bloodily retributive sectarian attack on the people who lived next door.

Although the immediate cause of the St. Bartholomew's Day Massacre does remain, as Pope John Paul II pointed out, somewhat obscure, his veiled language was also obfuscatory. Both Protestants and Catholics are considered Christians, of course, but it was not the "Christians" in general who were doing things counter to the teaching of the Gospel on that particular day. Those shedding blood in the name of God were very particularly Catholics.

WARS OF RELIGION

Both religions had their share of fanatic believers. Ever since the monk Martin Luther nailed his Ninety-Five Theses to the door of All Saint's Church in Wittenberg, Saxony, on All Hallow's Eve, 1517, religious resentment and violence had embroiled Europe. The Reformation begun by Martin Luther sought to address the extreme corruption of the Catholic Church at the time—the selling of indulgences and church positions, as well as the venality of many Catholic clergy. But after the Church acted with predictable censure—Luther was excommunicated and the Reformation condemned—various radical Protestant religious groups began to spring up.

One of the chief among these was begun by Frenchman John Calvin, who had fled to Geneva to escape Catholic persecution. One of the central tenets of Calvinism, as it came to be called, was that each person's salvation or damnation had been predetermined by God. Using clandestine printing presses and sending disciples back into France, Calvin targeted influential French aristocrats for conversion; they in turn converted others.

Calvinism became so widespread, particularly among the upper classes and skilled artisans of France, that by the early 1560s there were some 1,200 Reformed churches in the country. In the same period, more than 450 French

Calvinists had been executed as heretics by the Catholic Church. This persecution drove many French Calvinists—who were now being called Huguenots,
a name whose origins are uncertain, but which was intended initially as a slur
by French Catholics—into exile in the Netherlands, Switzerland, England, and
North America. It also gave those who remained a militant tenor. They began
to arm themselves and form small armies. Things came to a head in 1559, when
the accidental jousting death of King Henry II left a vacuum in the French
court. A Catholic faction represented by the Guise family fought openly against
a Huguenot faction of the House of Bourbon. Despite the efforts of Henry's
widow, Catherine de Medici, mother of the 11-year-old King Charles IX, open
warfare broke out, with the Protestants plotting to seize the young king and
hold him captive.

This plot was foiled, but what became known as the French Wars of Religion
began in 1562. Huguenots seized churches and destroyed Catholic statuary in
cities where the Huguenots were in the majority; Catholics attacked Huguenots
while they worshipped, at times burning their churches. Catherine de Medici's
attempt to moderate the situation by giving Huguenots limited freedom to worship did not please either side. Much blood was shed by the time the third clash
between Protestants and Catholics ended with the Peace of Saint-Germain in
August 1570, in which Huguenots were finally allowed to hold public office and
Catherine agreed to marry her daughter Marguerite de Valois, sister of King
Charles IX, to the prominent Huguenot, Henry of Bourbon, King of Navarre.

THE REVENGE OF GOD

Catherine and King Charles had, however, underestimated the anger of French
Catholics, particularly in Paris. After the signing of the Peace of Saint-Germain,
the King ordered the tearing down of the Cross of Gastines, which had been
erected by Catholics on the former site of the home of two Huguenots who had
been executed for their beliefs. This sparked a furious spate of mob violence
against Huguenots.

Catholics, too, were outraged by the upcoming marriage between Henry of
Navarre and Marguerite de Valois, which they considered a "mixed" marriage.
Radical preachers inveighed against it, saying that God would avenge himself

against such heresy; the Parliament decided to boycott the event; and the Pope refused to give his permission for the ceremony. It took all of Catherine de Medici's celebrated powers of persuasion to convince a French cardinal to marry the couple.

From the Huguenot point of view, however, the marriage was cause for great celebration—a sign that their struggles had not been in vain, that they were at last being legitimatized in the eyes of the King of France. The wedding was scheduled for August 18, 1572, and hundreds of well-to-do Huguenots flocked to Paris for the extended festivities, which involved jousting tournaments, costume balls, and rich feasts. The Huguenots were not unaware of the hostility against them in Paris—part of the reason they were there was to protect Henry of Navarre as well as the Admiral Gaspard de Coligny, the political and military leader of the Huguenots, against any assaults on their person. Although the wedding occurred without incident, Coligny himself was shot and seriously wounded by a gunman as he returned from a meeting with Charles IX on the morning of August 22. The would-be assassin escaped and the reasons for the shooting remain mysterious even nearly half a millennium later.

Coligny had been conferring with Charles about the possibility of the king giving French aid to the Protestant rebels battling Spain in their war for independence in the Netherlands, so one of the most persistent rumors has been that Catherine de Medici tried to have Coligny assassinated to keep him from dragging the impressionable twenty-two-year-old Charles into a dangerous foreign war. Yet Catherine (see "Catherine de Medici: 'I Am Surprised She Never

Did Worse'," page 46) may genuinely be innocent of these charges, since she had made repeated attempts to mediate differences between the Catholics and Huguenots during the Wars of Religion.

Other suspects in the shooting of Coligny would be the Guise family, longtime enemies of the Huguenots (Coligny was shot from the upstairs window of a house that belonged to the Guises) or possibly the Duke of Alba, the Spanish governor of the Netherlands, who wanted to eliminate Coligny as a threat to his suppression of the Dutch rebellion.

Whoever ordered it, the attempted assassination had immediate repercussions. The Huguenots were enraged and demanded justice from Charles and Catherine in the strongest possible terms. A rumor spread that a Huguenot army was posted just outside of Paris; this was not the case, but the rumor, writes Barbara Diefendorf, "appears to have been believed in the highest [French] circles." In fact, the Catholics began to suspect that the Huguenots were going to use this occasion to strike at the Catholic leadership. Another long-held theory claims that even the wedding of Henry of Navarre to Margaret itself was part of a secret plot by Catherine to lure high-ranking Huguenots to Paris, provoke them, and then use the excuse to wipe out their leadership. This has never been proven.

What does appear to be true is that on the evening of August 23, Charles IX and Catherine met and, possibly believing the rumor about the Huguenot army outside the city, decided to attack the Huguenots before the latter could attack them. As one contemporary Catholic writer put it: "[The French court] resolved to do to the Huguenots what the Huguenots wanted to do to the king. . . and as soon as possible."

"KILL, KILL, KILL THEM ALL"

The attack was set for sometime early the next morning as the bells of the church of Saint Germaine, the parish church of the kings of France, tolled heavily in the humid air. It was the feast of St. Bartholomew, the apostle who, tradition had it, had been flayed alive during his bloody martyrdom in Asia Minor. The city watch was told to seal off the gates of Paris. The King's Swiss Guard was apparently given a list of leading Huguenots in town and their lodgings.

CATHERINE DE MEDICI: "I AM SURPRISED SHE NEVER DID WORSE"

Whether or not she planned the massacre of the Huguenots before they even arrived in the city of Paris—and chances are she did not—Catherine de Medici had a reputation as one of the most Machiavellian women in sixteenth-century France. It was probably not unearned.

Born in Florence in 1519 into the powerful Medici family, she was orphaned before she was two months old when her young parents died, probably of syphilis. Catherine was brought up by an aunt. When she was only eight, civil war overturned the Medicis as the ruling family in Florence and crowds called for Catherine to be killed; this did not happen, but she was forced to ride on a donkey in front of a jeering crowd. It would be her first taste of civil violence, but certainly not her last.

CHARLES IX, KING OF FRANCE, WITH HIS MOTHER, CATHERINE DE MEDICI. THIS NINETEENTH CENTURY FRENCH PAINTING DEPICTS A MAN AND HIS OVERBEARING MOTHER, CAPTURING THE PREVAILING CONTEMPORARY VIEW THAT CATHERINE CONTROLLED THE COUNTRY THROUGH HER WEAKLING SON.

CHARLES IX (1550-1574), KING OF FRANCE, WITH HIS MOTHER CATHERINE DE MEDICIS (1519-1589), REGENT OF FRANCE FROM 1560-1574 (ENGRAVING), FRENCH SCHOOL, (NINETEENTH CENTURY) / PRIVATE COLLECTION / KEN WELSH / THE BRIDGEMAN ART LIBRARY INTERNATIONAL

Pope Clement VII, a Medici, called her to Rome and managed to marry her off to Henry, Duke of Orleans, in 1533. Both bride and bridegroom were fourteen years old. Catherine, while described as not particularly pretty ("small of stature, and thin, and without delicate features, but having the protuberant eyes peculiar to the Medici family," one account had it) was bright and ambitious. When Henry became king in 1547, Catherine became queen of France and would bear Henry ten children, seven of whom survived infancy.

After King Henry was accidentally killed jousting, Catherine's son, Francis, became king at age fifteen in 1559, but it was apparent that Catherine was the power behind the throne. When Francis died of disease the next year, his brother Charles IX took over at the tender age of eleven and Catherine—who slept in the boy's chamber with him—essentially ran the country. She tried to keep the powerful Guise family at bay as they battled the Huguenots, while at the same time not giving too much religious freedom to the Protestants, whom many of Catherine's fellow Catholics considered heretics.

Charles IX died, also of illness, in 1574, leaving Henry II, Catherine's third son, to rule France. Unlike his two brothers, Henry was a grown man when he came to the throne, but he still depended heavily on Catherine to do much of the governing of the country; Henry was pious and given to long pilgrimages and self-flagellation. By 1588, with religious wars still raging in France, Henry and Catherine had nearly lost control of the country. Catherine died of illness in early January 1589, and Henry was assassinated six months later by a crazed monk. He was succeeded by Henry of Navarre, who became Henry IV, and wrote sympathetically of Catherine:

> I ask you, what could a woman do, left by the death of her husband with five little children on her arms and two families of France who were thinking of grasping the crown—our own [the Bourbons] and the Guises. Was she not compelled to play strange parts to deceive first one and then the other, in order to guard, as she did, her sons, who successively reigned through the wise conduct of that shrewd woman? I am surprised that she never did worse.

The Duke of Guise led a group of armed men to the residence where Admiral Coligny recovered from his wounds. In the first murder of the day, the men stormed up the stairs, broke into Coligny's room, hacked him to death with swords, then threw his body out the window so that Guise could make sure that he was dead. Guise then led his men after other targets, while the King's guards roamed through the darkness seeking out other Huguenots on their list.

THE HUGUENOTS WERE SUBJECTED TO BIZARRE AND SICKENING PERVERSIONS OF RELIGIOUS RITES—INFANTS WERE "BAPTIZED" IN THE BLOOD OF THEIR PARENTS BEFORE BEING KILLED THEMSELVES.

The commotion these men made on their mission caused other Frenchmen to awake and grab their own arms, thinking they were under attack. But Guise shouted that he and his men had been given carte blanche by the King of France himself to kill Huguenots. The Parisian mob took this as permission to set off on its own missions of slaughter. Chains were placed across Parisian streets to block them off and armed men stormed the houses of Huguenots—in particular those among Henry of Navarre's party, but also simple merchants and clerks in Paris, people who had lived there all their lives. They were dragged from their beds and beaten or stabbed to death. The mob sought to humiliate them, forcing them to say Catholic prayers or burn their own Protestant books before they were killed. The Huguenots were subjected to bizarre and sickening perversions of religious rites—infants were "baptized" in the blood of their parents before being killed themselves.

Protestant minister Simon Goulart, who survived the slaughter, wrote:

Militia captains and district officials went with their men from house to house, wherever they thought they might find Huguenots, breaking down the doors and cruelly massacring whoever they found, without regard to sex or age . . . calling out "Kill, kill, kill them all; the king commands it." Carts piled high with dead bodies of noble ladies, women, girls, men, and boys were brought down and emptied into the river, which was covered with dead bodies and red with blood, which also ran in other places in the city, such as the courtyard of the Louvre and surrounding areas.

Goulart gives the number of dead in Paris alone as 10,000, which is a great exaggeration, but he accurately notes the names of numerous Huguenot officials who perished. He also notes that the Catholics committed especially horrible atrocities when they caught Huguenot women. One noble lady had her hands cut off so that her assailants could more easily steal her gold bracelets; she then died screaming as a butcher ran her through with a meat skewer. Another woman, about to give birth, faced an even worse fate when enraged members of a mob burst into her room:

ON THE NIGHT OF THE ST. BARTHOLOMEW'S DAY MASSACRE, THE DUKE OF GUISE VIEWS THE CRUMPLED AND SLASHED CORPSE OF ADMIRAL DE COLIGNY, THE MOST PROMINENT HUGUENOT CASUALTY OF THE EVENING.

The midwife, seeing they wanted also to massacre the pregnant woman, begged them insistently to wait until she had delivered the child . . . After having wrangled about this for a time, they took this poor [woman], already half dead with fright, and plunged a knife up to its hilt in her anus. Feeling herself mortally wounded, but nonetheless desiring to bring forth her fruit, she fled to the attic, where they pursued her and gave another dagger blow to her belly, then threw her out the window into the street.

"HAD I NOT FEARED OFFENDING GOD"

The massacre in Paris continued for three days. The Catholics wore white arm-bands and sometimes a white cross so they could recognize each other during the killings, hunting down Huguenots as if they were terrified animals. (The roman-tic painting by John Everett Millais, *A Huguenot on St. Bartholomew's Day* [1853] shows a Huguenot youth refusing the white armband that his terrified girlfriend is trying to force on him, preferring martyrdom to renouncing his religion.)

One well-to-do Huguenot woman, Charlotte d'Arbaleste, happened to be visiting Paris on business when the massacre broke out. She was twenty-two years old, already a widow and no stranger to sectarian violence—her husband had been killed in the last War of Religion. While she was still in bed early on the morning of St. Bartholomew's Day, "one of my kitchen servants, a Protestant and native Parisian, came to find me and, very frightened, told me that they were killing everyone." D'Arbaleste looked out her window to see "an agitated popu-lace and several platoons of soldiers, each wearing a white cross on his hat."

Aware of her situation, d'Arbaleste's uncle, a Huguenot bishop, sent word to her that he was sending someone to escort her out of danger, but when the uncle went out on the street himself, he was nearly killed, only escaping with his life when he agreed to make the sign of the cross. This, plus the fact that another uncle was murdered by a Catholic mob, caused the bishop "to forget about me entirely," d'Arbaleste writes ruefully.

It was now up to her to try to make her way out of Paris along with her three-year-old daughter. She first went to the home of a relative who held the position of a magistrate in the king's household, one Monsieur de Perreuse. Perreuse was a Catholic, but nonetheless—in one of the acts of mercy and humanity that did sparkle through those awful days in Paris—took in Charlotte and, eventually, more than forty fugitives. D'Arbaleste stayed with Perreuse for three days. Her mother came secretly to visit her and told her that the Duke of Guise's men were looking for her, that the only way she could save herself was to bribe them with gold crowns, and then go to Mass, as several of her brothers had done.

But d'Arbaleste refused to do this, despite the fact that day and night, hiding in an attic in Perreuse's home, she heard "such strange cries of men, women, and children being killed in the streets below that I was unable to think clearly and

[was] almost in despair. Had I not feared offending God, I almost would have preferred to jump to my death than to fall alive into the hands of the populace . . ."

Eventually, Charlotte d'Arbaleste escaped Paris and after several months of travail eventually made it to a fortified Huguenot city in northeastern France. In the meantime, Charles IX issued a statement on August 28 that he had acted only because he had discovered a Huguenot plot against himself and the royal family. Nothing that happened, Charles wrote, "is to nullify the edict of pacification, which, to the contrary, I want observed as strictly as before."

> ... WHEN D'ARBALESTE'S UNCLE, A HUGUENOT BISHOP, WENT OUT ON THE STREET HIMSELF, HE WAS NEARLY KILLED, ONLY ESCAPING WITH HIS LIFE WHEN HE AGREED TO MAKE THE SIGN OF THE CROSS.

In other words, the murders of the Admiral and others were an answer to a Huguenot plot, only. The Peace of Saint-Germain still held. Charles had copies of his statement sent to provincial governments in the hopes of forestalling sectarian violence there, but he was far too late.

"A REAL TORTURE TO THEM"

There have long been rumors that Charles accompanied his written letter with oral orders to kill "any Huguenot found outside his home," but this is not very likely. Historians today believe that Charles ordered the initial killings of the Huguenots in Paris only after very severe pressure was put upon him by his mother and members of his royal council.

Still, many Catholics in outlying cities had been waiting for a long time to get revenge on the Huguenots, and those Catholics were able to convince themselves that Charles really did desire these heretics dead. The killings were the most terrible in cities like Orleans, Meaux, and Troyes, which had seen the worst violence during the Wars of Religion and had sizeable Huguenot minorities. In Troyes, the citizens did not even wait, as soon as first word of the massacres in Paris reached them, two days after St. Bartholomew's Day, they began killing Huguenots on the street.

Religious hatred was often used to settle old scores. A Huguenot named Pierre Blancpignon, who made pewterware, was dragged outside his house by a Catholic mob, one of whose members was Jean Despine, whom Blancpignon had previously arrested for theft. When he saw Despine, an observer wrote, "Blancpignon walked out with his hands clasped together and his eyes raised to heaven," ready to be killed. Despine ran him through with a sword, another man struck him with a dagger, then the mob set upon him: "Thus, with blows from swords, daggers, knives and stones, he was killed and slaughtered and then stripped naked and dragged into the river near the Comporte gate, where there is more garbage and filth than water."

A woman who was killed in much the same way shouted before her death: "You reenact Christ's Passion, but God will exact vengeance." It did her no good—her naked body joined the others floating in the Loire.

In Orleans, the city provost stationed 600 archers around the city, trapping the Huguenots inside. One observer wrote that the mob that then formed at first satisfied itself with pillaging and looting, but then began to massacre Huguenots wherever they could find them. In Orleans, perhaps 1,000 Huguenots died. More would certainly have done so, but they began to "repent."

"On Sunday, all the churches were filled with people," wrote a contemporary observer. "Thousands of widows and orphans, youths and little children, who customarily went to Protestant services, went instead to Mass. They presented themselves en masse for Communion . . . and [were forced] to sign a formula of abjuration. These abjurations were a real torture to them." Even worse, children were re-baptized, this time as Catholics.

In Rouen, out of 16,000 Huguenots, several hundred died but 12,000 either converted to Catholicism or went into exile. The slaughter and mass conversions in the countryside went on from August to October.

"A BLOODY AND TREACHEROUS RELIGION"

No one will ever know how many people died in the St. Bartholomew's Day Massacre and the massacres that followed close on its heels. The best estimate (albeit a conservative one) is from 5,000 to 6,000. But the massacre had far wider repercussions even than the horrible sight of thousands of dead Huguenots floating in France's rivers. Afterward, both sides began to use the story to push their agenda.

In the immediate aftermath, the militant Catholics who had done the killing were triumphant. The severed head of Admiral Coligny was sent to Pope Gregory XIII, who in turn sent King Charles IX a golden rose in thanks. The Pope then ordered a *Te Deum* to be sung in thanksgiving, a practice that was kept up for a number of years. When he realized that many Catholics celebrated the fate of the Huguenots, Charles, who had initially been a reluctant participant in the whole affair, cast himself as a heroic figure, even having a medal struck that showed him as Hercules fighting Hydra-headed heresy. However, more moderate French Catholics were horrified by the killings and began a movement, calling themselves the *Politiques*, which sought to place national interest over narrow sectarianism, one that would eventually help France's growth as a nation state.

Internationally, the violence against the Huguenots, as portrayed in numerous Huguenot pamphlets, some of which considerably exaggerated the numbers of dead, caused Protestants to come out firmly against Catholicism. It also swayed the mind of Queen Elizabeth I of England when it came to secretly supporting the Protestant rebels in the Netherlands.

If the goal of the French killers those bloody days in August 1572 was to weaken the Huguenots in France, they were successful. Hundreds of prominent Huguenot leaders were killed, many thousands more were forcibly baptized as Catholics, and thousands of Huguenots went into exile. The Huguenots, while not destroyed as a religious force in France, were severely crippled.

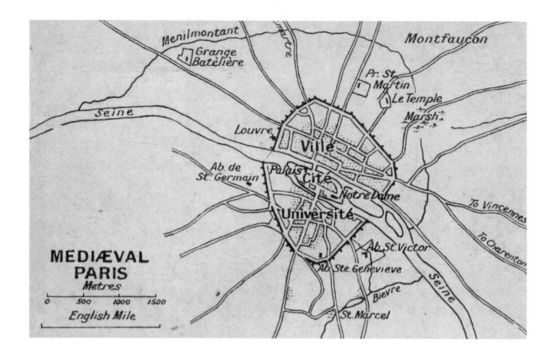

A MAP OF THE MEDIEVAL CITY OF PARIS. MUCH OF THE SLAUGHTER ON THE NIGHT OF THE ST. BARTHOLOMEW'S DAY MASSACRE TOOK PLACE WITHIN THE CONFINES OF THE OLD CITY OF PARIS, WHOSE NARROW STREETS COULD BE EASILY ROPED OFF BY THOSE MURDERING THE HUGUENOTS.

COURTESY OF THE UNIVERSITY OF TEXAS LIBRARIES, THE UNIVERSITY OF TEXAS AT AUSTIN

However, the true and lasting effect of the St. Bartholomew's Day Massacre was, one historian has written, to mark "Protestant minds [with] the indelible conviction that Catholicism was a bloody and treacherous religion." It is no wonder that the Massacre continues to evoke the horror of religious intolerance and no wonder John Paul II, so many centuries after that bloody day, still felt the need to address the event, and to hope for the "fully Christian reconciliation" that had been beyond the capabilities and imaginations of the militant Catholics and Protestants of the late sixteenth century.

ONE HUGUENOT RECANTS

In a document luridly called *Confession of his Descent into Popery*, a Huguenot minister, Hugues Surreau Du Rosier, described the enormous pressure of the massacre on his beliefs. Du Rosier was pastor of a small church outside of Paris. When he heard about the killings, he decided to flee the country.

> When I was leaving, in thinking about the difficulties I would have to face, I decided to half pretend to be a papist by wearing the insignia [the cross] they wore on their hats. . . The following day, on my arrival in the first city on my route, I was asked who I was and found myself completely at a loss. I did not have the wits to say what I planned and said something completely inappropriate, which made them suspicious of me.

Du Rosier admitted his religion in front of a judge and was thrown in prison to await almost certain death. "I resolved at first to endure whatever death they had to offer," he wrote, but soon realized that this courage "was but a puff of smoke." Du Rosier began to think about the severe nature of this persecution:

> I had always believed the past calamities [attacks on the Huguenots] to be so many visitations and rods by which God purged his church and had always judged them to be clear signs marking out the children of God. But inasmuch as the [the current massacre] could be seen to entirely ruin the church, without the least hope for its reestablishment, I began to see it as evidence of God's indignation. . . .

Lost and alone, Du Rosier felt God's grace leaving him, and so he recanted and survived. Later, he returned to the Huguenot church—as many thousands of Huguenots who had recanted under duress did.

CHAPTER 4

"THE GHASTLIEST FORMS THAT WERE EVER SEEN ALIVE"

THE BLACK HOLE OF CALCUTTA, 1756

IT WASN'T EVEN A HOLE, NOR DID AS MANY PEOPLE DIE HERE
AS HISTORY HAS LONG THOUGHT, BUT THE BRITISH USED IT
AS AN EXCUSE TO CONQUER AN INDIAN EMPIRE

A MAP OF INDIA, CIRCA 1760, SHORTLY AFTER THE INCIDENT OF THE BLACK HOLE OF CALCUTTA. THE TITLE—"INDIA IN THE TIME OF CLIVE"—REFERS TO ROBERT CLIVE, A LIEUTENANT COLONIAL IN THE BRITISH EAST INDIA COMPANY WHO BEGAN THE CONQUEST OF INDIA IN THE LATE 1750S.

COURTESY OF THE UNIVERSITY OF TEXAS LIBRARIES. THE UNIVERSITY OF TEXAS AT AUSTIN

THE STORY OF THE BLACK HOLE OF CALCUTTA, AS THE INDIAN historian Nirad C. Chaudhuri nicely put it, "threw a moral halo over the British conquest of India." Mark Twain called the Black Hole "the first brick, the Foundation Stone, upon which was reared a mighty Empire—the Indian Empire of Great Britain." The incident was taught to British school children for two hundred years, became a part of the English language—the term "hole" used to describe solitary imprisonment comes from the Black Hole of Calcutta—and entered the annals of Imperial England's poetry, especially William Ernest Henley's muscular 1875 paean to British manliness, "Invictus":

> Out of the night that covers me
> Black as the Pit from pole to pole.
> I thank whatever gods may be
> For my unconquerable soul.

INDIA

In the time of Clive

1760

English Miles

50 100   200   300

Before June 26, 1756, the extent of Great Britain's power and wealth in the Indian subcontinent had been represented by the British East India Company, which poured back into Great Britain spices, precious metals, and silks from trading with the Mughal Empire. It was a commercial enterprise, not a governmental one. But then came the night when 146 people (supposedly) were squeezed into a (supposedly) 18- by 14-foot (5.5 × 4.3 m) room and left to suffer a nightmare of the damned. When only twenty-three of them came staggering out alive the next morning, the British Empire in India was born.

"FREEDOM ANSWERABLE TO THEIR OWN DESIRES"

In the early seventeenth century, the people of Great Britain and the rest of Europe hungered for spices now considered commonplace—cloves, pepper, and, especially, nutmeg, which was considered an aphrodisiac as well as a possible cure for everything from boils to the plague. At that time, the main supply of nutmeg and other spices came from the Moluccas, or Spice, Islands, in Indonesia, which were firmly in the hands of the Dutch East India Company.

The British East India Company, despite numerous pitched battles fought against the Dutch, was unable to gain ascendancy in the Moluccas and hence turned to the subcontinent of India, hoping to gain a foothold there. In 1615, the East India Company, backed by King James I, signed a treaty with Mughal Emperor Nuruddin Salim Jahangir to build factories and trading posts in Surat, a port in western India, as well as other areas. Furthermore, the Emperor promised: "I have commanded all my governors and captains to give [Company merchants] freedom answerable to their own desires; to buy, sell, and to transport into their country at their own desire."

And "their own desire" was great. Over the next 100 years, the East India Company profited greatly from its trade in India and by the beginning of the eighteenth century had become a quasi-governmental entity, by charter of the king able to acquire territory, mint money, command armies, build fortresses, and make war and peace. Thousands of young Britons, seeking sunny climes and rosy fortunes, spread out across India in the employ of the Company, setting up great trading centers—known in Company parlance as "presidencies"—in Madras, Mumbai, and Calcutta. However, this was commercial expansion, not empire-building, as the land these great trading entities stood on—the rich homes of the British, the factories and stores, the wharves and warehouses—was only leased from the Mughal owners. "Our business is only trade and security, not conquest," the Company said in one reassuring missive to Mughal royalty.

Despite the fact that there was money to be made, adventure to be had, and beautiful woman to be found—many British quickly married, or at least found mistresses, once in India—there was peril in an Indian posting for the Company. There were shipwrecks on the way over, blazing hot weather once there, tropical diseases, and occasional pitched battles with local princes, as well as the French and Portuguese. It sometimes seemed to those British who lived there that the trading city of Calcutta, located in eastern India on the bank of the River Hooghly, comprised all these problems rolled into one.

THE TWO-MONSOON RULE

Calcutta, founded by the legendary East India Company factor, Job Charnock, was in some ways hell on Earth. It was situated a little too far up the Hooghly from the ocean to allow big ships to get near; and before the river was dredged, dangerous sandbars gutted many a merchant vessel. Three miles (4.8 km) from Calcutta was a saltwater lake that overflowed during the monsoon season, causing fish to spill out for miles around. When the waters receded, dead fish lay everywhere. Their "thick, stinking vapors" sickened people. Cholera and typhus were endemic. European life expectancy was such that people who survived two monsoons, or three years, were considered quite lucky (it was dubbed "the two-monsoon rule"). Infant mortality, high at the time, was even worse in Calcutta—only one in twenty British newborns survived infancy.

And yet, there was money to be made in Calcutta. Calico, silks, tea, spices, saltpeter (for use in making gunpowder), and precious gemstones filled the Company warehouses along the Hooghly and were transferred to ships that carried the goods out to the Bay of Bengal and then across the Indian Ocean to Great Britain. Although "trade and security" were indeed the main business of the Company, it was obvious that protection was needed for its rich stockpiles of goods and thus a Company militia was born, peopled by Portuguese and Dutch mercenaries, as well as Indians, and officered by the British.

In the early part of the eighteenth century, the British constructed a fort on the banks of the Hooghly, which they called Fort William after King William III. It contained the so-called Government House, where the main warehouse and business offices of the East India Company were located, as well as a pleasant park where visitors could stroll. There was also a parade ground surrounded by barracks; these barracks contained a small guardhouse or jail—really a walled-off corner of the veranda, with two barred grills for windows—that usually housed a few miscreants who were mainly Company soldiers sleeping off their hangovers. It was jokingly called the Black Hole.

"GOD SAVE US FROM HIM"

As the eighteenth century wore on, the already-fading Mughal Dynasty had begun to fade even further, and France and Britain, both of whom had sizeable trading contingents (with private armies attached), began increasingly to compete to fill the vacuum of power. When the Seven Years War began in 1756, with Britain and France officially at war, these private armies were supplemented with government forces.

> . . . THE BARRACKS CONTAINED A SMALL GUARDHOUSE OR JAIL——REALLY A WALLED-OFF CORNER OF THE VERANDA, WITH TWO BARRED GRILLS FOR WINDOWS——THAT USUALLY HOUSED A FEW MISCREANTS WHO WERE MAINLY COMPANY SOLDIERS SLEEPING OFF THEIR HANGOVERS. IT WAS JOKINGLY CALLED THE BLACK HOLE.

The spreading warfare in India was of concern to the British in Calcutta, especially because the now-fifty-year-old Fort William was in some disrepair. One engineer wrote that "it does not look like a place capable of prolonged resistance." The torrential monsoon rains and hot tropical sun had worn down the stone and mortar of the walls and, over the years, numerous gates and doors had been cut into the walls, so that workers might more readily access the Company warehouse. This made entry into the fort an easy feat for a determined invader.

In the light of hostilities with the French, the British quite naturally decided to make some repairs to Fort William.

However, this construction, which began in 1755, did not sit well with the new *nawab* (an Urdu term that means viceroy or governor) of Bengal, Siraj-al-Dawlah (whom the British, since they could not pronounce his name, often referred to mockingly as Sir Roger Dowett). Siraj-al-Dawlah ascended the throne in April 1756 in what one historian has called "the usual bloodbath"; because he was only a grandson of the previous nawab, not a son, he felt compelled to eliminate potential rivals.

Reviews of Siraj were decidedly negative. Robert Clive, the future British conqueror of India, called him "a monster of vice, cruelty and depravity," and even though Clive had reason to be prejudiced against the new nawab, it does appear that Siraj—all of twenty-three years old when he took the throne—was murderous (he was also "remarkable for the beauty of his person," according to one contemporary British writer).

His own cousin claimed that Siraj "did not know the distinction between vice and virtue . . . and carried defilement wherever he went . . . and people meeting him by chance used to say: 'God save us from him.'" (There are also contemporary accounts that Siraj's mind had been addled by extreme amounts of alcohol and drugs, even though he had sworn on a Koran to his grandfather never to touch the stuff again when he became nawab.)

However flawed the new nawab's personality might be, he did have a legitimate gripe with the British. They had supported a rival of Siraj's for the throne and then, when Siraj came into power, did not pay him the proper respect and give him the kind of monetary tribute he expected. And for years, they had been cheating the nawabs of Bengal out of certain taxes, claiming that they had received a waiver from the grand Mughal in Delhi. This in fact was true, but the British were arrogant about it, treating Siraj like a petty provincial prince. They calculated he would not dare do anything about this provocation, because he and his family had gained immense wealth from the British traders, but that was based on the supposition that they were dealing with a rational person. In Siraj, they were not. He ordered Governor Roger Drake, the Englishman in charge of Calcutta, to stop reinforcing Fort William, and when Governor Drake refused, the fates of the British in Calcutta—and for that matter, the fate of Siraj and all of India—were sealed.

THE ATTACK COMES

The nawab's capital city was Murshidabad, about 160 miles (257.5 km) up the Hooghly River from Calcutta, and there Siraj promptly organized an army of 18,000 horsemen, 30,000 infantry, 500 elephants, and 2,000 camels. At the end of May, the nawab headed south toward Calcutta. Those watching the procession of his army said it took ten hours to pass by one spot. As Siraj reached British trading posts, he captured them and took the British owners hostage.

News of this reached Calcutta, but Governor Drake did little to prepare the city for a siege—he stockpiled some food and ordered his officers to be in a state of readiness, but did not impart any sense of urgency. There was no defense plan.

Fifty cannons, which had been unloaded from a ship three years before for the defense of the fort, had simply sat rusting in a warehouse and now were useless. There were large supplies of gunpowder, nearly all of it, however, damp.

The garrison of soldiers amounted to about 300, both British and Indian, as well as mercenaries of all nationalities. An additional seventy soldiers were in the hospital with various diseases. By June 8, Drake, now growing more alarmed as Siraj's army got closer and closer, begged the captains of the Company ships in the harbor to send in crewmembers to partake in the defense of the Fort. Other defenders were found in the so-called "Black Town," the shantytown area of Calcutta. All in all, those manning the ramparts of Fort William numbered perhaps 550.

By June 12, Siraj and his army were outside Calcutta and the British were in a fever of preparation. Despite the fact that daily temperatures reached 100°F (39°C; the monsoon was only a few days off and Indian weather was at its most formidable), men, women, and children stuffed mattresses in cracks in the fortress walls, prepared bandages, and shored up defenses as best they could.

On the morning of June 16, the attack came. With drums pounding and scimitars waving, a vast force of Indians soldiers crashed out of the jungle 200 yards (182.9 m) from one of the fort's strong points, which was held by only twenty-four soldiers, three British, and the rest recruited Indian mercenaries. Wave after wave of Bengal troops were repulsed with heavy losses, in part caused by the highly accurate cannon fire of the *Prince George*, a British ship in the harbor. The soldiers in the redoubt fired their muskets frantically and bravely, pouring water over them to cool them in the immense heat, but the invaders nearly overwhelmed them until more cannon fire drove them at last back into the jungle.

A further attack that afternoon was broken up by cannon fire, one blast of which so frightened two elephants that they ran amok, tearing up the ranks of Siraj's troops. Eight hundred of the nawab's men lost their lives that day, as opposed to a handful of the fort's defenders.

"A HELLISH CACOPHONY"

Fort William could not possibly hold out for long, however. The forces of the nawab moved through Black Town, burning shanties and killing all before them, as hundreds of refugees flocked to the fort. Attack after attack was met bravely

by Fort William's defenders—most of them young merchants who had never before fired a shot in anger—but gradually, one by one, they were killed. The nawab's cannon found the range and sent iron balls hurtling directly through the crumbling walls of the fort, tearing apart women and children who huddled on the parade ground in terror.

As flames rose all around the fort, shimmering like mirages in the intense heat, one observer wrote of the incessant "hellish cacophony" of shouts, screams, shots, and collapsing buildings. Elephants brayed and trumpeted, a sound especially unnerving to the British. The nawab's soldiers took the high houses surrounding the fort, whose roofs and uppermost windows overlooked the walls, and began an incessant and highly dangerous sniping fire, so that one risked one's life to walk anywhere in the open.

When word leaked out that the fort's supply of dry powder was nearly at an end, chaos ensued. The only possible chance of safety now lay in the British vessels at anchor in the harbor, and a mob began to race down to the wharves to find boats that might take them out to the ships. Roughly 200 women and children found their way onto a boat meant to hold forty. As the boat slowly made its way into the river, soldiers of the nawab shot fire arrows into it from a rooftop, setting women's dresses on fire, causing them to jump screaming into the river's swift currents. The boat overturned, and all 200 drowned.

To make matters worse for the beleaguered city, Governor Drake, along with the military commander of Fort William and other high British officials, now raced in full view of the populace down to the docks and boarded a boat that took them out to a waiting British warship. This escape and abandonment of duty on Drake's part was to go down as one of the most ignominious in British history and he was sacked by the Company as soon as he got back to Britain. But the rest of the fort's British population, seeing Drake flee, decided to flee themselves, while they could.

That left one unusual man in control of the fort and its now 170 fighting men: John Zephaniah Holwell.

"OUR PRESUMPTION IN DEFENDING THE FORT"

The forty-five-year-old Holwell was Chief Magistrate of Calcutta, a man with a somewhat shady background (see "Will the Real J.Z. Holwell Please Stand Up," page 67) who, in the way of Britishers with difficult backgrounds at the time, had found himself making a new start with the East India Company in Calcutta. Holwell was intensely ambitious and also very brave; when Governor Drake abandoned the fort, he decided to take charge and organize the few remaining soldiers for a last stand. The fact that this was pointless did not seem to bother him—historian Jan Dalley believes he may have expected rescue from the ships in the harbor and wanted to be seen as a heroic figure holding off the nawab's forces.

THE ESCAPE AND ABANDONMENT OF DUTY ON GOVERNOR DRAKE'S PART WAS TO GO DOWN AS ONE OF THE MOST IGNOMINIOUS IN BRITISH HISTORY AND HE WAS SACKED BY THE COMPANY AS SOON AS HE GOT BACK TO BRITAIN.

Holwell's men, firing with their last powder, accounted for hundreds of dead Bengals, but it did not change the outcome of the story. When Holwell at last surrendered on June 20, Calcutta fell and was immediately swarmed over by looters. Holwell was called in front of Siraj and given a dressing-down—the nawab, according to another British prisoner who was present, "expressed much resentment at our presumption in defending the Fort against his army with so few men." Siraj also said that the British were "fools" to have forced him to destroy such a fine city.

REFERENCES

A. *King's Bastion*
B. *Queen's Bastion*
C. *Prince of Wales's Bastion*
D. *Duke of York's Bastion*
E. *Duke of Gloucester's Demi Bastion*
F. *Duke of Cumberland's Demi Bastion*
G. *Royal Gate*
H. *Treasury Gate*
I. *Plassey Gate*

K. *St. George's Gate*
L. *Calcutta Gate*
M. *Water Gate*
N. *Forts Ravelin*
O. *Pocock's Ravelin*
P. *Clive's Ravelin*
Q. *Smith's Ravelin*
R. *Vansillart's Ravelin*
S. *Carlton Counterguard*

REFERENCES

T. *World's Counterguard*
U. *Conway's Redoubt*
V. *Argyll's Redoubt*
W. *Commanding Officer's House*
X. *Main Guard*
Y. *Artillery Barracks*
Z. *Arsenal and Armoury*
aaaa. *Casemates in the Gorges of the Bastions*
b. *Barracks for Soldiers*

cc. *Officers' Barracks*
d. *Soldiers' Barracks*
eeee. *Old Powder Magazines*
f. *New Powder Magazine for 22*
g. *Magazine for Grain*
h. *Ordnance Store House*
iii. *Casemates for 800 Men*
k. *New Officers' Barracks*
l. *Reservoir*

PLAN of FORT WILLIAM

A PLAN OF FORT WILLIAM, CIRCA
1762-1799. CONSTRUCTED BY THE
BRITISH, IT WAS NAMED AFTER
KING WILLIAM III AND CONTAINED
THE MAIN WAREHOUSES AND
BUSINESS OFFICE OF THE EAST
INDIA COMPANY.

© THE BRITISH LIBRARY/ HIP/
THE IMAGE WORKS

With that, he irritably sent Holwell back to join the other prisoners, who were being forced to sit in the middle of the burnt-out parade ground, surrounded by corpses and debris. There were 146 of them, according to Holwell's count, "those who had borne arms," as he was later to write, "[and those of] all sorts and conditions, black, brown, and white."

There was one woman present, Mary Carey, the Eurasian wife of British sailor, Peter Carey, who had fought bravely in the siege and who was now badly wounded. In fact, many of the prisoners were wounded. Night fell and still they sat on the parade ground, in stifling 100°F (39°C) heat—for it was literally the hottest night of the year, the night before the monsoon would hit and the weather would break—until finally, they were told to get up. It appeared to Holwell that they were to be taken into the barracks that lined the parade ground and he expected happily to spend a night in relative comfort.

WILL THE REAL J.Z. HOLWELL PLEASE STAND UP

John Zephaniah Holwell was born in Dublin in 1711 and grew up in London. His lineage is somewhat distinguished—his grandfather was a noted scholar and mathematician, his father a fairly well-to-do merchant. He went to school in Holland for a while, learning to do sums and keep books, but apparently decided to pursue a career as a doctor, as records have him serving a medical apprenticeship at Guy's Hospital in South London.

Next Holwell took a job as a surgeon aboard an British East India ship bound for Calcutta—this was in 1732—and he knocked around a good bit in the Indies, mastering Arabic and perfecting his skill as a surgeon. Finally, in 1742, he was named a surgeon with the Company at Calcutta, taking the place of a man who had died of fever. There was nothing mysterious about this nor was there in the fact that by the time of Siraj-al-Dawlah's attack, Holwell had been named Chief Magistrate, but there are apparently hints in the records of financial malfeasance—Robert Clive wrote that Holwell was "unfit to preside where integrity as well as capacity is equally necessary." There were also rumors that Holwell, while a regular churchgoer with his wife and children, had affairs with other men's wives.

All of this suspicion continued after the Black Hole of Calcutta. There were those who doubted the veracity of his story from the very beginning and there were those who were jealous of his appointment to temporarily take the place of Robert Clive when the latter was absent as acting Governor of Bengal. This appointment was short-lived, however—another man was placed in the job, and once again there were vague stories attributing financial irregularities to Holwell. These were never proven, and Holwell lived on to a ripe old age of eighty-seven, publishing books on India, Hinduism, and other subjects. Whatever he did in life, Holwell ended up a survivor.

Instead, to his horror, the guards "ordered us to go into the room at the southernmost end, commonly called the Black Hole prison, whilst others from the court of guards, with clubs and drawn scimitars, pressed upon those of us next to them. This stroke was so sudden and unexpected and the throng and the pressure so great upon us there was no resisting it."

Slowly, slowly, with Holwell at the front, the 146 prisoners were pushed into the Black Hole guardhouse, which measured 18 by 14 feet (5.5 × 4.3 m), and which was meant to hold, at most, five or six people. When the last person was pushed inside, the door slammed shut and this mass of sweltering humanity began collectively gasping for the little oxygen that entered the room through two small grilled windows high up on the wall.

THE BLACK HOLE OF CALCUTTA

What follows we know from a letter Holwell later wrote—a letter that was intended for publication and was indeed published under the title *A Genuine Narrative of the Deplorable Deaths of the English Gentlemen and Others Who Were Suffocated in the Black Hole*. It is a controversial account and subject to much dispute over the years (see "The Black Hole Revisited," page 70), especially concerning the number of people who were crushed into the tiny room—there were almost certainly nowhere near as many as Holwell claims. However, just as certainly, there were far too many for the size of the room, and the deaths that followed are some of the most horrible one can imagine.

Holwell had the luck to be standing near one of the windows and so was able to breathe in a little of the thick and humid night air, but those standing farther inside of the room had no chance at all. After a few minutes of gasping, panic set in. People at first shouted and begged the guards to open the doors, offering them wild bribes, but the guards refused to listen. Then there was an attempt to push toward the windows, but because the room was so dense with humanity, all this succeeded in doing was pack people further.

Men began to die one by one, their internal organs crushed. They could not move and so their corpses were simply held upright by the back. Some found that they could move their arms enough to take off their hats and wave them

THIS BRITISH LITHOGRAPH PRESENTED THE HELL OF THE BLACK HOLE TO A HORRIFIED BRITISH PUBLIC. ALSO, THE STORY WAS VASTLY EXAGGERATED BY JOHN HOLWELL, THE SHADY CHIEF MAGISTRATE OF CALCUTTA, WHO WAS TAKEN PRISONER AND WROTE ABOUT THE EXPERIENCE AFTERWARD.

THE BLACK HOLE REVISITED

John Holwell's account of that horrifying night in the Black Hole of Calcutta—the account that so roused the British public to rage and provided the moral excuse for British empire builders to take over India—cannot be completely accurate, as many writers have attested over the centuries.

For one thing, it has been proven through scientific experiments that 146 people simply cannot fit into a room measuring 18 by 14 feet (5.5 × 4.3 m), no matter how hard you shove them with rifle butts. In 1915, the English scholar J.H. Little published an influential article entitled *The Black Hole—The Question of Holwell's Veracity,* in which he claimed that Holwell had essentially made up the entire incident in order to pass himself off as a hero.

However, other scholars, like Jan Dalley and the Indian historian Brijen Gupta, feel that, although Holwell exaggerated, there was substantial truth to his story. And there were other survivor accounts, especially by Captain James Mills and a soldier named John Cooke, that agree with Holwell's, at least as to the essence of what happened.

It boils down to a numbers game. Holwell, whether deliberately or simply in miscalculation, vastly overestimated the number of people placed in the Black Hole. We will never know for sure, but best estimates are that about sixty-five people were placed in the Hole—still a staggering number in a room that size—and that forty-three of them died. Forty-three is the number of Fort William garrison members unaccounted for after Siraj-al-Dawlah's attack, and it is fairly certain that Holwell's count of twenty-three survivors is correct.

AS A PART OF THIS SERIES "THE WONDERFUL WORLD OF BRITAIN," POPULAR ENGLISH ILLUSTRATOR PETER JACKSON CAPTURED THE NOT-SO-WONDERFUL WORLD OF THE BLACK HOLE, WHERE TWO HIGHLY STEREOTYPED INDIANS CALLOUSLY IGNORE THE PLEAS OF THE DYING ENGLISH.

THE BLACK HOLE OF CALCUTTA

above their heads, to create a little breeze, but then many of these, too, died, so that it appeared that they were frozen in a ghastly charade of waving their hats to someone across the room.

As more and more people died, there was shouting and screaming in the room, followed by long periods of silence, followed by more swearing, begging, and crying. People nearest the door implored the soldiers to waken the nawab—surely he could not have meant for them to die this way—but they were told that the nawab was asleep and could not be disturbed.

People struggled to take off their clothes to cool their skin but found that the sweat dripping off their bare flesh made contact with the bare skin of others disagreeable in the extreme. Holwell kept his clothes on and at one point started sucking on his sweat-soaked shirt in order to get some moisture; he felt a movement at his side and realized that a soldier next to him was sucking on his other sleeve. Others pressed together, licking at each other's hair and necks. People began to vomit and urinate, and their bodily fluids made the floor slippery, so that people shuffled their feet in a macabre dance as they tried to stay upright. The stench of the place was indescribable.

Holwell did not know many of the people there, but a few scenes stood out for him—Mary Carey holding her husband as he died slowly in her arms; a father and a son, Ralph and John Bellamy, holding hands as they both fell into unconsciousness and then death. Finally, Holwell himself passed out, but he was grabbed by two friends and held upright, and mercifully was in a semi-dazed condition for much of the rest of the night.

"THE GHASTLIEST FORMS"

Finally, about five o'clock in the morning on June 21, a senior officer of the nawab was told what was happening and he went to Siraj and informed him. Siraj, who had indeed been asleep and who had not ordered this punishment for the prisoners, immediately ordered that they be released.

Just about six o'clock in the morning, the guards attempted to open the door, which pushed inward. Unfortunately, there were so many dead bodies against it that it would not open, no matter how many guards threw their weight on it. The enfeebled survivors inside were forced to pull corpses away from the door until, finally, eleven hours after they were imprisoned, twenty-two men and one woman came crawling and staggering out, "the ghastliest forms that were ever seen alive," Holwell wrote.

These few survivors gasped for fresh air on the parade ground as the guards pulled out the bodies of those who had died and dumped them unceremoniously in a ditch and covered them with earth. For some reason, every single survivor had a horrible case of pus-filled boils covering their skins, which merely added to their misery. Although Siraj had not ordered their ordeal, he wasn't especially sympathetic to them, either, calling the barely conscious Holwell before him and quizzing about the whereabouts of a supposed treasure the East India Company had hidden in Calcutta. He offered no solicitations about what had happened, although he did, apparently, proffer Holwell a glass of water.

. . . THE GUARDS ATTEMPTED TO OPEN THE DOOR, WHICH PUSHED INWARD. UNFORTUNATELY, THERE WERE SO MANY DEAD BODIES AGAINST IT THAT IT WOULD NOT OPEN, NO MATTER HOW MANY GUARDS THREW THEIR WEIGHT ON IT.

But Siraj was nothing if not capricious. A month after the horrible night in the Black Hole, he released his captives, including Holwell, who traveled to the safety of a Dutch-held city and returned home to Great Britain the following year. Preceding him, however, was *A Genuine Narrative of the Deplorable Deaths of the English Gentlemen and Others Who Were Suffocated in the Black Hole*, which was widely read in London and caused great outrage.

In 1757, Robert Clive, a lieutenant colonel in the East India Company, gathered together a powerful force and easily defeated Siraj at the battle of Plassey—Siraj was shortly thereafter killed by members of his own army—after which Clive installed a puppet prince as Nawab of Bengal. The British conquest of India had begun and, because of the Black Hole of Calcutta, there was not a British person anywhere who would gainsay it. Whatever truly happened that horrible night became, as Jan Dalley has written, "a turning point, a moment in which the relationship between the British and the Indians, a commercial relationship based solely on mutual interest, began to shift inexorably towards control and empire." Starting in 1858, India was directly ruled by the British Crown as a colonial possession, each of its provinces administered by a British governor or lieutenant governor. India would not gain independence until 1947.

The Black Hole itself soon disappeared as Calcutta was rebuilt and by the beginning of the nineteenth century no trace of it remained. However, the famous Lord Curzon, who was Viceroy of India beginning in 1899, insisted on finding the approximate spot and erecting a monument to the event. On it he described those who had died such a horrible death that night as "men whose life-blood cemented the foundations of the British Empire in India."

CHAPTER 5

"A SHRIEK OF BLANK DESPAIR"

THE MOUNTAIN MEADOWS MASSACRE, UTAH, 1857

MORMONS JEALOUSLY GUARDING THEIR WESTERN KINGDOM
SLAUGHTERED INNOCENT CIVILIANS IN A MASSACRE THAT
RESONATES THROUGH THE UNITED STATES TO THIS DAY

T HERE WERE THOSE WHO SAID GOD DELIBERATELY CREATED Mountain Meadows as a resting spot for the weary human beings trekking across the United States to the promised land of California in the mid-nineteenth century. Located some 300 miles (482.8 km) southwest of Salt Lake City, at the southern edge of the Wasatch Mountain foothills, Mountain Meadows was a valley five miles (8 km) long and only a few hundred yards (around 300 m) wide, fed by mountain streams that caused the grass to grow tall and green, and the pinion trees to sprout thickly on the slopes of the rounded hills that overlooked it. Before they got to Mountain Meadows, the settlers in their creaking wagon trains trekked for miles (kilometers) through arid rocky wastes. Afterward, they faced the rigors of the Mojave Desert. But for a few brief days at the Meadows, while their livestock fed and watered and their children played, it was as if they were being given a foretaste of the paradise of California.

One of the worst civilian massacres in U.S. history took place in this peaceful valley on September 11, 1857—a crime of religious zealotry that would not be equaled until other religious zealots flew airplanes into

THE FOUNDER OF THE MORMON RELIGION, JOSEPH SMITH WAS A CHARISMATIC BUT CONTROVERSIAL FIGURE WHO CLAIMED TO BE A PROPHET BUT WHOSE POLICIES ULTIMATELY LED TO HIS ASSASSINATION.

PORTRAIT OF JOSEPH SMITH (OIL ON CANVAS), AMERICAN SCHOOL, (19TH CENTURY)/ NATIONAL GALLERY OF ART, WASHINGTON DC, USA/ THE BRIDGEMAN ART LIBRARY INTERNATIONAL

U.S. public buildings on another September 11, almost a century and a half later. A special report to Congress called this killing of 120 men, women, and children of a peaceful wagon train "a hellish atrocity."

To make matters more shocking, the murderers were members of the all-powerful Mormon Church. Their actions that day caused a deep rift of distrust to open up between the rest of the United States and the Church of the Latter-day Saints, a chasm that continues as the ever-expanding and powerful Mormon Church still attempts to absolve itself of responsibility in the matter.

JOSEPH SMITH, PROPHET OF GOD

The trail that led to the bloody grass of Mountain Meadows began directly with Joseph Smith, the founding father of the Mormon religion. Smith was born in Vermont in 1805, but moved to western New York with his farmer father, mother, and eight siblings by the time he was fifteen. Smith grew up in an area that was rife with religious zealotry, so much so that it was called "the Burned-Over District" because so many evangelists, revival meetings, and religious renewals had hit the downtrodden people, causing the religion to be "burnt out of them." It was not burnt out of Joseph Smith, however.

As a seventeen-year-old, praying in his upstairs bedroom, he was visited by a figure bathed in light "as bright as the midday sun." This spirit or angel, whose name was Moroni, told Smith "God had work for [him] to do." More visitations in ensuing years led Joseph to discover, buried on a snowy hillside, the golden tablets upon which was engraved what would become the nucleus of the Mormon religion. By 1832, Smith had translated (or made up out of whole cloth, according to scoffers) *The Book of Mormon*, which held that two tribes of Israelites had been brought by God to North America 600 years before the birth of Christ. These people had at first built a powerful civilization but had then turned away from God and gradually regressed into being the Native Americans, whom Europeans had first found on the continent.

The Angel Moroni was the last of God's true prophets in the United States; he had safeguarded the story of the Mormons until Smith could reveal it to the world. Perhaps unsurprisingly, the fantastic tales of the *Book of Mormon* met a ready audience and the ranks of the religion Smith began calling the Church

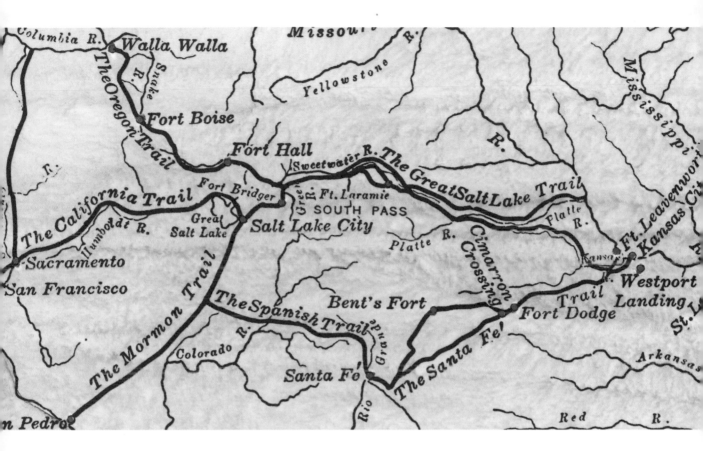

of Jesus Christ of the Latter-day Saints began growing. Just as unsurprisingly, Smith and his followers began to meet with resistance for their unorthodox views and habits.

PERSECUTION, POLYGAMY, AND DEATH

Forced to leave western New York by Christians who felt they were blasphemers, Smith and his Saints went to Kirtland, Ohio, on the southern shores of Lake Erie, to found a fresh Mormon community. The Saints believed it essential that a new Zion be built in the U.S. wilderness to create Mormon paradise on Earth that would be echoed in heaven.

At first, Smith and his 2,000 followers were met with open arms in Kirtland, but soon they had worn out their welcome. Smith—a handsome, charismatic figure whose likenesses bear a strong resemblance to photographs of the young

A MAP OF THE MAIN TRAILS WESTWARD IN THE MID-NINETEENTH CENTURY. ON THEIR WAY OVERLAND TO THE PROMISED LAND OF CALIFORNIA, THE FANCHER PARTY OF ARKANSAS EMIGRANTS MADE THE MISTAKE OF TAKING THE WRONG TRAIL TO CALIFORNIA.

Elvis Presley—began to espouse the philosophy of polygamy (he would take on forty-nine wives in all), although he called it "celestial marriage." This practice became a cause for great jealousy in and out of the Mormon Church, and in frontier communities where there were relatively few women.

As the panic of 1837 hit the United States, a bank Joseph Smith opened spread useless paper currency throughout the area. Facing criminal charges, he fled Kirtland in the middle of the night, first for Missouri and then for Illinois. The story was the same everywhere—as the ranks of the Mormons grew larger and larger (swelled with converts now arriving from England who had been converted by early Mormon missionaries), people began to resent them, and violence broke out. The lieutenant governor of Missouri said publicly: "Mormons are the common enemies of mankind and ought to be destroyed." A band of vigilantes attacked a Mormon settlement at Haun's Mill, Missouri, in 1838, and gunned down a family, including a pleading ten-year-old boy, in cold blood. "Nits grow lice," one of the killers reportedly said, as he put a bullet in the child's head.

SMITH BEGAN TO SELECT TOP-SECRET GROUPS TO SURROUND HIM. CHIEF AMONG THESE WAS THE SONS OF DAN, OR DANITES. THESE MEN WERE, ESSENTIALLY, ASSASSINS.

Under real threats such as these (and under many imagined ones), Joseph Smith created an armed force called the Army of God (whose 2,000 troops were a quarter of the size of the standing U.S. army at the time), styled himself a general, and wore a uniform of his own design. He also began to select top-secret groups to surround him. Chief among these was the Sons of Dan, or Danites. These men were, essentially, assassins. Taking their name from the biblical prophet Daniel, they dealt out vengeance in the form of "blood atonement" to people both inside and outside the Saints who had in some way crossed Smith or his religion.

As Smith made his policies of plural marriage official in 1843, more and more people became offended by his persistently shady business dealings and his bloody vigilante groups. Arrested by authorities, Smith was killed by an enraged mob while still in jail, and once again, the Latter-day Saints would move—this time to Utah, under the leadership of the steely-eyed Brigham Young.

"THE BLOOD OF THE PROPHET"

The stocky, redheaded, thirty-eight-year-old Brigham Young was a natural successor to Joseph Smith. A dynamic speaker who had made numerous successful recruiting missions to Great Britain on behalf of the church, Young would rule with absolute authority and an iron fist. One of his first acts, according to the Danite soldier John D. Lee, who would figure heavily in the Mountain Meadows Massacre, was to swear "by the eternal Heavens that I have unsheathed my sword, and I will never return it until the blood of the Prophet Joseph [Smith] . . . is avenged." But even Young knew they could not stay in Illinois and prosper. He needed to create his new Zion, his new city of heaven, farther west, in an unpopulated territory. Thus, Young led his people in an exodus and settled them in the arid country around the Great Salt Lake in present-day Utah, in the summer of 1847. It was not the biblically well-provisioned area many of the Saints had envisioned, but Young insisted they begin irrigating the country on the very afternoon they arrived, and gradually the outlines of the future Salt Lake City grew.

Two years later, when gold was discovered in the United States, Brigham Young controlled land that became a crucial link between California and the rest of the country. Young's Mormons controlled all access into and out of Utah: every mountain pass, every ford. By the early 1850s, he had essentially created his own theocracy, apart from and beyond the control of the federal government. Finally President Milliard Fillmore was forced to bow to the inevitable and make the Mormon leader governor of the new Utah Territory.

IN A PHOTO TAKEN AROUND 1850, BRIGHAM YOUNG, LEADER OF THE MORMONS AFTER JOSEPH SMITH'S DEATH, PEERS SHREWDLY AT THE CAMERA. YOUNG'S IRON-FISTED LEADERSHIP HELPED FOUND THE EMPIRE OF THE CHURCH OF THE LATTER-DAY SAINTS IN UTAH, BUT PUT HIM ON A COLLISION COURSE WITH THE U.S. GOVERNMENT.
UTAH STATE HISTORICAL SOCIETY

CELESTIAL MARRIAGE: SEALED FOR ETERNITY

Along with blood atonement, the concept of polygamy—otherwise known as celestial marriage or plural marriage—caused a great deal of controversy among the U.S. public and was, in reality, a disastrous public relations fiasco for the Mormon Church. The concept of plural marriage has been rejected by the Mormon Church since the beginning of the twentieth century, but in the nineteenth century it caught the imagination of the U.S. public, both prurient and censorious.

Started by Joseph Smith, celestial marriage is based on the belief that women can't enter heaven unless brought there by a man. Therefore, the more wives a man brings to heaven, the better his standing there, both because he was able to save more people and because a man with many wives was considered a prosperous man. Once the Mormons moved to Utah, Brigham Young carefully controlled polygamy—at any given time, perhaps only twenty-five percent of Mormons were polygamists, but Young (who had about twenty wives himself) got to decide to whom they were married. The situation often got sticky because it was possible for a woman to be married on Earth to one man but "sealed" in eternity to another, whom the women thought had the better possibility of getting into heaven. Because Young was the one who arranged these secret "sealings" he was privy to insider knowledge of the private lives of most of the members of his flock.

In some ways, the Mountain Meadows Massacre was instigated by a scandalous polygamous situation—Parley Pratt's murder after stealing another man's wife. After Brigham Young's death, wiser heads in the church turned against celestial marriage, ultimately denouncing it in 1890 under pressure from the U.S. government.

A POLYGAMOUS MORMON FAMILT IS PICTURED IN THIS PHOTOGRAPH, CIRCA 1890. THE MORMONS REFERRED TO POLYGAMOUS MARRIAGES AS "CELESTIAL MARRIAGES," BUT ULTIMATELY DENOUNCED THEM AROUND THE TIME THIS PHOTO WAS TAKEN.

GETTY IMAGES

But, even then, Young and his Mormons acted as if they were above the law. A U.S. surveying party was attacked and massacred in 1853 because the Mormons did not like the government measuring their land. Federal judges were killed. An emigrant who had foolishly courted Brigham Young's daughter was butchered. In almost all these cases, the perpetrators were local Native Americans—or so it seemed. The victims were scalped or otherwise hacked-up in what was presumed to be Native American atrocity style and witnesses saw painted warriors running away.

As these incidents increased, outrage mounted back east, and the federal government, under President James Buchanan, decided to send an army out west to quell what Buchanan and others believed to be a virtual rebellion in Utah Territory. In doing so, they decided the fate of the peaceful wagon train that was making its way toward the not-so-welcoming community of Salt Lake City.

"THE BETTER, RICHER LIFE"

The wagon train was known as the Fancher Train, after its leader, Alexander Fancher, and it originated from Harrison County, Arkansas. On March 29, 1857, it left Arkansas, heading for California, where Fancher's brother, John, had already started a ranch. Alexander Fancher, forty-three years old, perhaps epitomizes the best of U.S. pioneer stock. Sober, industrious, a Mexican-American War veteran and born leader, the father of eight children, Fancher had already led one wagon train to California and had returned to form another group of friends and neighbors to take with him to the rich new farm and pastureland of California.

People begged to go with Fancher, and he was able to pick and choose those who accompanied him. They were people like himself from a select group of about twenty to thirty close-knit families, and they formed an optimistic convoy of westward emigrants who, one local newspaper writer said on their departure, "were looking for the better, richer life that they envisioned California would hold for them." And, according to research done by Sally Denton in her book *American Massacre*, they were already fairly wealthy: "They had converted their life-savings into gold and were transporting it . . . Among the valuables hidden in the floorboards of the wagons or in the tickings of the featherbeds was as much as $100,000 in gold coins."

As the Fancher Train left Arkansas it numbered roughly 200 men, women, and children, a group size that normally did not receive trouble from Native Americans. Even so, Fancher had made sure that all the men were well armed and knew how to use their weapons. They were not expecting major problems, however, nor were they, as Mormon disinformation later put out, wild and boisterous, "swearing and boasting . . . that Buchanan's whole army was coming right behind them, and would kill every God Damn Mormon in Utah." They were in fact ordinary families seeking a new start, nothing more or less.

But the deck was stacked against them. As the Fancher Train approached Salt Lake, the Mormon community was abuzz with rumors that a force of U.S. troopers was coming to remove Brigham Young from his position and forcibly install federal officials. (In fact, Buchanan's army was being formed, although it would not arrive in Utah Territory until November 1857, at which point a nearly bloodless war would be fought between the Mormons and the U.S. government.)

Even worse for the Fancher Train, a prominent Mormon named Parley Pratt had just been murdered in Arkansas by the husband of a woman Pratt had taken as his twelfth wife. This killing outraged the Mormon community and increased their already simmering levels of paranoia. "We have borne enough of their oppression and hellish abuse," cried Brigham Young at a Founder's Day celebration just a few weeks before the Fancher Train arrived in Salt Lake Valley, "and we will not bear any more of it."

Arriving in the Great Salt Lake basin in early August, the Fancher Train members found themselves in what amounted to a hostile camp. No amount of money could purchase needed supplies and thus, a planned weeklong rest was shortened to two days before the lumbering wagon train moved out again.

There were two routes into California from Utah, a northern one—the California Trail, through Salt Lake City and Nevada—and Southern Trail (the so-called Old Spanish Trail) through the Mojave Desert. The Fancher Train had been planning on taking the northern route, but were convinced by a Danite named Charles Rich—who rode into their camp near Salt Lake City giving them orders that they must leave the next day—that the Southern Trail was safer from Native Americans, and that there was more feed for the cattle along the way, especially in a sweet little valley called Mountain Meadows.

NONE WILL BE SPARED

As the Fancher Train headed south, a conspiracy swirled around them; the details remain unclear at times, but its outlines are sharply defined. On September 1, Brigham Young met with Paiute Indian leaders in Salt Lake City. Using his son as interpreter, Young told the tribal leaders that all the cattle on the Old Spanish Trail were theirs for the taking—a clear reference to the large and valuable herd that accompanied the Fancher Train. "The prophet's message to the Indian leaders was clear enough," writes Jon Krakauer in his book *Under the Banner of Heaven*: "He wanted them to attack the Fancher wagon train."

The very next day, the Paiutes left Salt Lake City and headed for southern Utah. In the meantime, the Fancher Train was passing near Cedar City, Utah, about thirty-five miles (56.3 km) from Mountain Meadows, on September 4. There they were refused food and cattle feed, as well, but directed to the Meadows as a place where they could at least rest and refresh themselves. Unbeknownst to them, the Danite John D. Lee had already arrived at Mountain Meadows with a mixed force of Paiutes and Mormons, the latter of whom painted their faces to make themselves look like Native Americans. They watched the Fancher Train enter the valley and make camp on the night of September 6. When full dark came, Lee and his men crept down from the hills and concealed themselves among nearby rocks and stands of brush.

Monday morning, September 7, 1857, broke bright and clear. The emigrants gathered brush and set up their cookfires, and soon the smell of coffee rose into the air. People warmed themselves by the fires and chatted. Then, recalled one survivor: "While eating a breakfast of rabbit and quail, a shot rang out and one of the children toppled over." A second volley of shots struck between ten and fifteen people. Seven were immediately killed; the others, including Alexander Fancher, were mortally wounded.

Although they were taken by complete surprise, the experienced men and women of the Fancher party sprang instantly into action. They circled the wagon trains, dug ditches behind them, both as firing trenches and to protect the women and children and wounded, and immediately returned fire. They assumed they were being attacked by Native Americans, could hear horrible howling cries, and could see dark-skinned men darting through the woods in the distance. Yet this seemed strange to them, because Paiutes of the region were far from bloodthirsty—they were in fact known as peaceable people who owned very few firearms.

The emigrants fought tenaciously, and their witheringly accurate fire—three Paiutes were immediately killed—had a telling effect. The Mormons and their Native American allies realized that destroying the Fancher Train was not going to be easy. The Paiutes in the hills told Lee and his men that they were going to leave—that this bloodletting was not what they had bargained for. Knowing he needed more reinforcements, Lee rode to Cedar City to recruit a new batch of Mormon men. According to Lee, he received three wagon-loads of "well-armed men" under the command of Major John Higbee. Higbee told him that this was no longer a mission to merely frighten or harass the Fancher Train, or rob them of their rich belongings. Higbee said that "it is the orders of the President [Brigham Young] that all emigrants must be put out of the way . . . none who are old enough to talk are to be spared."

"GOOD GOD, NO, MATT!"

In the meantime, the siege of the emigrants in Mountain Meadows had continued. Despite their brave stand, they were at a considerable disadvantage. They had the tactical error of not setting up camp near the stream that ran through the Meadows (because the ground around it was too wet), and so needed to traverse 100 open yards (91.4 m) under fire to get water. As the days wore on, the emigrants suffered more and more from thirst. Desperate, they dressed two little girls in "spotless white," and sent them to the stream with pails for water, but this appeal to the humanity of their enemy did no good—the girls were shot dead instantly.

By Wednesday, Lee had returned with his reinforcements and the volume of fire pouring down on the Fancher Train increased. More men and women were killed, and corpses lay swelling and stinking in the sun. In another desperate move, two men snuck out of the camp one night, attempting to find another emigrant train to summon help from. Successfully escaping their encirclement, they made their way out of the valley and rode until they came to a small campfire around which three men sat peacefully smoking. Thinking they might be men from another wagon train, one of the emigrants frantically spilled out their story of being attacked in Mountain Meadows. But the men around the campfire were Mormons—Danites, as it turned out—and the emigrant was awarded with a bullet in the chest. The other managed to elude them and race back to the encircled wagon train, where he poured out his story. If Fancher's party had ever had any doubt that it was Mormons, not Native Americans, behind their predicament, they did not now.

But when John D. Lee rode into their camp under a white flag on Friday, September 11, there was little they could do but trust him. They were nearly out of ammunition and dying of thirst. Lee told them that he was a major in the Mormon militia, that while the Native Americans had gone "hog wild," he would try to save them by taking them under the protection of himself and his men and leading them into Cedar City. All they had to do, he said, was give up their guns and ammunition so as not to inflame the Paiutes. Despite their suspicions of the Mormons, there was little else the emigrants could do—they had perhaps twenty rounds of ammunition left among them, as well as an increasing number of wounded who needed care. With Alexander Fancher dying, his nephew Matt was in charge of the party. Even though Fancher exclaimed deliriously: "Good God, no, Matt!" the decision was made, and the men in the Fancher party laid down their arms.

JOHN D. LEE, THE MORMON ELDER WHO LED THE ATTACK AT MOUNTAIN MEADOWS, WAS CONVICTED OF MURDER AND EXECUTED TWENTY YEARS AFTER THE MASSACRE. MANY REMAIN CONVINCED LEE WAS A SCAPEGOAT WHO HAD ACTED UNDER THE DIRECT ORDERS OF BRIGHAM YOUNG.

UTAH STATE HISTORICAL SOCIETY

THE MASSACRE

Once this fatal decision was made, Lee organized the emigrants into three parties. First went the wagons of wounded of both sexes, then the women and children, finally the men, walking single file about 10 feet (3 m) apart, each accompanied by a Mormon guard. These men were led by Major Higbee, sitting high on his horse. After about a mile (1.6 km) of walking, he stopped his horse near an open area surrounded by scrub oak. "Halt!" he shouted, and then fired his pistol in the air. "Do your duty!" And each Mormon then turned and shot the man he was guarding.

Pandemonium broke out, the emigrants attempted to flee, but were gunned down. Among the Fancher Train were so-called "apostate Mormons," who had given up their faith. These were singled out for the special treatment of blood atonement. Higbee, according to reports, approached one former Mormon he knew as the man lay wounded on the ground. "Higbee, I wouldn't do this to you," the man pleaded. "You would have done the same to me or just as bad," Higbee retorted, and then cut the man's throat.

As soon as the shooting started, the women and children in the wagons began to panic. Lee then gave the order to kill them. "From the survivors [in the wagon] went up such a piercing, heart-rending scream—such a shriek of blank despair" that everyone who heard it afterward remembered it. Sallie Baker, a child who survived, remembered how one Mormon gunman ran up to the wagon, raised his gun, and said: "Lord my God, Receive their spirits. It is for Thy kingdom that I do this." He then shot indiscriminately into the wagon. Another man shot two wounded men huddled together, killing them each with one shot. A fourteen-year-old boy was clubbed to death with the butt of a gun.

Two teenagers, Rachel and Ruth Dunlap, raced into a stand of trees, where witnesses said they were raped by Mormons and shot by Lee himself as they promised to "love him forever" if he spared their lives. Much of this killing was done with sword and knife, both by Paiutes and Mormons wearing warpaint, although one of the murderers later confessed that "mostly white men" had done the butchery. One young girl fell on her knees in front of a teenage Mormon boy, begging him to spare her. He said he would, but his father—whom some reports have as Lee—stabbed her to death as he held her.

A four-year-old girl remembered over half a century later seeing her mother "shot in the forehead and fall dead." Other witnesses watched "children clinging around the knees of their murderers, begging for mercy and offering themselves as slaves for life could they be spared. But their throats were cut from ear to ear in answer to their appeal." "Much later, one young survivor of the massacre was asked how she could remember everything in such detail. "You don't forget the horror," she replied. "And you wouldn't forget it either, if you saw your own mother topple over in the wagon beside you, with a big red splotch getting bigger and bigger on the front of her calico dress."

INNOCENT BLOOD

When most of the killings were finally over, there was left the matter of what to do with children who were considered to be of "innocent blood"—generally, under the age of eight. By this the Mormons meant that they had not yet attained the age of reason, and were thus innocent of whatever "crimes" their parents had committed, and in the eyes of God should be spared. However, it appears that several children of about eight became the last ones executed on the bloody meadow that day, when it was decided that they might be able to carry the tale of their terrible ordeal with them.

The rest of the children, about twenty in all, mainly seven years old and under, were led by wagon from the site of the massacre to a Mormon farm a few miles (kilometers) away. The screaming and wailing of the children, most of whom were soaked with the blood of their parents and many of whom were wounded grievously (two would later die) was unbearable to hear. The children were parceled out to Mormon families—in some cases the families of the men who had killed their parents and siblings—until the federal government tracked them down and repatriated them back to Arkansas in 1859. Astonishingly, the Mormons tried to demand money for taking care of their young victims.

The next day at Mountain Meadows, the Mormons moved among the stiff and twisted corpses, tearing clothes and jewelry off the bodies and ransacking the wagon trains for gold and useful goods. What they didn't take was given to the Paiutes. The Mormon militia then did a half-hearted job of burying the bodies—simply dumping them in ditches and tossing dirt on them—before swearing an oath to keep what had happened secret. Then they left what remained of the Fancher Train to the wolves and buzzards.

But the enormity of what had happened to these 120 men, women, and children could not be concealed and their killers, once the blood-lust left them, all seem to have realized it. Men like Higbee and his immediate superiors began by blaming the killings on the Paiutes, although, since the Mormons were in possession of the Fancher supplies, cattle, gold, and their surviving children, this was a little hard to believe. A few days after the massacre, Brigham Young wrote a letter dated before the killings, ordering southern Mormons not to harass the emigrants—an obvious attempt to prove his lack of involvement.

BLOOD ATONEMENT AND OTHER ATROCITIES

In 1856, Brigham Young preached to the faithful in Salt Lake City: "There are sins that men commit for which they cannot receive atonement in this world, or in that which is to come." The atonement of Jesus—his spilling his blood for them—does not apply. These were people, Young and other Mormons believed, who needed to be dealt with by the practice of "blood atonement"—not just by being killed, but by the practice of literally "having their blood spilled upon the ground."

The Danites, or Avenging Angels, terrified apostate Mormons by threatening blood atonement, which was usually done by slitting a victim's throat. Most blood atonement was involuntary, although there were times when repentant Mormons allowed themselves to be slaughtered to save their souls after they had committed a particularly heinous crime against the church. At the time of the Mountain Meadows Massacre, many of those present had their throats slit, and some historians have presented the entire affair as a kind of "blood atonement" for sins supposedly committed by the emigrants of the Fancher Train against the Mormons.

However, there were even more frightening atrocities against Mormons and non-Mormons in Utah during the mid-nineteenth century. The Mormon Bishop Warren Snow wanted to eliminate a younger man who was courting a woman whom Snow wanted for his wife, so he captured the man and had him castrated, nailing the poor unfortunate's private parts to a schoolhouse wall as a warning against sexual misconduct (or sexual competition). The man lived on, although he later died insane in a California mental hospital.

THE YOUNGEST SON OF ALEXANDER
FANCHER, KIT CARSON FANCHER
WAS FIVE YEARS OLD AT THE TIME
OF THE MOUNTAIN MEADOWS
MASSACRE. HE WATCHED HIS
FATHER DIE AT THE HANDS OF
MORMON ASSASSINS.

UTAH HISTORICAL SOCIETY

As reports by ensuing parties of emigrants reached the California newspapers and Washington, the U.S. public clamored for an investigation and the U.S. army sent Major James Carleton to look into the murders and gather up the surviving children. Even in 1859, Carleton found the scene of the massacre "horrible to look upon." He collected bushels of women's hair, which were lying, "in detached locks and masses" everywhere. Bones and skulls were scattered all over the area, as well as small pieces of cloth from children's clothes. A pathologist with Carleton noted that "many of the skulls bore marks of violence, being pierced with bullet holes, or shattered by heavy blows . . . or firearms disclosed close to the head."

This put the lie to Mormon claims that the victims had been killed by Native American arrows. Unfortunately, Carleton's report was insufficient to bring about a prosecution of those involved in the massacre, such was the power of the Mormon Church to block any investigation. Finally, twenty years after the massacre, the federal government brought charges for the killings against John D. Lee and four others, including Major Higbee. They only stuck against Lee, whom many were convinced was a convenient scapegoat to protect Brigham Young. Lee was convicted of murder, taken to Mountain Meadows, and, on March 23, shot by firing squad.

And there the matter lay closed—or so the Mormon Church hoped. But the massacre at Mountain Meadows has never disappeared, and has colored the relationship of the Mormon Church with the rest of the United States. Even at a time when it has distanced itself from polygamy and other controversial practices, the Mormon Church has not yet convincingly answered charges that it was fully involved in the deaths of the innocent emigrants passing through. It now admits that "local" Mormons took part in the massacre, not just Native Americans, but refuses to admit that Brigham Young ordered or had foreknowledge of the killings, as many historians believe he did. Until the true story behind Mountain Meadows is revealed, the reputation of the Mormon Church will remain controversial in the United States.

CHAPTER 6

"I LONG TO BE WADING IN GORE"

THE SAND CREEK MASSACRE, 1864

ONE OF THE MOST HORRIFIC OF INDIAN WAR MASSACRES, THIS SLAYING OF PEACEFUL CHEYENNE IN THEIR WINTER VILLAGE BY A COMPANY OF COLORADO MILITIA EXPLODED ALL CHANCE OF NATIVE AMERICANS AND WHITES COEXISTING PEACEFULLY

E ARLY ON THE FRIGID MORNING OF NOVEMBER 29, 1864, A Cheyenne woman left her lodge, blanket wrapped tightly around her shoulders, and walked sleepily off to find wood to kindle her breakfast fire. She was surrounded by about 100 white, conical dwellings belonging to her tribe, that of Chief Black Kettle, and she had no reason to feel alarmed when she heard a faint rumbling in the distance. Although a war had been waged between the Cheyenne and the white man this past summer, peace had arrived—and the Cheyenne were now in their winter quarters along the Sand Creek in Colorado Territory.

Thus the woman assumed the rumbling sound, growing ever louder, was that of a buffalo herd, and she was amazed at her village's stroke of luck—for meat had been rare that frigid winter and even now most of the men were out hunting. But then she heard the distinctive *crack* and *whap* of rifle bullets whizzing by and hitting the ground around her. As other Cheyenne began pouring out of their tents, shouts and screams rose into the air. The people began running, but the soldiers, wild-eyed, kicking and spurring their horses, were upon them.

MAP OF INDIAN TERRITORY, MID-NINETEENTH CENTURY. THE DARK AREAS ON THE MAP ARE INDIAN RESERVATIONS. THOUGH REFERRED TO ON THIS MAP AS A "BATTLE," WHAT REALLY HAPPENED AT SAND CREEK IN EASTERN COLORADO WAS A MASSACRE.

MINN.

GROS VENTRES, PIEGAN,
BLOOD, CROW

N. D.

SIOUX

CROW

ARIKARA,
GROS VENTRES,
MANDAN

Bismarck
FT. A. LINCOLN

FT.
RI

Missouri R.

Yellowstone R.

SIOUX

MIN

BATTLE OF CROW
LITTLE BIG HORN *

Rosebud R.

Tongue R.

Powder R.

S. D.
SIOUX

Missouri R.

SIOUX

Wood

FT. C. R. SMITH

WYO.

*Little
Big
Horn R.*

Big Horn R.

FT.
PHIL KEARNY

*Black
Hills*

Cheyenne R.

White R.

SHOSHONE
WAGON BOX BATTLE

* FT. RENO

Pine
Ridge Agency

* BATTLE OF
WOUNDED KNEE

Wounded Knee Creek

North Platte R.

GRATTAN'S DEFEAT *

FT. LARAMIE

NEBR.

• Ash Hollow

Platte R.

TREATY OF
HORSE CREEK

Horse Creek

COLO.

Republican R.

FT. L

BEECHER ISLAND *
FIGHT

KANS.

BATTLE OF
SAND CREEK *

• Sand Creek

Arkansas R.

BENT'S FORT

FT. LYON

TAH

N. M.

OKLA. ARAPAH

TEX.

Canadian R.

Rio Grande

BATTLE OF
THE WASHITA

* FT. C

ARAPAH

D BATTLES

What happened that day, and the next, would surpass in savagery any encounter between whites and Native Americans in the long and bloody history of the U.S. westward expansion. The first shots fired by the Third Colorado Regiment that grim and cold dawning would have enormous ramifications, far beyond the banks of the frozen Sand Creek, its sandy bluffs, and windswept prairies. The massacre that was about to ensue would make sure that the Plains Indians would fight to the death against the whites in the years after the Civil War, and would lead directly to other butchery, eleven years hence, at a place called Little Bighorn.

"THE CONCOURSE OF WHITES"

Before the cycle of violence started by the Sand Creek Massacre, the land between the Platte and Arkansas rivers, stretching all the way from central Kansas to the Rocky Mountains, had been the home of the Cheyenne and their allies, the Arapaho. The Cheyenne were a proud warrior people who fought with traditional enemies—the Sioux to the north, the Ute to the west, and the Comanche and Kiowa to the south—and hunted buffalo as they wandered their vast territory.

However, the Cheyenne had never had hostile intentions toward the whites, who began showing up early in the nineteenth century in the form of traders who sought to exchange guns, horses, and whiskey for furs. The Treaty of Fort Laramie, in 1851, had legally recognized that the Cheyenne and Arapaho were entitled to the land between the Platte and Arkansas, but unfortunately, gold changed this balance, as it often does. Gold was discovered around Pike's Peak in 1858 and suddenly a rush of miners poured into the area. Except that they weren't just traveling through on the way to California anymore, nor were they wandering fur traders or trappers, mountain men who often lived with and intermarried among the Cheyenne.

Instead, following the miners came merchants, farmers, schoolteachers, and soldiers. Communities rose up—including the city of Denver. At first, the Native Americans were welcoming. Their attitude could be summed up in the words of the Arapaho Chief Little Raven, who visited Denver and spoke to a local reporter. Little Raven "pledged his word for the preservation of peace and law and order by his people," he said. And he was glad that the white people were finding the gold that they valued so much. But, he told the reporter, he wanted to remind everyone that the land belonged to the Native Americans—and also to express the hope that the white people "should not stay around too long."

However, this was a fond hope, as even Little Raven must have known in his heart. The whites were there to stay, and criminal incidents—raping of Native American women, theft of Native American property—began to mount. The Cheyenne and Arapaho Indian agent William Bent—a man deeply trusted by the Cheyenne, into whose tribe he had married—wrote in 1859: "The concourse of whites . . . is constantly swelling and incapable of control or restraint by the government . . . These numerous and warlike Indians, pressed upon all around . . . are already compressed into a small circle of territory, destitute of food, and itself bisected athwart by a constantly marching line of emigrants. A desperate war of starvation and extinction is therefore imminent and inevitable, unless prompt measures shall prevent it."

"A STARVING CONDITION"

Prompt measures, at Bent's urgings, were taken. The federal government called for a conference to be held with the Cheyenne and Arapaho at Fort Wise (later Fort Lyon), the U.S. army outpost on the Upper Arkansas River that had formerly been William Bent's trading fort. In September 1860, Cheyenne chiefs Black Kettle and White Antelope and the Arapaho Little Raven, as well as other subchiefs of the tribes, agreed to a treaty in which they would be placed on a reservation in southeastern Colorado, thus ceding much of their traditional hunting grounds. In return, however, the U.S. government would provide each tribe (the Arapaho and the Cheyenne) with $15,000 a year for fifteen years, purchase livestock and farm implements for them, and essentially teach them to become farmers. Every single Indian would receive forty acres (0.2 km²) of land.

The Fort Wise Treaty might have temporarily lessened the growing tensions between whites and Indians, but it was never actually put into effect. After the treaty was signed, in February 1861, the United States plunged into the Civil War. The Union controlled Colorado Territory and the Confederates attempted an invasion from Texas. A group of Coloradan and New Mexican volunteers moved

A PORTRAIT OF THE CHEYENNE AND ARAPAHO CHIEFS WHO MET PEACEFULLY WITH THE WHITES IN DENVER IN 1864. BLACK KETTLE, SEATED FAR LEFT, SURVIVED THE MASSACRE AT SAND CREEK. WHITE ANTELOPE, SEATED BESIDE HIM, WAS MURDERED AS HE SANG HIS DEATH SONG.

DENVER PUBLIC LIBRARY, COLORADO HISTORICAL SOCIETY, AND DENVER ART MUSEUM

heroically to join Union forces resisting the rebel attack. One company, led by a former chaplain named John Chivington (see "The Fighting Parson," page 99) flanked the Confederate invasion force in New Mexico, caught its entire supply train in a canyon, and destroyed it, forcing the Rebels to withdraw. The Union Southwest was saved; John Chivington returned to Denver a hero, and was appointed colonel in charge of the military district of Colorado.

Chivington, who was often described as a "bull" of a man, over 6 feet (1.8 m) tall, barrel-chested, and loud, was given the task of protecting Colorado Territory from Confederate incursion, but he was more interested in keeping it safe from the Cheyenne. Chivington had his eye on a postwar career in politics and was an early supporter of statehood for Colorado. He sided with the burgeoning white population against the Native Americans, whom settlers began to feel were becoming more and more of a problem. As the war went on and Washington made no move to fulfill the obligations of the Fort Wise Treaty, settlers spoke of seeing Cheyenne, who were on the warpath against the Ute and the Kiowa, traveling through on horseback holding lances onto which were tied dripping and bloody scalps. This was not exactly a reassuring sight, even if the Native Americans didn't molest the settlers.

The problem was that the Native Americans had little food. The buffalo were fast disappearing and more and more white settlers were moving onto Native American land—and yet no reservation had been set up for the Cheyenne. And so Native Americans began raiding cattle herds belonging to whites. Troops were sent out, but usually found that the cattle had been butchered by the time they even got close to the Native Americans. A sympathetic Indian agent wrote: "Most of the depredations committed by [the Cheyenne] are from starvation. It is hard to make them understand that they have no right to take from them that have, when in a starving condition."

THE CHEYENNE WAR

By late 1863, most people in Denver, including Colonel John Chivington and Colorado Territory Governor John Evans, had heard rumors that thousands of Cheyenne (some even gathering with their traditional enemy, the Sioux) were joining forces to "exterminate" the whites in the spring of 1864. This was not true, but rage, fear, and paranoia against the Cheyenne began to reach a fever pitch. A newspaper in Denver called for "the extermination of the red devils" and suggested that able-bodied men in the city "take a few months off and dedicate that time to wiping out the Indians."

Colonel Chivington began to send his horse soldiers out across Colorado Territory, in response to continued incidents of stolen cattle. When they made attempts to disarm traveling bands of Native American warriors, skirmishes ensued. Between April and May of 1864, Chivington's troops engaged the Cheyenne in three small battles, burned three of their villages, and shot dead a chief who was attempting to parlay with them under a flag of truce. Chivington's orders to his captains were continually inflammatory. "Do not encumber your command with prisoner Indians," one such directive read.

His public utterances were much the same. Speaking to a gathering of church deacons in Denver, Chivington told them: "It is simply not possible for Indians to obey or even understand any treaty. I am fully satisfied, gentlemen, that to kill them is the only way we will ever have peace and quiet in Colorado."

The Cheyenne began to attack isolated settlements, killing and mutilating whites (see "They Killed and Scalped Mr. Eubanks," page 101). Soldiers responded by seeking out Native Americans wherever they could find them and killing them, whether or not they were guilty of atrocities. In the meantime, Governor Evans petitioned the federal government to allow him to raise a small army of "hundred-day" volunteers, whom he could use to augment his regular military force.

Finally, in September 1864, chiefs such as Black Kettle and White Antelope sought peace for their groups of Cheyenne and Arapaho, which numbered perhaps 600 to 800 men, women, and children. They arrived in Denver bringing with them white captives as a sign of good faith, and parlayed with Governor Evans and Colonel Chivington. Although no actual peace treaty was signed, the Native Americans informed the white men that they were done fighting and wanted to be put under the protection of the military, to keep them from being attacked by other whites. They were advised to go to their winter camps at about forty miles (64 km) from Fort Lyon, so that soldiers could protect them if necessary. Then all shook hands, had a photograph taken together, and disbanded.

"I HAVE COME TO KILL INDIANS"

Despite this apparently amicable meeting, Chivington still sought to make war on the Cheyenne. He simply didn't trust the Cheyenne—he thought they were pursuing what he called their "war in the summer, peace in the winter" policy, wherein they could wait out the frozen months without fear of attack, and then go on the warpath as spring arrived. Also, Governor Evans had finally received permission and funds to raise a regiment of short-term soldiers, but their enlistment was only for 100 days; after that, the so-called Third Regiment were to be disbanded. This group of mainly Denver layabouts and workers were becoming known derisively as "the Bloodless Third" and the "Hundred Dazers," and Chivington seems to have wanted to put them to work.

But the driving force behind the forthcoming bloodletting was Chivington's ambition and personality. He had convinced himself the only way to succeed politically in Colorado was to exterminate the Cheyenne. Therefore he decided to ignore the fact that the Cheyenne nearest to him were the very ones who had

THE FIGHTING PARSON

John Chivington was born on an Ohio farm in 1821. Because his father died when he was five, the family was poor, and Chivington was only able to go to school occasionally. He began running a small lumberyard but found himself drawn to the clergy and was ordained a minister in 1844.

Chivington was what used to be called a "frontier preacher." He moved with his wife and children from Ohio to Illinois to Missouri to Kansas, establishing churches and often filling the position of town sheriff. At one point, facing a turbulent congregation in Missouri, he preached a sermon with a Bible and two six-shooters side-by-side on the pulpit. "By the grace of God and these two revolvers, I am going to preach today," he said, earning himself the nickname "the Fighting Parson."

By the time the Civil War broke out, Chivington was a pastor in Denver. The Colorado Territorial governor offered him a commission as a chaplain in the Union Army, but he turned it down, asking instead for a "fighting" commission. He won his reputation against the invading Rebel army in New Mexico, was appointed head of military affairs in Colorado, and his career seemed to be on the rise. But then Sand Creek happened. At first, as he presented his version of the action at Sand Creek, Chivington was hailed as a hero, but then stories of atrocities and drunken troopers began to leak out, and even though Chivington resigned, he was forced to face a Congressional investigation. No criminal charges were ever brought against him, but a judge publicly called Sand Creek "a cowardly and cold-blooded slaughter, sufficient to cover its perpetrators with indelible infamy." In 1865, Chivington headed to Nebraska, where he worked for a few years as a freight hauler. He then began his wanderings—to California, back to Ohio— working as a newspaper editor and farmer. Perhaps thinking himself far enough away from Colorado, he ran for a state legislature seat in Ohio, but his opponents brought up the massacre and he was forced to withdraw. Friends in Denver got him a job as a deputy sheriff—dealing with town drunks and petty criminals—and this is how Chivington finished out the days before his death from cancer in 1892.

JOHN CHIVINGTON, THE "FIGHTING PARSON" WHO LED THE COLORADO MILITIA AT THE SAND CREEK MASSACRE, WAS FORCED TO RESIGN HIS COMMISSION AS WORD OF THE MASSACRE LEAKED OUT, BUT HE WAS NEVER PUNISHED FOR HIS CRIMES.

COLONEL JOHN MILTON CHIVINGTON (LITHO), AMERICAN SCHOOL, (19TH CENTURY) / PRIVATE COLLECTION / PETER NEWARK AMERICAN PICTURES / THE BRIDGEMAN ART LIBRARY come in peace and set off on an expedition to "punish" them on November 14, 1864. He had with him about 700 troopers—the entire Third Regiment, plus three companies of the Colorado First.

Although Chivington told his commanding officer that he didn't know where the Native Americans were and wasn't sure he could catch up with them, he headed directly toward Sand Creek, about forty miles (64.4 km) from Fort Lyon. It was a hard march for the soldiers, through thick, drifting snow and frigid temperatures. At one point, Chivington stopped at a stage post along the Arkansas River, where he had dinner with fellow officers and some civilians. The army men talked about how many scalps they were going to take. Chivington pushed his chair back from the table after his dinner and said: "Well, I long to be wading in gore."

Not all of the officers who were with Chivington agreed with what he was doing, however. Captain Silas Soule, Lieutenant Joseph Cramer, and Lieutenant James Connor told Chivington that an attack on the Native Americans would violate the spirit of the agreement reached in Denver in September and would be "murder in every sense of the word." Naturally, Chivington reacted violently when he heard this. He shouted in Lieutenant Cramer's face: "Damn any man who sympathizes with the Indians. I have come to kill Indians and believe it is right and honorable to use any means under God's heaven to kill Indians."

Despite their misgivings, Soule, Cramer, and Connor were forced to go along on the expedition. However, they agreed privately that they would not allow men under their command to engage in combat unless in self-defense.

"NOTHING LIVES LONG"

By about 8:00 p.m. on November 28, Chivington's column had reached a point not far from Black Kettle's camp. Their campfires were ordered snuffed out and the men moved out into the clear, chilly night in columns of fours, bringing with them four mountain howitzers. Needing a guide, Chivington had forced a rancher named Robert Bent, the half-Cheyenne son of the Indian agent William Bent, to lead the column. As it happened, both of his brothers—Charles and George—were at Sand Creek with Black Kettle's people.

"THEY KILLED AND SCALPED MR. EUBANKS"

Although there were not as many Native American atrocities as the panicked citizens in Denver might believe, more isolated settlers were vulnerable during the high summer of the Cheyenne War.

In August 1864, Cheyenne warriors attacked a tiny frontier settlement in Kansas and one of the women whom they captured was a seventeen-year-old girl named Laura Roper. She had been visiting some neighbors, Mr. and Mrs. Eubanks and their two young daughters, on a warm Sunday afternoon. It was such a nice day that the Eubanks offered to accompany her partway home and she accepted. As they were walking through some woods they heard yelling behind them. Roper then gave this account of what happened next:

> We knew at once [the yelling] was Indians. The little girl began to cry and Mr. Eubanks took us off the road and into the brush to hide. Not being able to quiet the child he stuffed his handkerchief into her mouth so tightly that she could not cry out. We then kept very quiet until they had passed, yelling as only Indians can, expecting to overtake us soon.

> Mr. Eubanks had just taken the handkerchief out of the little girl's mouth when he heard them returning. The child screamed from fright and the Indians were upon us in an instant. They killed and scalped Mr. Eubanks before our eyes, leaving his body where it fell. We were then put upon horses and our hands tied behind our backs. [The Indians] headed off towards some of our neighbors. A woman lived in the first house was simple-minded. She was so crazed with fright when the Indians came that she tried to fight them, scratching and biting. They shot her and took her boy, and another, both about nine years old, with them . . . They led my horse past the woman's body. She was not dead yet for as I passed she crossed her feet one over the other.

Laura Roper was brought back to the whites a few months later as a conciliatory gesture by a Cheyenne chief named Left Hand. Mrs. Eubanks had been sold to the Sioux, but was rescued by soldiers the following year, with one of her daughters. The other child was rescued from a different tribe, but died of disease before Mrs. Eubanks could reach her.

The Native American encampment was in a horseshoe bend of the Sand Creek, which was dry except for a frozen trickle running down the middle. There were 600 Cheyenne camped there, two-thirds of them women and children. A small group of Arapaho had pitched their lodges a few miles away. The Native Americans felt so safe they kept no night watch at all, which is why the first thing most of them heard, early on the morning of the 29th, was the sound of hoofs thundering, followed by gunshots. Coming upon the sleeping village at dawn, Chivington had ordered three companies to dash across the creek to cut off the Native Americans from their all-important pony herd—he did not want these unparalleled horsemen to have a chance to get up on their steeds to fight. Once the pony herd was cut off, these troopers swung in the direction of the village, dismounted, and began pouring rifle fire indiscriminately into the lodges.

Chivington in the meantime ordered men of his Third Regiment to attack, shouting to them to "remember the murdered women and children," who had been the victims of Cheyenne attacks. Two of his howitzers opened up, pouring canister shot into the group of scattering Native Americans, who by this time had raced out of their tents in panic. Most of the men in the village were absent on a buffalo hunt, but a few of those who were present formed a battle line and began to fight back. They had very few guns, however, and their bows and arrows were no match for rifles and howitzers. White Antelope, the great Cheyenne chief, walked out into the middle of Sand Creek and stood there, unarmed, with his arms folded over his chest, trying to show the soldiers that he had no intention of fighting them. They shot him down, and as he lay in the snow dying he sang his death song:

Nothing lives long.
Only the earth and the mountains.

Soldiers swarmed over his body and cut off his nose, ears, and testicles—the latter to make a tobacco pouch.

Black Kettle took out a large U.S. flag he had been given and attached it, along with a white flag, to a long lodgepole, and raised it above his tent, but it did no good. He kept telling his people that the camp was under protection, but

then the soldiers began closing in and firing on women and children, and Black Kettle could see the situation was hopeless. He started to run along with the rest of the Native Americans, but there was almost nowhere they could go.

About a hundred Native Americans raced into the nearly dry creek bed, where high bluffs at first gave them some protection against the bullets. They dug shallow trenches in the sand and hid there, but the soldiers found them, and surrounded the trenches, and began firing. An eyewitness named John Smith, a white interpreter, testified afterward that the soldiers "fired [on the Indians] until they had almost completely destroyed them. I think I saw altogether seventy dead bodies lying there; the greater portion women and children."

"MUTILATED THEIR BODIES IN EVERY SENSE OF THE WORD"

With the Native Americans panicked and running, the attack became a route. Chivington did little to control his men and they ran amok in small groups through the village, shooting anything that moved. One eyewitness reported:

> I saw one squaw lying on the bank whose leg had been broken by a shell; a solder came up to her with a drawn saber; she raised her arm to protect herself, when he struck, breaking her arm; she rolled over and raised her other arm, when he struck, breaking it, and then left

THIS NINETEENTH-CENTURY SKETCH SHOWS THE POSITION OF THE CHEYENNE TEEPEES AND THE ATTACKING SOLDIERS AT SAND CREEK. THE SOLDIERS WHO KILLED THE CHEYENNE LEFT THE CHILDREN FOR LAST, KILLING THEM AS THEY ROAMED THEIR VILLAGE IN SEARCH OF THEIR PARENTS.

her without killing her. There were some thirty or forty squaws collected in a hole for protection; they sent out a little girl about six year old with a white flag on a stick; she had not proceeded but a few steps when she was shot and killed. All the squaws in that hole were afterwards killed . . . The squaws offered no resistance. Every one I saw dead was scalped.

It was rumored that many of the men of the Third Colorado—the so-called "Bloodless Third" regiment of volunteers—were drunk during the attack at Sand Creek. This has never been proven, but certainly they acted like wild men, possessed of an insane rage. John Smith testified: "All matter of depredations were inflicted on [the Indians]. They were scalped, their brains knocked out; the [soldiers] used their knives, ripped open women, clubbed little children, knocked them in the head with their guns, beat their brains out, mutilated their bodies in every sense of the word."

Another soldier reported that the bodies of the Indians "were horribly cut up, skulls broken in a good many. I judge they were broken in after they were killed, as they were shot besides. I do not think I saw any but what was scalped; saw fingers cut off, saw several bodies with privates cut off, women as well as men." Many of the officers indulged in wholesale scalping. Some soldiers cut out the privates of dead squaws and used them to adorn their hats or draped them across saddle horns.

Saddest of all was the fate of the young children whose parents had been killed. They were generally left till last, and there are many stories of toddlers roaming the village amid the wholesale slaughter and mutilation, until someone noticed them. Then:

There was one little child, probably just big enough to walk through the sand. The little fellow was perfectly naked, traveling on the sand. I saw one man get off his horse, at a distance of about seventy-five yards [68.6 m], and draw up his rifle and fire. He missed the child. Another man came up and said: "Let me try to kill the son-of-a-bitch; I can hit

him." He got down off his horse, kneeled down, and fired at the little child, but he missed him. A third fellow came up and made a similar remark, and fired, and the little fellow dropped.

"THE EMBLEM OF JUSTICE AND HUMANITY"

The killing took the rest of the day and the morning of the following day. On the evening of the 29th, Colonel Chivington wrote his superior officer, claiming that he had won a great victory, saying that he had killed some 500 Native Americans after attacking a village filled with 1,000 Native Americans warriors. (Best estimates place the Native American death toll at Sand Creek at about 150, two-thirds of them women and children. Nine white soldiers died.)

Ever mindful of publicity, he sent a messenger to the *Rocky Mountain News* in Denver, reporting that his victory "was one of the bloodiest Indians battles ever fought on the Plains." He claimed that he had killed Black Kettle, which wasn't true. Black Kettle and other survivors crawled out of holes they had dug in the river bank after nightfall and made a dreadful forced march through the bitter cold "most of it on foot," as George Bent, one of the half-breed Bent brothers remembered, "without food, ill-clad, and encumbered with women

TAKEN SOMETIME IN THE 1870S, THIS IS A PICTURE OF AN ARAPAHO CHILD TAKEN AFTER THE SAND CREEK MASSACRE AND RAISED BY WHITES.

DENVER PUBLIC LIBRARY

and children." They traveled fifty miles (80.5 km) before they reached the safety of the warriors in their buffalo camp. When the warriors heard what happened, their grief was so great that they wailed, and took out knives and gashed their skin. All of the Bent brothers now renounced the blood of their white father, William Bent, and joined the Cheyenne to fight the white men.

Though Chivington hadn't killed Black Kettle, he had killed White Antelope, Standing in the Water, One-Eye, War Bonnet, Two Thighs, Bear Man, Yellow Shield, and Yellow Wolf—every chief who wanted to coexist peacefully with the whites. "In a few hours of madness at Sand Creek," writes Dee Brown in his classic *Bury My Heart at Wounded Knee*, "Chivington and his soldiers destroyed the lives or the power of every Cheyenne and Arapaho who had held out for peace with the white man." In a gathering of the Cheyenne shortly after Sand Creek, the Indians rejected the failed policies of Black Kettle and flocked to the militant society of Cheyenne warriors, the Dog Soldiers, and their chief Tall Bull, as well as to the fierce Roman Nose and his band of warriors.

The Sioux now joined forces with the Cheyenne and Arapaho—something the whites had always feared—and in January 1865 launched a series of retaliatory raids against the whites. They killed soldiers and settlers, burned the entire town of Julesburg and scalped its inhabitants, and raided up and down the Platte River, eventually killing hundreds of settlers and soldiers. It was the beginning of a bloody conflict that would reach its full fruition in June 1876, when the Sioux and Cheyenne attacked and destroyed the command of George Custer at Little Bighorn. Because of the massacre at Sand Creek, any hope of finding a rational solution as to how whites were to live with Native Americans had disappeared.

Back in Denver, the Third Colorado, led by John Chivington, paraded through the streets with their bloody trophies held high, but it was to be Chivington's last moment of triumph. When stories began to trickle out about the atrocities at Sand Creek—many of them leaked by the officers who had refused to partake in the killing—Chivington was forced to resign his commission. A Congressional investigation took testimony from many of the attackers, including Chivington, who claimed that he saw few, if any, women and children killed, and also claimed he was justified in his attack on the camp because of a

BECAUSE OF THE MASSACRE AT SAND CREEK, ANY HOPE OF FINDING A RATIONAL SOLUTION TO THE PROBLEM OF HOW WHITES WERE TO LIVE WITH NATIVE AMERICANS HAD DISAPPEARED.

white scalp supposedly found in one of the lodges. The committee had no power to take action against Chivington, but it roundly condemned him: "Wearing the uniform of the United States, which should be the emblem of justice and humanity . . . he surprised and murdered, in cold blood, the unsuspecting men, women, and children of Sand Creek, who had every reason to believe they were under the protection of United States authorities."

CHAPTER 7

A BLOODY EASTER SUNDAY

THE COLFAX MASSACRE, LOUISIANA, 1873

THIS LITTLE-KNOWN AND MURDEROUS EPISODE IN RECONSTRUCTION HISTORY SET BACK THE CAUSE OF CIVIL RIGHTS IN AMERICA FOR A CENTURY

O N AN APRIL DAY IN 1865, IN A PRIVATE HOME IN THE VILLAGE of Appomattox Court House, Virginia, General Robert E. Lee surrendered his Army of Virginia to General Ulysses S. Grant. Grant was short, solid, mud-spattered, and informal; Lee was six feet (1.8 m) tall, erect, wearing a dazzling uniform from which hung a jeweled sword. They treated each other with the courtliness of old comrades in arms and honored foes, and after a short period of time had worked out a surrender agreement that signified the end of a war that had taken 620,000 lives and torn the United States apart.

Ever since, schoolchildren have learned that the meeting at Appomattox ended the Civil War. In fact, as historian William Gillette has written, "Appomattox signified much but settled little." Slavery was now dead, but what would become of the slaves who were now emancipated but without livelihoods and homes and who were living surrounded by their former masters?

Far less known than that poignant day at Appomattox would be another day in April, an Easter Sunday eight years later, when the simmering tensions left by the issues that Appomattox had not even come close to solving erupted in violence in a Louisiana county named for Ulysses S. Grant. The

THIS 1873 IMAGE FROM *HARPER'S WEEKLY* SHOWS AFRICAN AMERICANS REMOVING THE DEAD FOLLOWING THE COLFAX MASSACRE. AT LEAST SIXTY WERE KILLED DURING THE MASSACRE OR DIED LATER OF THEIR WOUNDS.

GETTY IMAGES

result was sixty black men massacred in cold blood and a Supreme Court decision that would stymie the cause of Reconstruction in the South and set back the civil rights movement 100 years.

"WITH MALICE TOWARD NONE"

The word "reconstruction" simply means "to build again," but after the Civil War there was nothing simple about the policy of Reconstruction. Even while the war was being waged in its final year, the North, under Republican President Abraham Lincoln, debated how to treat its soon-to-be vanquished foe. Lincoln, in his second inaugural address given just a month before both Appomattox and his assassination, signaled that he was willing to be charitable toward the South when he closed with the famous words:

> With malice toward none, with charity for all, with firmness in the right as God gives us to see the right, let us strive on to finish the work we are in, to bind up the nation's wounds, to care for him who shall have borne the battle and for his widow and his orphan, to do all which may achieve and cherish a just and lasting peace among ourselves and with all nations.

But there were others, known as "Radical Republicans," who were pushing for a much firmer hand when it came to the terms by which the defeated Southern states would be let back into the Union and to the rights to be extended to "freedmen," the 4 million former slaves. Lincoln had wanted to extend the right to vote to freedmen, but also to allow Southern states back into the Union once only 10 percent of their white voters took an oath of allegiance to the Union and pledged to agree to the emancipation of the slaves.

He also wanted, importantly, to reimburse the Southerners for the loss of slaves. As abhorrent as this policy seemed to Northern abolitionists and radical Republicans, he understood that without their slave "property" Southern planters and farmers would be ruined and that their resentment would do much to keep the nation from healing.

However, Radical Republicans repudiated both the policies of Lincoln and Andrew Johnson, who became president after Lincoln was killed. Johnson, originally from Tennessee, offered a pardon to all Southerners except leading Confederate generals, and authorized them to create new state governments. Freedmen were excluded from the process. Most of these new governments immediately enacted so-called Black Codes, which limited the ability of freedmen to find work outside of their former plantations, refused them the right to vote, and failed to provide public funds for their education.

Radical Republicans overrode Johnson's vetoes of their legislation, overturned his programs, and came within one vote of impeaching him. They divided Southern states into five military districts, forced them to repeal the Black Codes, and mandated that each state agree, as a precondition for re-entering the Union, to give blacks full emancipation, including the right to vote. As a part of this agreement, they were required to ratify the 14th Amendment to the Constitution, passed in 1866, which guaranteed blacks the same rights of citizenship as whites.

Reluctantly, Southern states complied. Blacks began to send legislators to Congress, elect mayors and state assemblymen, and find their way into the U.S. political system.

"THE INVISIBLE EMPIRE OF THE SOUTH"

There now began the bloody and violent period in the South that has been called the second Civil War. Whites, most of them former Confederate soldiers, formed paramilitary organizations. Chief among these was the Ku Klux Klan, which began in Tennessee in 1865 and evolved into a terrorist group led by Nathan Bedford Forrest, a former Confederate general. The Klan called itself "the Invisible Empire of the South" and began, early after the war, to target blacks and white Republicans, at first by fomenting riots. In Memphis in 1866, a Klan-inspired riot killed forty-six blacks and wounded seventy others. Two months later in New Orleans, a white mob attacked blacks attending a suffrage convention and killed thirty-seven of them.

In 1868, as Ulysses S. Grant was running for president on the Republican ticket, the Klan attempted to keep black voters (the vast majority of them Republican) away from the polling places. The numbers are astonishing—2,000 murders committed in Kansas in connection with the election, and 1,000 in Louisiana. A special Klan terrorist tactic was the assassination and beatings (see "The Ordeal of Abram Colby," page 115) of black politicians. Even so, Grant won an easy victory in 1868 and again in 1872, and was instrumental in passing laws that outlawed the Ku Klux Klan. However, with other distractions, he did not rigorously pursue prosecution of the Klan, and the Klan and similar organizations only grew stronger as whites fought to retake control of Southern states from blacks and liberal Republicans. By 1870, white Democrats had returned to power in Alabama, Virginia, Tennessee, North Carolina, and Georgia. But nowhere was the power struggle more vicious than in Louisiana.

The Republicans had been more successful in hanging onto control in Louisiana for several reasons. Blacks outnumbered whites in that state, particularly in the populous counties (parishes, as they are called in Louisiana). Also, the black population of New Orleans, Louisiana's chief city, was more powerful and sophisticated than that of other southern cities. Finally, New Orleans, as a port city, was controlled directly by its powerful custom house, where jobs were handed out by political patronage. Because the chief custom collector was James F. Casey, who was married to a sister of Julia Grant, wife of President Grant, he wielded an enormous amount of power in the Republican cause. And this power was not always used wisely.

When the Radical Republicans wanted to oust Louisiana Governor Henry Clay Warmoth (who had supported certain Democratic causes and whom Grant disliked personally), they held a state convention in Warmoth's absence, and federal troops, armed with rifles and two Gatling guns, kept the Governor from attending. In the Louisiana gubernatorial election of 1872, the radical Republican candidate, Illinois carpetbagger William Kellog, defeated Democrat John McEnery, although the election was marked by such violence and voter fraud it is hard to determine who actually won. In response, McEnery formed his own state legislature and his own militia, which in March of 1873 attempted to seize control of police stations in and around New Orleans.

"WE THE WHITE PEOPLE OF LOUISIANA"

The federal government made attempts to restore order in Louisiana but the Grant administration began to waffle, afraid that too strong or violent a response would provoke Southern whites even further. So for months, Louisiana was governed by two sets of governors and legislatures. Mayhem was in the air. The platform of the state Democratic Party opened with the words: "We, the White People of Louisiana," and one influential New Orleans paper claimed that "a war of the races" was imminent.

This unrest now spread outward from the major cities to the countryside and reached a quiet town called Colfax in the Grant Parish, on the Red River in the northern part of Louisiana. Colfax had been named after Grant's first-term vice-president Schuyler Colfax and the county itself was named after Ulysses S. Grant. It was one of a number of Louisiana parishes created after the Civil War to build local support for the Republican administration in Washington. Almost all of the land of Grant Parish had originally been a part of the huge

plantation belonging to the Calhoun family. It was fertile "bottom land" between the Red River and the piney hills of the Louisiana backwoods country.

Colfax was the country seat; it consisted of a collection of tumble-down cabins, many of them slave cabins from pre–Civil War times, which were inhabited by blacks. Most of the blacks were former slaves who now farmed small patches of land and worked in various conditions of indentured servitude for whites, who owned large parcels of land in the area.

Yet things were not quite unchanged since the days of slavery. Blacks earned a wage, even if a poor one, and could save a little money. A black Union army veteran opened his own general store; more black men formed political clubs and voted in local and national elections, beginning in 1868. Blacks began to acquire minor political positions: justice of the peace, constable, county surveyor.

Many of the whites in Grant Parish, heavily outnumbered by the black population, approved of these changes, seeing them as a microcosm of the way Reconstruction should work. The white Republican sheriff, Delos White, originally from New York, said of the "sober and industrious" blacks of the parish that "with any kind of favorable chance, they will outstrip the whites in material prosperity."

Naturally, this did not sit well with local whites who belonged to the paramilitary organizations springing up—not just the Klan, but groups like the White League and the Knights of the White Gardenia, whose purpose, as its bylaws said, was "the better preservation of the white race and to see that the white blood was handed down unmixed with the offensive globule of African blood." Some of these men, led by a Colfax citizen and Confederate Army vet-

THE ORDEAL OF ABRAM COLBY

Abram Colby was born into slavery in the state of Georgia, educated himself, and was elected to the state legislature of Georgia after the Civil War. He was an uncommonly brave man, both a political organizer and radical Republican at a time when the Ku Klux Klan was killing such men by the hundreds. We have a first-hand record of what happened to Colby because he was called to Washington to testify in front of a Congressional committee that was investigating violence against blacks in the South in 1872.

Colby testified that, on October 29, 1869, "Klansmen broke my door open, took me out of bed, took me to the woods, and whipped me three hours or more. They said to me, 'Do you think you will ever vote another damned Radical ticket?' I said, 'If there was an election tomorrow, I would vote the Radical ticket.'"

The Klansmen replied by continuing to whip him with sticks and belts with straps and buckles. In a telling bit of testimony, one Congressman asked Colby, "What is the character of the men who were engaged in whipping you?" And Colby replied:

Some are first-class men of our town. One is a lawyer, one a doctor, and some are farmers. They had their pistols and they took me in my night-clothes and they carried me from home. They hit me [with] five-thousand blows . . . They said I had voted for Grant and carried the Negroes against them . . . The worst thing was my mother, wife, and daughter were in the room when they came. My little daughter begged them not to carry me away. They drew a gun and actually frightened her to death. She never got over it until she died. That was the part that grieves me the most.

Colby's testimony not only shows the vicious cruelty of the Klan, but that at this stage they were not simply young thugs out rampaging, but prominent members of communities. Colby was badly injured by the assault—"they broke something inside me," he told Congress—but he was re-elected to Congress during the next election, despite the fact that the Klan peppered his home with bullets. Even so, as he told Congress, he believed that "no man can make a free speech in my county. I do not believe it can be done anywhere in Georgia [by] a Republican, either white or colored."

Sadly, until the 1960s and later, Colby was right.

eran named Christopher Columbus Nash, arrived on Delos White's doorstep one fall night in 1871 and blew his head off when he answered the door.

It was representative of the times that, at the moment of White's murder, the captain of the Louisiana State Militia company stationed in Colfax was a black man named William Ward, a former Union army soldier. After White's death, Ward fearlessly arrested Nash and others who had been in on the murder. Shortly thereafter, Ward and members of his 72-man, all-black company exchanged gunfire near Colfax with hooded riders from the Ku Klux Klan, killing one and capturing another. Whites began to claim that blacks had instituted a "reign of terror" in Colfax and cheered when a judge dismissed all charges against Nash and those arrested with him in November 1871. A year later, as Louisiana fell apart into warring factions, each belonging to a different governor, there were ready-made armed forces now about to face off in Colfax.

"HE'S DEAD AS HELL!"

By the early winter of 1873, Colfax reflected the violence going on in Louisiana between factions that supported the governments of McEnery and Kellog. In the elections for sheriff and other officers of Grant Parish in November 1872, both sides claimed victory, but Henry Clay Warmoth, the lame duck governor, declared that the Democrats were the victors—these included Christopher Columbus Nash, who was named sheriff of Grant Parish.

But in January 1873, when Kellog was sworn in as governor, he ousted the Democrats and named his own Republican slate. The Democrats refused to give up their offices and thus the Republicans pulled off a daring move. On the night of March 25, a group of white and black Republicans, including William Ward, climbed into the Grant Parish courthouse, formerly a large stable belonging to the Calhoun plantation, and occupied it. The next day, they swore themselves into office—a white Republican named Dan Shaw became sheriff—and sent a messenger bearing their oaths of office to the secretary of state in the Louisiana capital of Baton Rouge. The secretary filed the oaths and those who held the courthouse were now officially sworn in.

But it wasn't going to be that easy. Enraged Democrats, led by Nash and other ex-Confederates, gathered and decided that they were going to retake the

MAP OF LOUISIANA SHOWING GRANT COUNTY, WITH COLFAX SQUARELY IN THE CENTER OF IT. GRANT COUNTY WAS NAMED AFTER PRESIDENT ULYSSES S. GRANT.

COURTESY OF THE UNIVERSITY OF TEXAS LIBRARIES, THE UNIVERSITY OF TEXAS AT AUSTIN

courthouse, with force of arms if need be. They put out a call for all white men who sympathized with their cause to meet at the courthouse in April. Upon hearing of this, Ward, who had been removed from his position as head of the militia by former Governor Warmoth, managed to find two dozen poorly armed black men to cordon the courthouse.

Another group of black Republicans also formed a posse and forced a prominent Democratic attorney to leave his home in Colfax, in order to search it for papers and a seal they believed stolen from the courthouse. While searching, they came upon a tiny coffin containing the embalmed body of the man's infant daughter, who had died some six years earlier and whose body had been kept in the home. They dumped the corpse out onto the porch, an act of unthinking callousness that enraged the whites who heard about it.

More and more armed whites began to appear in the field around Colfax and the courthouse, where they skirmished with Ward's men. On the night of April 5, a black man named McKinney, who supported Ward, was at his home three miles (4.8 km) from Colfax repairing a fence when a group of a dozen white riders came storming up, their horses leaping the fence and surrounding the terrified McKinney. As his wife and young son watched from the front porch, one of the men leaned over from the saddle and fired two shots directly into McKinney's head. The black man let out an unearthly scream and collapsed as his killer yelled, "I got him! He's dead as hell!" The riders did a kind of victory dance around the body, shouting and making their horses prance, and then took off, disappearing into the dusk.

As word spread among the local black population of McKinney's murder, black families as well as more armed black men began to make their way to the courthouse in Colfax. By Easter Sunday, April 13, there were 150 black men and about the same number of black women and children in the courthouse. There were also a handful of whites.

"WE ARE GOING TO STAND WHERE WE ARE"

On the morning of Easter Sunday, April 13, a force of 165 white horsemen gathered in a field not far from Colfax. Half of them were ex-Confederate soldiers who had seen a good deal of combat in the Civil War. They brought with them shotguns, muzzle-loading Enfield rifles, pistols, and hunting knives. They also had a small cannon, which they carried on a horse-drawn cart.

The men were led by Christopher Columbus Nash and other ex-Confederate officers, most of whom were members of the Ku Klux Klan. One such man, named David Paul, had the horsemen line up in front of him, and then made a speech. "Boys," he told them, "this is a struggle for white supremacy. There are one hundred and sixty-five of us to go into Colfax this morning. God only knows who will come out. Those who do will be prosecuted for treason and the punishment for treason is death."

He then told the assembled men that anyone who didn't want to follow him unquestioningly should step out of line and leave. Twenty-five men, sobered by what he had just said, did so. That left the force 140-men-strong. With Nash in the lead, they rode out with the Red River on their right, moving through the fields of the old Calhoun plantation, until they were about three-quarters of a mile (1.2 km) away from the Colfax courthouse. At this point, Nash took four of his men and rode under a white flag in the direction of the courthouse and asked for a parley. Those defending the courthouse sent out an ex-slave named Levi Allen.

Nash asked him: "What do you depend on doing in there?"

To which Allen replied: "We are doing nothing more than we were doing before—standing still, as we've been standing."

"We want that courthouse," Nash told him.

"We are going to stand where we are until we get some United States' troops or some assistance," Allen replied.

Attempting to strike a deal, Nash then told Allen that if the blacks holding Colfax left their arms behind and marched away from the village, they would not be harmed, but Allen did not believe him.

"Colored men have been hurt," Allen replied. "I am afraid to trust the word of any of you."

Nash stared at him grimly. "Then go back in there and tell your people that I advise them to get out. You have thirty minutes to remove your women and children."

With nothing further to say, both men turned and rode away.

BLOODY SUNDAY

Back in Colfax, the black defenders sent their women and children fleeing away through the woods. They also advised the few whites who were there, including Sheriff Dan Shaw, to leave, and these men did—for they would be special targets for Nash's embittered ex-Confederates. Then William Ward took stock of his men. There were 150 of them, but only a half (by some accounts, just a third) of them actually had guns, and these guns were mainly shotguns—inaccurate at all but the shortest range—and old fowling pieces.

To help defend themselves, they had dug a trench in a semicircle around the courthouse, but the trench was only two feet (61 cm) deep and offered little protection from a determined attack. They had improvised homemade cannons from old steam pipes, but when they tested one of them, it blew to pieces, injuring two men.

At noon, Nash's men moved out, led by a skirmish line of the men who had the best rifles, breech-loading repeaters that could do heavy damage to the enemy. They used military tactics the ex-soldiers were familiar with, including sending out small forces to cover their flanks. When the skirmish line came within 300 yards (274.3 m) of the trenches dug by the Colfax defenders, they stopped and waited until the cannon was brought up. Its first booming shot signaled the opening of hostilities. The skirmish line opened up a few moments later, sending bullets whizzing above the heads of the black men crouching in their shallow trenches; these returned fire sporadically, trying to save ammunition.

For two hours, both sides skirmished in this way without doing much damage—the cannon was too far away to really hurt the courthouse defenders, just as the attacking whites were out of the range of the blacks' shotguns and rifles. But then Nash's men found a gap in the levee near the Red River, behind and to the left flank of the black forces. They pulled their cannon to this weak spot, loaded it with buckshot, and then blasted the unsuspecting defenders from behind. The shot immediately killed one man, who stood up, with his intestines hanging out, and then fell in a heap to the ground. It panicked many of the black defenders in the trench, who raced for the cover of the courthouse building. The whites chased after them, firing their guns and shouting the high-pitched Rebel yell that had become famous during the Civil War. They pulled their cannon with them until it was eighty yards (73.2 m) in front of the courthouse and fired four more shots at the black defenders who were trying to cram through the courthouse's narrow front door.

Those blacks who were unable to make it through the pileup at the front door of the courthouse fled into the woods behind it, where many of the women and children waited. They were pursued by white fighters who swarmed among them, killing as many as they could. One of the blacks, a former slave, was overtaken by his former master. "Master Johnnie, don't kill me!" he begged. The man shouted, "God damn you, I told you what I would do if I caught you here!" He shot and killed the man.

Once the blacks had raced into the thick woods, where they were not easily pursued, the whites left them alone for the moment, and turned their attention to the men trapped in the courthouse.

THE SLAUGHTER

Nash had several choices—he could simply besiege the place, but that would take quite a while and reinforcements might arrive for the defenders. He could assault it, but that would certainly result in great loss of life among the whites. Finally, he decided the best option was to burn it down. Impressing a black man they had captured into service, they made him rush to the courthouse when the attention of the defenders was elsewhere and throw a burning torch on the dry cypress shingles of the roof, which immediately went up in flames. The defenders, who had no water, attempted to climb into the rafters to knock out the burning shingles, but they were shot and killed by Nash's men.

With fire blazing and smoke filling the courthouse, some of the blacks decided to give up. A dozen of them left the courthouse, waving pieces of paper or handkerchiefs in token of surrender. As soon as they were outside, the whites opened fire, killing several at close range. Six others raced and hid beneath a nearby warehouse, where they were surrounded, dragged out, and murdered, some with knives slashing their throats.

By this time, dusk was falling. The last remaining blacks in the courthouse, who had been crouched beneath the floorboards, were told that they would not be harmed if they gave themselves up—it was either that or be burned to death. With little choice, they allowed themselves to be taken prisoner. But they were far from safe. A man named Jim Yawn, whose brother was the Klansman killed earlier by William Ward's forces, searched the prisoners until he found the man whom he thought had fired the shotgun blast that had done it.

"I got you!" he shouted triumphantly. He dragged the man away by the collar of his coat, pulled out his gun, and shot him.

Rain began to fall as night came on, putting out the smoldering fire on the courthouse roof. The whites had lost one man, and had two wounded seriously (who would die later). Dead blacks littered the courthouse grounds. By 9:00 p.m., most of the whites were ready to leave, but there remained the question of what to do with the sixty or so blacks they had with them as prisoners.

Surprisingly, Nash wanted to let them go. He said to the assembled black men: "If we turn you lose, will you stop this damn foolishness?" The men promised they would—they said they would even kill William Ward, who had escaped, if he ever came back. It appears that Nash still wanted to be sheriff of Colfax and felt that killing this many people in cold blood would jeopardize his chances. But the other whites with him didn't want to let them go. They told Nash that if he did so, he wouldn't live two weeks, that some freedmen, once safe, would plot to kill him out of revenge.

Even so, Nash insisted that the blacks not be killed, but, significantly, he did not stay around to make sure that his orders were followed, instead riding off up the river. By this time it was 10:00 p.m. The blacks were told by the whites guarding them, who were led by an ex-Confederate officer named Bill

Cruikshank, that they were being transferred to a nearby jail in the town of Alexandria; for the night, they would be held in the nearby sugar house of the old plantation. The whites marched them in pairs down the road to the sugar-house, with two white men on horses on either side of each pair of black men. Cruikshank insisted that two black men he knew, Levi Nelson and William Williams, accompany him. After they had gone only a few hundred yards (274 m or so), Cruikshank ordered Nelson and Williams to line up one behind the other, then he pulled out his gun and shot them—he was apparently trying to see if one bullet could kill two men. Nelson received only a minor wound and played dead. Williams, shot in the stomach, began moaning, and another white man walked up and shot him six times.

NASH INSISTED THAT THE BLACKS NOT BE KILLED, BUT, SIGNIFICANTLY, HE DID NOT STAY AROUND TO MAKE SURE THAT HIS ORDERS WERE FOLLOWED, INSTEAD RIDING OFF UP THE RIVER.

Up and down the line, shots and screams rang out. A former slave named Wash Brannon was shot along with a friend. The friend was killed but Brannon played dead, even when a white ran his horse over him several times. Another ex-Confederate solder took aim at a former slave he hated. The slave shouted: "If you shoot me, you're shooting an innocent man!" and jumped out of the way, racing into the underbrush. The shot meant to kill him killed another man. Another white suddenly announced, "I can take five!" He lined up five shaking blacks and attempted to kill them with one shot. "It took two," recalled a white participant in the slaughter. "After that, it was like popcorn in a skillet." Shots rang out up and down the line, and blacks began to fall.

At the front of the line, two blacks named Benjamin Brim and Baptiste Mills walked with their captor. They heard shots and Brim asked the white man guarding them:

"Are you shooting the prisoners?"

"Shut up," the man snarled at him. "We're only shooting the wounded."

But a few seconds later, Brim heard the sound of a revolver being cocked. He turned his head in time to receive a bullet in the face, which entered just below his left eye and knocked him over. Lying facedown on the ground, he was shot again. Mills was shot as well, but managed to get up and stagger away. Brim lay on the ground as whites on horseback raced past him, shouting and shooting. He tried to be still, but blood pouring from his facial wound was nearly drowning him. He snorted to blow it out of his nose and a white rider heard him.

"This nigger's not dead," he shouted. He fired again into Brim's back. Still Brim lived. When all was quiet, he dragged himself into a ditch by the side of the road, covered himself with long grass, and passed out. When he came to, it was to the sound of footsteps and excited voices. It was the white people of Grant Parish. They had come to Colfax to loot the homes of the freedmen and were now returning home with wagons piled high with bedding and furniture, leading captured mule and cattle behind them.

"CARPETBAG MISRULE"

Two days later, on April 15, two deputy U.S. marshals, having heard about the slaughter, came riding into Colfax. They were stunned at the bodies lying everywhere, many of them partially eaten by dogs, some of them disemboweled and disfigured, beaten beyond recognition.

In the days before the marshals arrived, women whose husbands lay dead around the courthouse had come out of the woods to try to identify their bodies, only to be taunted by the whites who remained nearby (one white fighter, hearing the wailing of women who had lost their husbands, had remarked: "Listen to those cows bellowing over the dead bulls."). But the whites had been unsuccessful in getting any of the black men to come out and bury the dead because most of those who had run away were too frightened to return.

Since the whites would not touch dead black men, the evidence of the massacre was there for the deputy marshals to see. They counted sixty dead men. Five of these they turned over to their families for burial, the rest they interred in a mass grave. (There have been other estimates of the number of dead, including blacks who may have temporarily reached safety but died later of wounds, which have reached as high as 150.)

"THE GROUND WAS THICKLY STREWN WITH DEAD"

One of the deputy marshals who first came upon the bodies that surrounded Colfax court house in April 15 was a man named T.W. DeKlyne. He wrote this report, which captures with firsthand immediacy the shocking nature of the slaughter.

> The ground was thickly strewn with dead. We were unable to find the body of a single white man or to ascertain the loss of whites. Many [of the blacks] were shot in the back of the head and neck; one man still lay with his hands clasped in supplication; the face of another was completely flattened by the blows of a gun, the broken stock of a double-barreled shotgun being on the ground near him; another had been cut across the stomach with a knife after being shot; and almost all had from three to a dozen wounds. Many of them had their brains literally blown out.

The other deputy marshal, William Wright, who wrote of "the unusual marks of violence upon the bodies . . . have been in battle fields after a fight; the wounds in this case were different than those given in a regular fight."

Both Wright and DeKlyne's reports were used, to little avail, in the trials against those accused of the crimes.

The Colfax Massacre was now over, but its repercussions were just begin-ning. Outrage mounted among blacks and Radical Republicans over the massacre, and the courageous U.S. attorney in New Orleans, a man named Jim Beckworth, finally persuaded a federal grand jury to indict nearly 100 of the white attackers that day. Because most of the attackers, protected by the local white population, could not be found and brought to justice, only nine men were tried in front of a biracial jury in 1874. After two trials, the first ending in a hung jury, only three of these men were convicted. These included Bill Cruikshank, who had begun the massacre. However, the men were found guilty not of murder, but only of con-spiring to violate the civil rights of the black men they had killed, a conviction that brought with it a sentence of, at most, ten years in prison.

The defenders of the three convicted men took this verdict all the way to the U.S. Supreme Court, which in 1876, issued its shocking and far-reaching deci-sion *U.S. v. Cruikshank*. A 5,000-word opinion written by Chief Justice Morrison Waite delivered the chilling conclusion that federal statutes recently enacted to protect the civil rights of citizens only prohibited the violation of the rights of blacks by the states themselves, not by individuals. Thus the men had been pros-ecuted in the wrong venue—the state of Louisiana should have punished the criminals, not the federal government. Ignoring the fact that so many black citi-zens were massacred at Colfax, the decision, writes distinguished Reconstruction historian Eric Foner, "hammered the final nail into the coffin of federal efforts to protect the rights of black citizens in the South. Reconstruction effectively ended a year later, and the Jim Crow era began."

Well into the twentieth century, the bones of those massacred freedmen buried at Colfax have turned up during various building projects; at one point, skulls and other skeletal remains were placed into a cardboard box and stuck in the corner of a local newspaper office. But no attempt to bury them or memori-alize those slaughtered has been made. However, in 1921, a 12-foot (3.7 m) marble obelisk was erected "in loving remembrance" of the three whites who had died "fighting for White Supremacy." And in 1951, the state of Louisiana authorized a 7-foot (2.1 m)-high aluminum sign to be fixed in concrete just outside the Colfax courthouse. It reads: "On this site occurred the Colfax riot in which three white men and 150 Negroes were slain. This event on April 13, 1873, marked the end of carpetbag misrule in the south."

The plaque is wrong in almost every way—the number of black dead is misstated, and what happened at Colfax was not a "riot" caused by "carpetbag misrule" (i.e., Northern agitators). It was a massacre of U.S. citizens defending their rights, a slaughter that set back the cause of civil rights in the South a good hundred years.

The damage that *U.S. v. Cruikshank* did would not even begin to be undone until *Brown v. Board of Education*, the landmark 1954 Supreme Court ruling outlawing school segregation. Until then, the state of Louisiana would spend an average of 10 times more for the education of white students than of black students. And that was just on the level of education. In almost every area—employment, housing, health services—blacks were ignored and exploited by the white state governments in Louisiana, Mississippi, and other southern states, which would not see their first black congressmen since Reconstruction until pressure was brought to bear from the civil rights movement of the 1960s. This often violent and always repressive racial segregation was not a result of "carpetbag misrule," but of the kind of racism that led to the horrible bloodletting at Colfax.

CHAPTER 8

MARTYRS' DAY

THE ARMENIAN GENOCIDE, 1915–1917

THE FIRST MASS KILLING OF WHAT WOULD BECOME
THE BLOODIEST CENTURY IN HUMAN EXISTENCE; THE
TURKISH GENOCIDE OF THE ARMENIANS, WHICH DEVASTATED
AN ANCIENT PEOPLE AND A WAY OF LIFE

"THE MASSACRE OF THE
ARMENIANS BY THE TURKS." A
1916 ILLUSTRATION IN A FRENCH
NEWSPAPER IS IMAGINED, BUT
CAPTURES THE SAVAGERY OF THE
BEGINNING OF THE ARMENIAN
GENOCIDE AS WELL AS PORTRAYING
THE WORLD'S SYMPATHY FOR THE
PLIGHT OF THE ARMENIANS.

MASSACRE OF THE ARMENIANS BY THE
TURKS, FROM 'LE PETIT JOURNAL', 12TH
DECEMBER 1915 (COLOR LITHO), FRENCH
SCHOOL, (20TH CENTURY) / PRIVATE
COLLECTION / ARCHIVES CHARMET / THE
BRIDGEMAN ART LIBRARY

THE MASSACRE OF MORE THAN ONE MILLION ARMENIANS IN Turkey and the Syrian Desert during the First World War and just afterward has been called the twentieth century's first genocide. However some scholars point to the German slaughter of about 60,000 Herero people of Namibia, Africa (1904–1907) as the first state-sponsored ethnic killing to qualify for the term "genocide" (from the Greek *genos*, meaning "race" or "tribe" and the Latin suffix *cide*, "to kill") in modern times.

Certainly the Armenian slaughter was the largest mass killing until Adolf Hitler's Holocaust. And it was, as the historian Richard Rubenstein writes, "the first full-fledged attempt by a modern state to practice disciplined, methodically organized genocide." The fact that the Turks essentially got away with it may even have inspired Hitler, who told his generals on the eve of the invasion of Poland, which began World War II: "Who, after all, speaks today of the annihilation of the Armenians?"

The genocide of the Armenians is famous not just for how many people the Turks murdered, but for the continuing denial for nearly a century by the Turkish government that such a mass killing ever took place. Theirs has been the most successful genocide denial in history, which means that the story

of the Armenian holocaust—commemorated by Armenians every April 24, the day the genocide began in 1915—needs to be told over and over again, lest its real horrors are befogged by the Turkish attempt to reshape the past.

"Given such intransigence," writes scholar Roger W. Smith, "healing and closure can take place only by the world recognizing and acknowledging the historical reality of the Armenian genocide."

"MY MOST LOYAL MILLET"

As of World War I, there were an estimated 1.5 to 2 million Armenians in Turkey. The ancestors of the Armenians who lived there in 1914 had inhabited the area for 8,000 years; the first Armenian state was established 200 years before the birth of Christ. The Armenians were well-known traders, whose country spanned a large central plateau in what is now eastern Turkey, abutting Syria to the south, Persia to the east, and Russia to the north. Because of its location, the ancient homeland of the Armenians had long been a crossroads of cultures and colliding armies. The Romans conquered the Armenians in the first century CE, and between the fourth and fifteenth centuries, their land was conquered in turn by the Persians, Arabs, Mongols, and finally, the Turks.

For a long time, Armenians lived fairly peaceably under Turkish rules. They were a quiet people with a distinct culture, Nestorian Christians in a Muslim land who were tolerated and even accepted—one mid-nineteenth-century Turkish sultan referred to them as "my most loyal *millet*," *millet* meaning "nation" or "religious group" within the Ottoman nation. However, importantly, the Turks never regarded them as first-class citizens. They could not testify in court cases or bear arms and were more severely taxed than the average Ottoman citizen.

During an era that that saw numerous successful revolutions, this state of affairs could not continue for long and by the late nineteenth century, Armenian political parties began to form. They began to agitate for change, even an independent Armenian nation, but the response of the Turkish Sultan Abdul Hamid II was to repress any dissent. Turkish troops used Kurdish mercenaries to brutally attack Armenian villages. The Armenians armed themselves and fought back, but to little avail. During 1894–1898, there may have been hundreds of thousands of Armenians killed, enough to bring the censure of some Western powers on Abdul Hamid.

The Ottoman Empire was crumbling, however, rife with corruption and unable to modernize. In 1908, a new political party known as the Committee of Union and Progress (CUP) made a bid to overthrow the Ottoman government. A bitter civil war broke out between the CUP forces and those of Abdul Hamid. The Armenians, generally sympathetic to CUP, lost 30,000 people to a massacre by forces of the Sultan near the city of Adana in 1909. But by 1913, the new party, now led by a triumvirate of three men—Enver Pasha, Ahmed Cemal Pasha, and Mehmed Talaat Pasha—had taken power. All three were in their thirties and their party, known popularly as the Young Turks, promised new religious and civil freedoms to all minorities of Turkey, including the Jews, Albanians, Bulgars, various Christian sects, and the largest ethnic group of all, the Armenians.

"A SPECIAL ARMENIAN QUESTION"

Armenians were at first optimistic about the new government, but there were warning signs that the Young Turks were not about to change any of the policies of the old Ottoman Empire when it came to this ancient ethnic group. Referring to what he called "a special Armenian question," prominent CUP leader Murat Bey said that Armenians "wish with true naiveté to cause a new Armenia to arise from the debris of the present Ottoman Empire. This idée fixe, this maladroit project, pushes them to criminal resolutions . . . They are past masters in the practice of deceit . . . which gives rise to the expression 'Armenianism.'"

Resembling to a startling extent the pronouncements the Nazis would later make about Germany's Jews, this type of statement by the Young Turks alarmed many prominent Armenians. Some Young Turks even claimed that Armenian revolutionaries of the 1890s had deliberately provoked the Ottoman government into murdering hundreds of thousands of their fellow citizens to curry sympathy with Western powers. In fact, intervention by other countries was one of the chief fears of the Young Turks, who thought that if the Armenians continued to complain of ethnic killings (which persisted after the Young Turk victory, with Kurds and Turkish peasants attacking Armenian villages), Great Britain or

Russia might invade. They also felt that the significant cultural differences between the Armenians and the Turks would impede their dream of a homogenous, pan-Turkic empire.

When World War I broke out in August of 1914, the Young Turks found the excuse they needed to eliminate the Armenians. The new Turkish government signed a pact with Germany, becoming a part of the Central Powers fighting against Britain, France, Russia, and eventually the United States. After a disastrously failed Turkish offensive against Russia in the Caucasus Mountains in December 1914 (when it is estimated that only 10,000 out of a Turkish army of 100,000 survived), Russia began to move into eastern Turkey. Turkey responded by claiming that it needed to remove Armenians from the region to "protect" them. They also claimed that many Armenians were engaged in a vast conspiracy with the Russians to overthrow the Turkish state.

Many Armenians, afraid of what the Young Turks might do, had sided with the Russians. But even before the disastrous Turkish defeat in the Caucasus, the genocide was being planned. It would be run from the Ministry of the Interior, headed by Talaat Pasha, but the two men behind the idea were Drs. Nazim Bey and Behaeddin Shakir, Young Turks who were chief, if behind-the-scenes, advisors to the ruling triumvirate. In a speech delivered to a closed session of the Central Committee of CUP, Nazim Bey said:

> If we remain satisfied with the sort of local massacres which took place in Adana and elsewhere in 1909 . . . if this purge is not general and final, it will inevitably lead to problems. Therefore, it is absolutely

necessary to eliminate the Armenian people in its entirety, so there is no further Armenian on this earth and the very concept of Armenia is extinguished.

Enver Pasha founded an organization called *Teshkilati Mahsusa* (Special Organization); its job was to systematically eliminate the Armenians. Enver Pasha and his advisors decided that the genocide would take three forms. First, Armenian politicians and prominent thinkers and leaders, mainly based in Constantinople, would be rounded up and killed. Second, those Armenians who had already been conscripted into the Turkish army to fight the Russians would be disarmed and turned into labor battalions, where they would be worked to death, or summarily executed. Male Armenian civilians between the age of twenty and sixty-five would be stripped of their private weapons, forced into labor gangs, and killed. Finally, the remaining Armenian population of non-conscription-aged men, women, and children, would be "deported" (sent on forced marches) to the Syrian Desert. Those who did not die of thirst, hunger, and exposure would be massacred once there.

And who would the killers of the Special Organization be? They would be paramilitary groups recruited by the Young Turks, composed of thugs and outlaws known as *chetes* (some released specially from prison for the purpose), many of whom were ultra-radical Muslims who believed in killing infidels, or unbelievers. A large portion of those involved in the killing were also Kurds, whom the Turks had traditionally enlisted to do their dirty work against the Armenians. These Special Organization killers—who also raped and robbed Armenians—are close in nature to the *Einsatzgruppen* the Germans employed to kill Jews in the early part of World War II, before they developed more efficient methods of mass extermination.

MARTYRS' DAY

On the night of Saturday, April 24, 1915, about 250 Armenian politicians, writers, artists, and other important cultural figures in Constantinople were rousted from their beds, where they had been, as one survivor—a priest named Krikoris

Balakian—later wrote, "snoring in a calm sleep—exhausted from their Easter celebrations." Turkish police put them in large red military buses and took them at first to a military barracks outside Constantinople, then finally to the prison Sirkedji, a place, Balakian wrote, "with gigantic fences and iron-bolted gates." They sat on wooden benches in the prison's central courtyard, too surprised even to talk as more and more of their colleague and friends were brought in. Balakian wrote: "Like some dream, it seemed as if in one night all the prominent Armenians of the capital . . . had made an appointment in those dim cells of the prison."

In the next few days, the men were stripped of their belongings and finally taken by bus to a steamship, which brought them across the Sea of Marmara (an extension of the Mediterranean that separates European Turkey from Asian Turkey) and then taken by special train deep into Asia Minor "where, except in a few rare cases, we would all meet our deaths," wrote Balakian. It was apparent to those being transported that they were being taken as far away as feasible from Constantinople to keep their fates secret from the large European diplomatic population there, which might sound an international alarm. As they continued by train, stops would be made and Turkish officials would call out the names of groups of Armenians, who would be taken away and never heard from again.

One such group, which included the well-known Armenian poet Daniel Varoujan, was taken to a creek by a band of *chetes*, who told them to undress and fold up their clothing. Then, wrote Balakian, who heard the story from a Turkish carriage driver who had driven the group there, "[the *chetes*] began to stab them to death, slashing their arms and legs and genitals and ripping apart their bodies." Varoujan attempted to defend himself and the killers tore out his entrails and gouged out his eyes.

Balakian's own group of deportees was held in a small prison until August of 1915, then taken out and tied together, to join another group of about 300 Armenians gathered from all across Turkey. He describes the weak, semi-starved men stumbling along through a "bright moonlight night" behind three carts filled with "spades, hoes, pickaxes, and shovels." Seemingly at random, the *chetes* accompanying them would savagely bludgeon individual Armenians to death with one of the implements from the carts. Dozens died in this way the first

night. The men continued to walk for days through the desert, where 200 of them died of starvation and dysentery. Balakian survived and even managed to escape, ending up in England, but the Armenian people had now lost what the Armenian-American writer Peter Balakian (who is related to Krikoris Balakian) described as "its most gifted voices of resistance." Eighty-two writers perished— an entire holocaust all of its own in terms of Armenian literature—as well as hundreds of teachers and religious leaders.

MAP OF ARMENIA. HISTORICALLY, THE CENTRAL PLATEAU OF ARMENIA WAS A CROSSROADS FOR INVADING ARMIES AND COLLIDING CULTURES.

LIBRARY OF CONGRESS

"I REMEMBER GOING AND GOING"

On May 27, 1915, an official Edict of Deportation was issued to Armenians by the Ministry of Interior. In most cases, those men who had not already been conscripted into labor gangs were marched away first from Armenian villages and killed. After the men were gone, the deportation began. The remaining Armenians in any given district left with few belongings, having in many cases been forced to give their houses and livestock to their Turkish neighbors. The Turks followed the Armenians with long sticks, waiting for them to defecate in order to probe the feces for swallowed gold. One ten-year-old Armenian deportee remembered a woman squatting by the side of the road while Turks hovered around her. "They won't even let me shit in peace," she shouted to the boy.

Most of the Armenians inhabiting the central plateau of Turkey, what is usually known as historic Armenia, were "deported in this fashion. They were told they were being sent to the Syrian Desert—destination Aleppo—to get out of the way of a supposed Russian invasion, but they quickly saw through this ruse. The Turks had failed to provide any provisions for the deportees, and often denied them what food and drinking water there was available in the area. Survivors' accounts testify to the severity of the journey:

> Anyone who would fall behind would be shot on the spot [remembered one survivor]. They took us through desolate places, through the deserts and mountain paths, so we would not be near any of the cities where we could get water or food. We got wet at night by the dew and were scorched by the sun during the day. I remember going and going.

Starving to death, their clothes in rags, barefooted, covered with lice, the Armenians trudged on, guarded by army soldiers and *chetes*. There were teenaged Armenian men among the women and children, disguised in women's clothing, with headscarves. One of them remembered: "I had a child on my back, had on women's clothes, my face was covered with mucus, and I was limping." To make matters even worse, the deportees began to see corpses lining the road, from the groups that had gone before them. One survivor recalled: "Before us the people of Zeitun were taken to Katma and had already started dying of starvation, so that when we got there we saw so many of them dead, in a sitting position. We saw bones everywhere and saw many others who were dying, or on the verge of death, simply sitting and waiting their turn."

All through the remote roads and mountain passes leading south to Syria lay the corpses, thousands upon thousands of them. This became a problem for Talaat Pasha at the Ministry of the Interior, who on December 19 sent a coded cable to all the *vali* (governors) of the *vilayet* (provinces) being emptied of Armenians:

> I have been advised that in certain areas unburied corpses are still to be seen.
>
> I ask you to issue the strictest instructions so that the corpses and their debris in your *vilayet* are buried. Henceforth any officials in *kazas* [subdistricts] in which corpses are found will be dismissed . . .

The pressure put on the *vali* by Talaat caused them to in turn instruct their police and *chetes* to bury the dead Armenians. "Contrary to my repeated instructions," wrote one *vali* in frustration, "I am told there is still far too large a number of corpses along the roads. It is surely superfluous to refer again to the obvious consequences of this."

"BARBAROUSLY MUTILATED"

Hundred of thousands of those sent south were deliberately starved to death, but just as many were violently murdered, both by the *chetes* who guarded the caravans and by the Kurds who were encouraged to raid the convoys at various points during the journey. Many men and women were sexually mutilated. They were killed with guns and swords and knives, but also with blunt instruments of all kinds. Men, women, and children were forced into caves, the entrances of which were then filled with brush, which was doused with kerosene and set alight. Those inside were asphyxiated by the smoke in what the writer Robert Frank has called "primitive gas chambers."

A PHOTOGRAPH OF ONLY THREE OF THE ESTIMATED ONE MILLION OR MORE ARMENIANS KILLED (IN THIS CASE, STARVED TO DEATH) BY THE TURKS.

The U.S. consul in Harput, in the center of historic Armenia, was Leslie Davis, who wrote long reports describing the carnage he witnessed. In the fall of 1915, he rode on horseback through the region, visiting dozens of Armenian towns. "All of the purely Armenian villages were in ruins and deserted," he wrote. Then he came upon the corpses. Riding around the beautiful azure waters of Lake Goeljuk, Davis and a friend saw, shimmering within the translucent lake, "hundreds of bodies and many bones." Leading down to the lake were deep ravines "triangular in shape and shut in on two sides by high precipitous banks which the people when attacked were unable to climb." Penned in, the Armenians were gunned down by the *chetes* and their bodies dumped in the lake.

Davis's sharp eye caught many things—a tree "with a large red spot on it" and riddled with bullet holes, which indicated that Armenians had been stood up against it and shot. The smell of the dead bodies scattered near the lake was so strong that Davis rode high up on a cliff top to escape it, but it was no use—it followed him everywhere. He found naked Armenian bodies (they had all been forced to undress) with "gaping bayonet wounds" and noted that in other cases the killing was done with "axes, cleavers, shovels, and pitchforks," in order to save bullets.

Traveling farther, Davis and his companion began to come upon hundreds, then thousands of dead bodies, almost all of them women and children who had been killed perhaps only a few days to a week before. Many of these showed signs of "the brutal mutilation that so many of the gendarmes inflicted on so many of the women and girls whom they killed." In all during his ride around Lake Goeljuk, Davis estimated that he had seen the bodies of about 10,000 Armenians, all of them victims of extreme violence.

"That which took place around beautiful Lake Goeljuk in the summer of 1915 was almost inconceivable," Davis wrote. "Thousands and thousands of Armenians, mostly innocent and helpless women and children, were butchered on its shores and barbarously mutilated." And this was in only one remote region.

"THE STARVING ARMENIANS"

Despite the Turkish government's best attempts to keep the genocide in remote areas, mass killings and deportations on a vast scale could not be hidden for long. Foreign consuls like Leslie Davis, on the ground in Turkey's smaller cities and towns, began to send in shocking reports of the deaths. Often forgotten now, the cause of the Armenians actually was given wide coverage, especially in the United States, where former president Theodore Roosevelt called the genocide "the greatest crime of the war." *The New York Times* published 145 articles on the slaughter of the Armenians in 1915 alone. Luminaries like Ezra Pound, Clara Barton, President Woodrow Wilson, and others attempted to keep the issue before the public eye, and by the end of World War I, the U.S. public had sent $100 million in aid to the people whose wretched pictures had been published in newspapers—"the starving Armenians" as they were invariably called.

Much of the credit for this response should go to Henry Morgenthau, U.S. ambassador to the Ottoman Empire. On July 16, 1915, he sent a telegram to the U.S. State Department, which read in part:

> Deportation and excesses against peaceful Armenians is increasing and from harrowing reports of eyewitnesses it appears that a campaign of race extermination is in progress under the pretext of reprisal against rebellion.

THE FIGHTERS OF VAN

Not all the Armenian population was taken off to their deaths without a fight.

In the province of Van, an important center of Armenian social, economic, and cultural life, Armenian fighters armed themselves during a five-week period from April to mid-May of 1915, and fought bravely against overwhelming odds.

In April, wrote one survivor, the Armenians of Van "gradually got news that the Turks wanted to finish off all the Armenians by massacring them." The Armenians in Van therefore decided to arm themselves; children even melted down brass candle holders to make bullets. Approximately 300 men with rifles and another 1,000 men and boys with nineteenth-century rifles, including flintlock muskets, protected 30,000 Armenians in two different walled towns.

The Armenians were as ingenious as they were brave. An Armenian professor made smokeless powder. Women made uniforms for the men. Children dug out Turkish bullets fired into the walls of the town, melted them and reshaped them for re-use by the Armenian fighters. At night, the Turks fired artillery into the towns aiming for lights, and the Armenians were able to get them to redirect their fire by tying lanterns to donkeys and dogs.

Things were looking desperate for the Armenian fighters, but then a mixed force of Russian and Armenian troops crossed the border from Russia and attacked the Turks, driving them away. But the Turks returned with reinforcements a month or so later, and the Armenians were forced to flee Van, heading into the primarily Armenian region of Russia around the Yerevan Plain. During this retreat, thousands of Armenians were killed by Turks and Kurds, but those who survived helped form the Soviet Republic of Armenia in 1918.

Morgenthau knew almost sooner than any other foreign observer just what the Turks were up to. He wrote in his memoirs that deporting the Armenians "represented a new method of massacre. When the Turkish authorities gave the orders for these deportations, they were merely giving the death warrants to a whole race; they understood this well, and, in their conversations with me, they made no particular attempt to conceal the fact."

From April to October of 1915, Morgenthau wrote, caravans of Armenians were seen "winding in and out of every valley and climbing up the sides of every mountain, moving on and on . . . every road led to death." He went to write:

> As the exiles moved, they left behind them another caravan—that of dead and unburied bodies, of old men and women dying in the last stages of typhus, dysentery, and cholera, of little children lying on their backs and setting up their last piteous wails for food and water. There were women who held up their babies to strangers, begging them to take them and save them from their tormentors.

Morgenthau made protestations directly to Talaat Pasha about the situation, but he responded with anger and indignation.

"Why are you so interested in the Armenians?" he asked Morgenthau one day. "You are a Jew, these people are Christians. Why can't you let us do with these Christians as we please?"

During another conversation, Talaat Pasha told Morgenthau: "It is no use for you to argue. We have already disposed of three-quarters of the Armenians."

HENRY MORGENTHAU, THE AMERICAN AMBASSADOR TO THE OTTOMAN EMPIRE, SAW WHAT WAS HAPPENING TO THE ARMENIANS AND ALERTED THE ADMINISTRATION OF WOODROW WILSON TO IT.

Unfortunately, while the American people responded with an outpouring of aid, the U.S. government under Woodrow Wilson did not act to stop the massacres by declaring war on Turkey—Wilson had made a pledge to keep the United States out of World War I, a pledge that he would have to break after a series of provocations by the Germans, but he refused to expand the war into Turkey for fear of overextending the U.S. armed forces.

DEIR EL-ZOR: "THE EPICENTER OF DEATH"

Those Armenians who survived their death march arrived at a remote place in the Syrian Desert called Deir el-Zor, which Peter Balakian calls "the epicenter of death." There the killing squads of *chetes* and Kurds smashed young children against rocks, burned hundreds of Armenians alive, asphyxiated others in caves (as recently as 1999, dozens of skeletons were found in these hard-to-locate rock dungeons), and mutilated men and women alike. Far from the eyes of the world, it was the ultimate Turkish act of violence against the Armenians.

After this, in early 1918, like a plague epidemic with nothing living left to feed on, the genocide of the Armenians wound itself down. Still, in the final months of the war, as the Russian Revolution forced Russia to make peace with the Central Powers, 50,000 to 100,000 Armenians were killed by Turkish troops in various Caucasus campaigns.

At war's end, perhaps 600,000 Armenians survived out of 1.5 to 2 million. Out of these, 250,000 had made their way into Russia. About 400,000 of the rest were scattered around Turkey, historic Armenia, and the Middle East. Many of them had been forcibly converted to Islam. Many more had either seen their children stolen or had given them up in the hopes of having them survive. Armenian woman captured by Turks and Kurds lived in virtual slavery to these men. But the heart of an entire people and an entire culture had been lost.

After the victorious British entered Turkey, they forced the sultan they had installed to try sixty-one members of the Young Turk regime for crimes against the Armenians. The only Turk to pay a high price for his crimes was Governor Yusuf Kemal Bey, who was hung, although he claimed he "was only following orders." The three chief Young Turks—Talaat, Enver, and Cemal—escaped Turkey on a German submarine at war's end.

THE ARMENIAN ASSASSINS

One March day in 1921, in the Charlottenberg district of Berlin, a stocky, well-dressed, middle-aged man walking down a quiet street was approached by a much younger man with wide dark eyes, who quickly pulled out a revolver as the older man passed and shot him in the back of the head. As his victim fell in a pool of blood, the young man cried out in broken German: "I foreigner, he foreigner, this no hurt Germany."

But he was arrested and taken to jail. The killer was Soghomon Tehlirian, an Armenian who had lost numerous members of his family in the recent genocide and had barely escaped with his life. His victim was Talaat Pasha, the Minister of the Interior who is thought to have been the architect of the genocide. Tehlirian was a member of a secret Armenian organization, the Armenian Revolutionary Federation (ARF), devoted to tracking down those who had instigated the genocide, particularly the Young Turk leaders, and bringing them to justice, especially since post-war tribunals had failed to do so. Tehlirian was tried in a Berlin court for his killing of Talaat, but the jury, having listened to Tehlirian describe the horrors he experienced during the genocide, acquitted him after only an hour of deliberation. Tehlirian afterward emigrated to the United States, where he lived until 1962 in California, a figure of great respect in the Armenian community.

His was only the first in a series of assassinations planned by ARF. In 1922, Cemal Pasha was found in Tiflis, in Soviet Georgia, and shot down on the steps of a public building by three Armenians, who escaped. Shortly thereafter, the former prime minister of the Ottoman Empire was assassinated in his car in Italy and later two more high officials of the Young Turks were killed in Berlin. In all cases, the assailants either escaped or were acquitted at trial.

MEHMED TALAAT PASHA. HEAD OF THE TURKISH MINISTRY OF THE INTERIOR, TALAAT PASHA WAS THE YOUNG TURK RESPONSIBLE FOR THE DAY-TO-DAY RUNNING OF THE GENOCIDE OF THE ARMENIANS. HE FLED TURKEY AFTER THE CENTRAL POWERS COLLAPSED AT THE END OF WORLD WAR I AND WAS KILLED IN BERLIN BY AN ARMENIAN ASSASSIN IN 1921.
GETTY IMAGES

ENVER PASHA. THE THIRD YOUNG
TURK OF THE TRIUMVIRATE THAT
RAN THE GOVERNMENT, ENVER
PASHA FOUNDED AN ORGANIZATION
CALLED *TESHKILATI MAHSUSA*
(SPECIAL ORGANIZATION) WHOSE
JOB WAS TO CARRY OUT THE
ELIMINATION OF THE ARMENIANS.

But for the Armenian people there would be no justice, and there is still none today. For ninety-four years, the Turkish government has continued to deny that a genocide occurred; their explanation for the deaths of thousands of Armenians was that they were engaged in a conspiracy against the Turkish government and thus deserved to be killed, although they were in the main killed by rogue elements within the Turkish army, and by Kurds.

The evidence is overwhelmingly against this explanation. In June 1998, the Association of Genocide Scholars passed an Armenian Genocide Resolution, calling on Turkey to atone. At the same time, 126 of these scholars placed an ad in the *New York Times* whose headline read: "126 Holocaust Scholars Affirm the Incontestable Fact of the Armenian Genocide and Urge Western Democracies to Officially Recognize It."

Western democracies, including the United States, have not done so, in large part because of global politics—Turkey is an important oil-producing country and a North Atlantic Treaty Organization (NATO) partner. Turkey not only denies the Armenian genocide, but does so aggressively; in the 1970s it successfully lobbied the U.S. Congress to not pass a bill recognizing April 24—Martyrs' Day—as a day commemorating the holocaust of the Armenians. Although President Bill Clinton issued a statement in 1995 remembering "the Armenians who perished, victims of massacres, in the last years of the Ottoman Empire" he would not use the word genocide to refer to it. And President Barack Obama, visiting Turkey in April of 2009, also refused to use the word genocide, although during his presidential campaign he strongly stated that he believed that a genocide is indeed what had occurred.

To answer the question, why so much emphasis on a single word, it is important to go back to Hitler's statement to his generals: "Who, after all, speaks today of the annihilation of the Armenians?" The Nazi holocaust of the Jews was to some extent inspired by and modeled after the then-"forgotten" Armenian genocide. In order to keep genocides from happening again and again, we need to call them by their proper name. As the holocaust scholar Deborah Lipstadt writes:

> Denial of genocide, whether that of the Turks against the Armenians, or the Nazis against the Jews is not an act of historical interpretation. Rather the deniers seek to sew confusion by appearing to be engaged in genuine scholarly effort … Denial of genocide strives to reshape history in order to demonize the victims and rehabilitate the perpetrators.

CHAPTER 9

"IF I HAD NOT SEEN IT WITH MY OWN EYES"

THE RAPE OF NANKING, CHINA, 1937–1938

THE ATROCITIES WROUGHT BY THE JAPANESE IN KILLING THOUSANDS OF CHINESE CITIZENS ADVERSELY AFFECTS RELATIONS BETWEEN THE TWO NATIONS TO THIS DAY

IN A SCENE ALL-TOO-TYPICAL DURING THE RAPE OF NANKING, A JAPANESE SOLDIER READIES HIMSELF TO CUT OFF THE HEAD OF A CHINESE PRISONER. THE JAPANESE WERE AVID PHOTOGRAPHERS OF SUCH BEHEADINGS AND OFTEN SENT SUCH PHOTOS BACK HOME TO LOVED ONES.

AFP/GETTY IMAGES

THE HISTORY OF THIS NOTORIOUS WORLD WAR II MASSACRE CAN be summed up as a tale told by two museums. The Yushukan Museum in Tokyo commemorates the Japanese victory in Nanking (now Nanjing) on December 13, 1937, with a video of Japanese shock infantry standing on the walls of the ancient city waving their Rising Sun flags in triumph and shouting "Banzai!" Then the video cuts to images of the same troops giving soup to elderly women and small children of the city, while a narrator explains in gentle tones that it was necessary for the Japanese to attack Nanking to stifle Chinese "terrorism."

The other museum is in Nanjing, China. The Massacre Memorial, built over a site where the Japanese executed and buried hundreds of innocent civilians, has graphic videos of the Japanese beheading the Chinese—decapitation being one of the primary Japanese means of dispatching Chinese during their occupation of Nanking—and in fact has a huge bronze of a decapitated head in its courtyard. The number 300,000 runs as a motif throughout the Massacre Memorial, emblazoned across the walls in different languages. This is the number accepted (in China) of those massacred by the Japanese. There is also the electronically amplified

sound of a drop of water falling every twelve seconds, to represent 300,000 deaths in six weeks, and perhaps subliminally remind patrons of the dripping of Chinese blood.

While these two museums diverge widely on their views of what happened in Nanking in the late fall and early winter of 1937–1938, most people in the world acknowledge that an unprecedented Japanese reign of terror occurred, one in which Chinese blood did not so much drip as gush. A Japanese reporter, witness to the early days of the slaughter, described walking one night through a field outside the Nanking walls and admiring the way moonlight gleamed off a dark pool in the distance. When he got closer, he realized he was looking at a vast pool of blood.

However, while many in Japan also accept this view (including Japanese soldiers who participated in the killings), the Japanese government has never officially recognized what happened, let alone made reparations for the brutal occupation that is aptly called the Rape of Nanking. During the occupation, not only were thousands of women of the city physically and sexually assaulted, but this ancient capital of China was left, as one historian has written, "a shattered and smoldering husk."

To this day, the grotesque shadow of the Rape of Nanking falls over any attempt of the two countries to put their contentious past behind them. It remains one of the main issues that China and Japan have been unable to reconcile, despite the fact that a recent poll has shown that most Japanese people want their government to take some responsibility for the atrocity that occurred at Nanking.

BODIES PILED LIKE FISH

As the 1930s began, the ultranationalists who had taken control of the Japanese government believed strongly that their nation had to aggressively seek new territory and raw materials to support its burgeoning population. China was an obvious first step in fulfilling these expansionist plans. Japan had long had aggressive intentions toward its massive neighbor to the west, winning large swathes of Japanese territory during the First Sino-Japanese War of 1894–1895.

In the early 1930s, taking advantage of the civil war going on in China between the Communist forces of Mao Zedong and the Nationalist army of Chiang Kai-shek, Japan conquered the province of Manchuria in a swift, five-month-long campaign. The Japanese turned it into the puppet state of Manchukuo, installing the last Chinese emperor, Pu Yi, as ruler. Ignoring protests from the League of Nations, from which it withdrew in 1933, Japan encroached farther into northern China, seeking to provoke a larger war with China.

This strategy came to fruition on the quiet night of July 7, 1937, when shots were fired at Japanese troops patrolling near Marco Polo Bridge on the outskirts of Beijing. One Japanese soldier went missing, then turned up unharmed, but the incident (which some historians believe the Japanese may have staged) was enough of a provocation to allow Japan to justify further invasion of China.

In August, the Japanese army and navy decided to occupy the major port city of Shanghai. Importantly, what followed in Nanking stemmed directly from the bloody battle for Shanghai. Here, the Japanese faced the elite troops of Chiang Kai-shek's Nationalist Army, who also outnumbered them, at one point by as much as ten to one. Beginning in mid-August, the fighting was house-to-house, and ferocious, with neither side backing down.

One Japanese recruit, landing in the city on September 3, later wrote: "As far as my eyes could see, there was corpse after corpse on top of the embankment . . . the bodies of thousands of soldiers were all piled up in a jumble like blue-fish tuna in a market." What the soldier saw was an entire Japanese division killed in combat with Chiang Kai-shek's army—the army the Japanese high command had boasted it could destroy in three months.

In mid-November, the Japanese finally seized Shanghai by outmaneuvering and flanking the Chinese, forcing them to withdraw to the west. By then, a rage born of humiliation had built among the officers and men of the elite Japanese 10th Army and the marines of the so-called Shanghai Expeditionary Force, who had seen the bulk of the fighting. One Japanese journalist accompanying the army wrote in his diary: "The reason that the [10th Army] is advancing to Nanking quite rapidly is due to the tacit consent among the officers and men that they could loot and rape as they wish."

THE ROAD TO NANKING

Nanking, the ancient capital of China, lies in a bend of the Yangtze River about 170 miles (273.6 km) northwest of Shanghai and has long been celebrated for its sophistication and cultivation—home to literary and artistic centers for centuries, and the birthplace of classic Chinese calligraphy. It was in Nanking that reformer Sun Yat-Sen became the first provisional president of the first Republic of China. In the fall of 1937, it was a city of some 600,000 inhabitants that combined the old—the towering Ming-era stone wall that encircled the city—with the new in the form of electric lights, pavement, and automobiles.

As the vengeful Japanese raced toward Nanking in a three-pronged movement meant to seal the city against the banks of the Yangtze, the exhausted Chinese army fell back before them. Thousands of veteran soldiers had been killed in Shanghai; raw recruits, some as young as twelve or thirteen, had been impressed from the countryside to replace them. Many of their officers had already fled into Nanking ahead of them, leaving the poorly trained recruits without any leadership at all.

Japanese forces were far better led and trained. The commander-in-chief of the Japanese army in the region was General Matsui Iwane, a devout Buddhist from a family of renowned scholars. However, he suffered from tuberculosis and was having an acute attack as the Japanese forged toward Nanking. In actual charge of their forces on the ground was Lieutenant General Prince Asaka Yasuhiko, Emperor Hirohito's uncle, who had had a dispute with the emperor and had been sent to the front to prove his loyalty.

Under Asaka's command, the 10th Army and Shanghai Expeditionary Force wreaked havoc on the road to Nanking. They executed those Chinese who did not flee, raped women, and plundered and burned down homes. A British journalist who followed in the wake of the Japanese reported:

Smoldering ruins and deserted streets present an eerie spectacle, the only living creatures being dogs unnaturally fattened by feasting on corpses. In the whole of Sungchiang, which should contain a densely packed population of approximately 100,000, I saw only five Chinese, who were old men, hiding in a French mission compound in tears.

"THE JAPANESE ARMY WOULD BE KIND AND GENEROUS"

By December 9, Japanese troops had entirely surrounded the city of Nanking, while inside chaos mounted. The town was filled with thousands of refugees who spread further panic among Nanking' s inhabitants by telling them stories of Japanese atrocities in the outlying areas.

About 90,000 Nationalist soldiers were in Nanking, some of them already stripping themselves of their uniforms and trying to blend in with the population, but others trying to prepare a defense under the command of General Tang Sheng-chih—Chiang Kai-shek and other Chinese officers had already fled across the broad Yangtze, announcing that the Chinese government would be transferred to the city of Chungking. But now there were few boats left to carry anyone across the river's swift currents; some desperate Chinese began to dive into the chilly waters in an attempt to swim across, but their sodden corpses soon floated back to shore.

The Japanese had been bombing the city steadily and indiscriminately for two months, and civilian casualties had the hospitals full to overflowing. As the Japanese settled into position outside the walls of the city, their planes flew over Nanking, but this time dropped another type of payload, leaflets that read, in Japanese and Chinese: "The Japanese Army would be kind and generous to innocent civilians and to Chinese troops with no sign of enmity, but would be relentlessly enraged by those who resist."

The Japanese set a deadline for the Chinese army to surrender, but General Tang refused to comply and fierce fighting broke out in the city's suburbs. In the meantime, those Westerners who still remained in Nanking (most had fled at the same time as Chiang Kai-shek) set up the International Committee for the Nanking Safety Zone to try to protect the city's citizens. The International Committee was led by John Rabe, a German businessman whose affiliation with the Nazi Party would presumably help protect any Chinese under his care, since Germany and Japan had signed a nonaggression pact in 1936. Along with the American doctor Robert S. Wilson, the American missionary Minnie Vautrin, and other members of the international community, Rabe created the Nanking Safety Zone in the western section of the city, an area of about 3.4 square miles (5.5 km²), within which were numerous refugee camps.

As the fighting around Nanking reached a crescendo, more refugees filtered into the Safety Zone. Then, on December 12, at five o'clock, General Tang ordered his men to retreat. Unfortunately, in the chaos, any withdrawal was bound to turn into a route, and so the Chinese troops raced for the waterfront, looting stores for food as they went, leaving the streets littered with "guns, grenades, swords, knapsacks, coats, shoes and helmets," one Western correspondent wrote.

On December 13, Japanese troops entered the city, while others ringed the top of Nanking's ancient wall celebrating. At first, the absence of gunfire brought what a *New York Times* reporter present called "a tremendous sense of relief." This would soon change to a feeling of utter horror.

"I KILLED THEM ALL!"

The first thing the Japanese army did was round up Chinese soldiers, both those who had surrendered and those who had attempted to hide by changing into civilian clothes and blending in with the cowering crowds of Nanking citizens (numbering perhaps half a million) still stuck in the city. The Japanese told these soldiers that they would be fed and taken to POW camps. In fact, Prince Asaka's headquarters had secretly ordered the deaths of all Chinese prisoners. There is some dispute as to whether Asaka knew of this order or not; he certainly knew of the ensuing massacre and did nothing to stop it.

The order reached battalion level commanders late on December 13. It read, in part: "All prisoners of war are to be executed. Method of execution: Divide the prisoners into groups of a dozen. Shoot to kill separately."

In fact, most of the Japanese troops in Nanking probably did not need an order to begin killing Chinese prisoners. It was not the policy of the Japanese to take POWs, for one thing; for another, the Japanese despised the Chinese for even surrendering, since they still outnumbered the Japanese, 90,000 to 50,000. One Japanese soldier remembered: "I thought, how could [the Chinese] become prisoners . . . without even trying to show any resistance?"

In any event, slaughter ensued as Japanese took Chinese soldiers to the riverbank of the Yangtze, grain fields, or ditches around the city and shot them. Nothing as neat as dividing into "groups of a dozen" occurred. One Japanese soldier recorded what happened in his diary.

December 16: We took about 5,000 prisoners of war . . . to the bank of the Yangtze and mowed them down with machine guns. Then we stabbed them with bayonets to our satisfaction. I probably bayoneted 30-odd hateful Chinese soldiers. Climbing up on a heap of dead bodies and bayoneting them gave me a courage, which made me feel I could even vanquish ogres. I stabbed them with all my might while hearing them groan. There were some old ones and kids. I killed them all. I even borrowed a sword and severed a head. It was the most unusual experience I've ever had.

Another soldier also participated in the bayoneting of those who did not die in the hail of machine gun fire, and remembered that the Chinese "screamed like mad men when I stabbed them . . . It was so loud. Their voices haunted me for a week . . . I didn't think much about the cruelty at the time. I just thought war was like that."

As the Japanese killed these men, they assigned Chinese laborers, referred to as coolies, the job of dragging the bodies to the wharves and throwing them into the river. One Japanese war correspondent who came upon the scene at night recreated its surreal horror:

On Hsiakwan wharves, there was the dark silhouette of a mountain made of dead bodies. About fifty to one hundred people were toiling there, dragging bodies from the mountain of corpses and throwing them into the Yangtze River. The bodies dripped blood, some of them still alive and moaning weakly, their limbs twitching. The laborers were busy working in total silence, as in a pantomime. In the dark, one could barely see the opposite side of the river. On the pier was a field of glistening mud under the moon's dim light. Wow! That's blood.

After a while, the coolies had finished their job of dragging corpses and the soldiers lined them up along the river. Rat-tat-tat machine gun fire could be heard. The coolies fell backwards into the river and were swallowed up by the raging currents.

"HEADS SHOULD BE CUT OFF LIKE THIS"

Too much killing, like anything else, brings with it a need for variety, and the Japanese soon tired of simply shooting men and then bayoneting them. Since the Japanese possessed—as officers' sidearms—fine samurai swords, beheading Chinese prisoners soon became a favored method of dispatching them. This was also a way for Japanese officers to inure, or desensitize, their greener soldiers to the bloodiness of up close and personal killing. So the Japanese began holding seminars on killing.

One new Japanese soldier recalled such a seminar, when a helpless Chinese prisoner was dragged to the edge of a pit and forced to his knees. The Japanese in charge, whose name was Tanaka, announced: "Heads should be cut off like this!" as he unsheathed his sword. Then:

> He scooped water from a bucket with a dipper, then poured it over both sides of the blade. Swishing off the water, he raised his sword in a long arc. Standing behind the prisoner, Tanaka steadied himself, legs spread, and cut off the man's head with a shout, "Yo!" The head flew more than a meter away. Blood spurted up in two fountains from the body and sprayed into the hole.

This scene was to repeat itself over and over again in the early days of the Rape of Nanking. The Japanese made a kind of fetish of beheading the Chinese, lining up rows of heads and taking snapshots to send back home. Sometimes they placed lit cigarettes between the lips, for a joke. Two soldiers supposedly engaged in a beheading contest, to see who would be first to kill 100 Chinese. Although this later turned out to be a fabrication of a Tokyo newspaper to increase circulation, just the fact that this would sell newspapers reveals a great deal (see "Iris Chang and Her Forgotten Holocaust," page 156).

It wasn't just beheading, of course. Soldiers were hardened by using bound Chinese captives for bayonet practice, burying them alive, burning them to death, smashing in their heads with axes, and setting dogs on them. One soldier, looking at his comrades, thought: "They had evil eyes. They weren't human eyes, but the eyes of leopards or tigers."

The seminars in killing were having the desired effect. A Chinese soldier who was able to escape the Japanese told of them castrating Chinese men and then eating their penises in the belief that they might increase their virility—a story that sounds farfetched unless one realizes that the Japanese would have a history of cannibalizing their enemies in World War II (see "The Dark Secret," page 160).

JAPANESE SOLDIERS ARE SHOWN BURYING CHINESE PRISONORS ALIVE DURING THE RAPE OF NANKING.

THE RAPE OF NANKING

After this initial rush of bloodletting the Japanese turned to what the author Iris Chang called "one of the greatest mass rapes in world history," probably greater than any such incident with the exception of the mass rape of Bengali women by Pakistani soldiers in Bangladesh in 1971. The number of rapes is estimated at 20,000 to 80,000; it is difficult to get a much closer estimate.

IRIS CHANG AND HER FORGOTTEN HOLOCAUST

In the fall 1997, a twenty-nine-year-old Chinese American woman named Iris Chang published a book called *The Rape of Nanking: The Forgotten Holocaust of World War II*, which brought the simmering controversy over the massacre to full boil. In the book, which was widely read and reviewed in the United States and elsewhere, Chang passionately attacked the Japanese for their actions, and included graphic stories of the violence as well as interviews with victims. Chang was also the first one to fully uncover and portray the Nazi John Rabe's role in saving Chinese during the Rape.

The book was a direct shot at the Japanese government and Chang came under considerable criticism for it. Her massacre figures were disputed and the accuracy of some of the stories she told was questioned. One such tale—the reported contest between two Japanese officers to see who could cut off the most Chinese heads—turned out to have been an invention of the Japanese news media of the time. There were those who felt such inconsistencies in Chang's book played into the heads of Japanese conservatives, who could now claim that Chang's larger picture of the Rape of Nanking was inaccurate and that she was a Chinese attempting to get back at the Japanese through her book.

However, *The Rape of Nanking: The Forgotten Holocaust of World War II* was mainly accurate and served the purpose of bringing this story before the public eye again, putting pressure on the Japanese to answer for their actions. Chang herself, however, was marked forever by the vitriolic attacks on her. In 2004, while researching a book on another Japanese atrocity, the Bataan Death March, she suffered a nervous breakdown and took her own life.

IRIS CHANG, THE CHINESE-AMERICAN AUTHOR OF *THE RAPE OF NANKING*, PICTURED HERE IN SEPTEMBER 2001. CHANG'S BOOK BROUGHT THE MASSACRE TO THE PUBLIC EYE, PUTTING PRESSURE ON THE JAPANESE TO ANSWER FOR THEIR ACTIONS. CHANG COMMITTED SUICIDE IN 2004, WHILE SHE WAS RESEARCHING A BOOK ON ANOTHER JAPANESE ATROCITY, THE BATAAN DEATH MARCH.

ASSOCIATED PRESS

A large number of the women raped were then killed. A certain number committed suicide. Many of those who survived refused to speak of their ordeal later, and some even drowned the half-Japanese babies they gave birth to. And while many former Japanese soldiers admitted freely to participating in mass murders, they fell silent with interviewers when the subject turned to rape.

Most Western journalists fled the city within a few days and were not witness to the mass rapes, which the Westerners running the Nanking Safety Zone later reported. The victims ran the gamut from girls as young as six to women as old as seventy. Housewives were raped; so were Buddhist nuns. The Japanese relentlessly searched the city for men to kill and women to rape. When they found women, they dragged them outside and gang-raped them, in broad daylight, in the middle of public streets. If they resisted, they and their families were killed. One Japanese soldier raped a sixty-year-old woman and then told her to "clean off his penis with her mouth." Another raped a woman in front of her husband. When he protested, they "stuck a wire through his nose and tied the other end of the wire to a tree," and then bayoneted him to death.

Worse things happened—fathers were forced to rape their daughters, sons their mothers. The Japanese specialized in horrific vaginal mutilation, involving firecrackers, sharpened bamboo stakes, and bayonets. The only hope for most women in Nanking was to reach the Safety Zone, run by John Rabe and the other Westerners of the International Committee. The Japanese nominally respected this Zone—and, ironically, the swastika that flew over it—into which

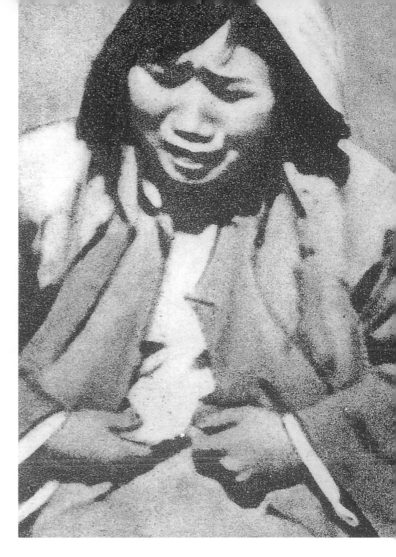

A CHINESE WOMAN GANG-RAPED BY JAPANESE SOLDIERS IN NANKING (A PHOTO TAKEN FROM A CAPTURED JAPANESE SOLDIER). THOUSANDS OF CHINESE WOMEN WERE RAPED, THEN KILLED OR MUTILATED, DURING EARLY DAYS OF THE JAPANESE OCCUPATION OF NANKING.

GERMAN BUSINESSMAN JOHN RABE, THIRD FROM LEFT, PICTURED IN NANKING WITH OTHER WESTERNERS IN 1938. DESPITE HIS AFFILIATION WITH THE NAZI PARTY, RABE'S EFFORTS AT SETTING UP SAFE ZONES FOR CHINESE REFUGEES SAVED THOUSANDS OF LIVES.

ASSOCIATED PRESS

more than 300,000 refugees had crammed themselves by mid-January. In reality, however, the Japanese made numerous incursions into it, seeking Chinese soldiers and, increasingly, women.

John Rabe wrote a letter to Adolf Hitler in an attempt to get him to intervene to stop the rape and massacre. Rabe had a misguided belief that the Fuhrer cared about the immorality of mass murder. He wrote: "If I had not seen [the behavior of Japanese soldiers] with my own eyes, I would not have believed it . . . We found corpses of women on beer glasses and others who had been lanced by bamboo shoots. I saw some of the victims with my own eyes—I talked to some of them right before their deaths."

"TERROR IN THE FACES"

Members of the International Committee acted with extraordinary bravery to try to keep as many Chinese alive as possible. Doctors, like Robert Wilson, operated on hundreds of mutilated women and children brought to them. Others, like John Rabe, used a combination of bribery and bravado to keep the Japanese as far away as possible.

Wilhelmina Vautrin (whom most people called Minnie) protected thousands of Chinese women during the Rape of Nanking. Fifty-one years old in 1937, she grew up on a poor farm in Illinois. She worked her way through college and became a missionary to China, eventually ending up in Nanking, where she became dean of studies at Ginling Women's Arts and Science College, a job she loved and where she was loved in return by her Chinese students. Vautrin refused to flee Nanking as the Japanese approached. Ginling was within the Safety Zone and refugees overwhelmed Vautrin. "From 8:30 this morning until 6 this evening, excepting for the noon meal, I have stood at the front gate while the refugees poured in. There is terror in the faces of many of the women—last night was a terrible night in the city and many young women were taken from their homes by soldiers."

Vautrin fed and clothed the women—many of whom had blackened their faces and cut their hair in an attempt to look old or ugly—and protected them as best she could. Still, individually and in packs, the Japanese would climb the fences of the college or bully their way through the gates to abduct women and rape them. This was known on the campus as "the lottery."

Vautrin prevented many of the rapes, even though she was slapped and beaten by Japanese soldiers, and threatened with guns and bayonets, some of which were stained with fresh blood. By January, Japanese officials were making a concerted attempt to "register" Vautrin's women, ostensibly to keep track of their welfare, but really to recruit them into the squalid military brothels where they would become known as Comfort Girls.

Thousands of women stayed under Vautrin's protection, sleeping "shoulder to shoulder on bare cement floors, in winter," as she wrote in her diary. She protected them throughout the worst days of the Rape of Nanking and afterward, but finally the responsibility—and the horrors she had seen—became too

THE DARK SECRET

Many have disputed claims of Japanese cannibalism during the Rape of Nanking, but Allied authorities knew and kept secret that the Japanese ate Allied prisoners and combat dead during the course of World War II.

These instances of cannibalism were brought before Judge William F. Webb, chairman of the War Crimes Committee of the International Military Tribunal for the Far East immediately after the war. The documents presented to Webb make riveting, if horrifying, reading. Here is one such combat report from a U.S. unit in New Guinea:

> Sergeant H.B. reported missing in action on 19 January 1943 was found in a mutilated condition on 23 January 1943. The body was identified by Pfc. Other [sic] E. Dickson who swore that the body was found in the following condition: "The flesh part of the thighs and each leg had been cut away. The abdominal cavity had been opened . . . Pfc. Dickson further stated that a stew pot in a nearby Japanese bunker contained the heart and liver of approximate size of that of a human.

Numerous reports like these, from U.S., Australian, and British soldiers, crossed Webb's desk. Webb also saw an even more horrifying report that Japanese prison camp guards used Indian prisoners as human cattle, culling the ones they wanted to eat and even cutting flesh from their bodies while they were still alive. Most of these instances happened when Japanese troops were cut off from their supply lines and extreme hunger forced them into cannibalism.

Ultimately, Webb did not prosecute the Japanese for these crimes, because of what was considered the pressing necessity to keep this horror from the families whose loved ones had been eaten.

much for her. In May 1940, she had a nervous breakdown and was sent back to the United States for medical help. During the voyage across the Pacific, she tried to kill herself by jumping off the ship. Once home, she was hospitalized and came out seemingly more healthy, but she was unable to finally shake the demons that had plagued her since Nanking. She committed suicide in 1941 by sealing her doors and windows with tape and gassing herself.

SHIRKING RESPONSIBILITY

Gradually, the worst horrors of the Rape of Nanking came to an end and Nanking settled into the dreary life of an occupied city—the Japanese would hold it until war's end. People drifted back from hiding places in the countryside, looking for work. Often the Japanese paid them in opium, or heroin cigarettes, so that a large percentage of the population of Nanking became enslaved to drugs.

The horrors were not over. The Japanese had secret laboratories where they experimented on Chinese prisoners, subjecting them to different strains of bacterial infection and poison gas, and then burning the corpses of these poor unfortunates in large incinerators. However, the tsunami of atrocity had retreated, pulling its wretched detritus with it.

In 1945, the Japanese surrendered and the war ended. The troops occupying Nanking went back home—and then what? What did the world know about what had happened in Nanking, and the thousands who had died there? During the early stages of the Rape of Nanking, Western journalists had published stories with titles like "Nanking Massacre Story: Japanese Troops Kill Thousands" and "Terror in Nanking," but these had been overwhelmed by the larger stories and manifold atrocities of World War II itself, especially the Holocaust.

GENERAL MATSUI IWANE, HEAD OF JAPANESE FORCES AT NANKING, HEARS THE SENTENCE OF DEATH PASSED UPON HIM AT THE INTERNATIONAL MILITARY TRIBUNAL IN TOKYO IN 1948. THOUGH IWANE WASN'T PRESENT DURING MOST OF THE ATROCITIES, HE ASSUMED RESPONSIBILITY FOR THEM AS DE FACTO JAPANESE LEADER.

When the International Military Tribunal for the Far East met in Tokyo in 1946, it heard the testimony of members of the International Committee, saw photographs, and watched film. General Matsui Iwane, de facto head of Japanese forces at Nanking, was sentenced to death and hanged, even though he had been ill for most of the Rape, but Prince Asaka, as a member of the Japanese royal family, was spared. In trials held in China, four Japanese officers who took part in the massacre were also executed, but the vast majority of those who had participated never spent a moment in court.

As time went on, Japan was rehabilitated in Western eyes, becoming an economic powerhouse, while China, under the control of Mao Zedong and the Communists, became vilified. Even if they knew what had happened at Nanking, people in the West cared less and less. China never forgot about the Rape of Nanking, although it served a variety of political purposes. During the Korean War, when feelings against the United States ran high, the Red Chinese used the graphic film and snapshots secretly taken by U.S. missionaries (and presented as evidence in front of the International Military Tribunal) as "proof" that these missionaries had stood idly by, snapping pictures, while Chinese died by the thousands.

THE CHINESE SEEM TO HAVE BEEN GENUINELY SURPRISED WHEN THE JAPANESE REFUSED TO ACKNOWLEDGE THE ATROCITIES ITS ARMY PERPETRATED IN CHINA, ESPECIALLY THE RAPE OF NANKING.

However, beginning in the 1970s, the Chinese government actually sought reconciliation with Japan as a way of moving into a future that included a shared economic relationship. The Chinese seem to have been genuinely surprised when the Japanese refused to acknowledge the atrocities its army perpetrated in China, especially the Rape of Nanking. In fact, it was apparent by the 1980s that a whitewash was in progress, with the Japanese attempting, as one historian has written, "to beautify [their] war memory and shirk Japanese responsibility."

In November 2007, on the 70th anniversary of the Rape of Nanking, 100 Japanese lawmakers from their ruling party said that documents from Japanese government archives showed that only 20,000 Chinese were killed. (While the Chinese place the death toll at 300,000, historians from other countries generally give the figure at 100,000 to 200,000.)

One Japanese lawmaker said: "We conclude that the death toll in the Nanking advance was nothing more or less than the death toll that would be expected in a normal battle." He also claimed that there was no massacre at Nanking. This flew in the face of research by scholars the world over, including scholars from Japan itself, and also ignored first-hand testimony both from the killers and those Chinese who survived. While there are inconsistencies and exaggerations in portrayals of the Japanese actions at Nanking, it is certain that a major bloodletting occurred there—a horrible violation of human life and dignity. Although Japan and China have had diplomatic and trade relations since 1972, tensions run high between these close geographic neighbors, particularly as China grows in industrial might and increasingly gains economic parity with Japan. Until Japan takes responsibility in some official capacity for the Rape of Nanking, these two countries will continue to be at odds.

CHAPTER 10

WOLVES AT THE GRAVE

KATYŃ FOREST, APRIL–MAY, 1940

SOVIET SECRET POLICE KILLED THOUSANDS OF POLISH
OFFICERS IN A MASSACRE THAT ROBBED THE NATION OF
ITS BEST AND BRIGHTEST AND WAS KEPT A DARK
SECRET FOR NEARLY FIFTY YEARS

THE EXECUTION/BURIAL SITES
AT KATYŃ. THIS DRAWING SHOWS
HOW CLOSE THE EIGHT MASS
GRAVES WERE TO THE GNIEZDOVO
RAIL STATION AND ALSO DEPICTS
THE NKVD SUMMER PLACE AND
THE OLDER GRAVES OF RUSSIAN
DISSENTERS MURDERED IN
EARLIER PURGES.

IN EARLY FEBRUARY 1943, A WOLF PADDED SILENTLY THROUGH THE frozen landscape of the Katyń Forest, whose tall conifers populate the high banks overlooking the Dnieper River, near Smolensk, in western Russia. After the German invasion of Russia in June 1941, the area had been occupied by the Wehrmacht's 537th Signal Regiment, commanded by Colonel Friedrich Ahrens, who headquartered himself in a dacha formerly inhabited by the *Narodnyy Komissariat Vnutrennikh Del* (or NKVD), the Russian secret police. Duty in the Katyń (pronounced *Cat'-in*) Forest was quiet and fairly routine, but there were days when the snow and ice-enshrouded forest seemed menacing to Ahrens and his men—local villagers told them the woods had been a place where Bolsheviks had, decades earlier, brought political prisoners to be executed.

On that February day, the wolf was probably not hunting randomly. It headed toward an area where it had doubtless been before, a hidden clearing in a remote part of the forest known to local villagers as Goats' Hills. Once there, the wolf began to dig deeply in a sandy expanse dotted with young pines and birches. Before long it had found what it was looking for—the skeleton of a human being—and began to pull and tear at it. Finally, an arm broke off and, holding the prize in its mouth, the wolf loped away through the trees.

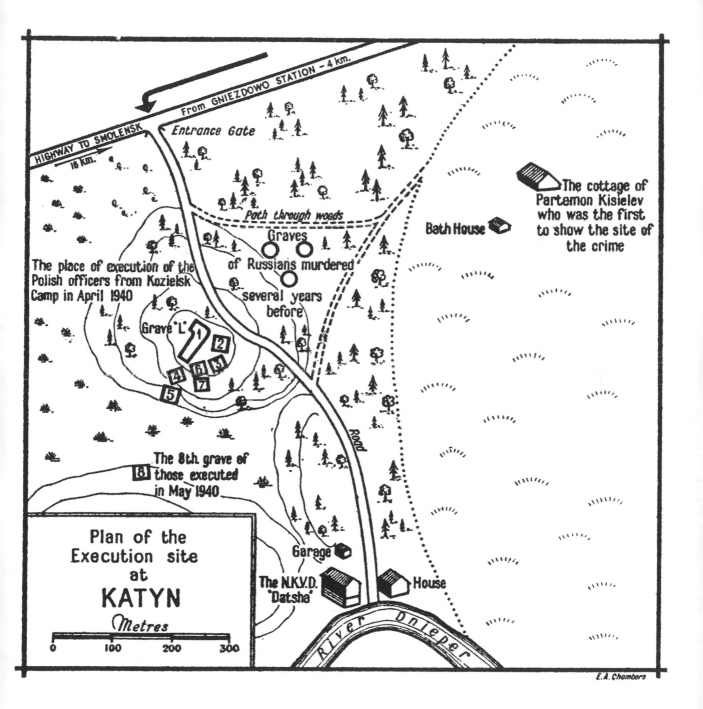

Plan of the Execution site at **KATYN**

The next day, four Russian prisoners of war on a detail to hunt wood for the 537th, discovered the disturbed skeleton, which they saw was wearing the uniform of a Polish officer. Debating among themselves, they decided to keep the find secret from the Germans, but they spoke of it in a nearby village, and word filtered back to Colonel Ahrens through informers. Four weeks after the wolf's dig, a temporary thaw uncovered a large portion of the sandy area, and Ahrens and his officers entered the forest to view it. After the war, Ahrens testified, "one could see that they were graves and that the wolf had been digging for bones."

There were a lot of bones in Katyń. The graves discovered by the Germans contained the remains of 4,000 Polish officers who were executed by the NKVD on direct orders of Joseph Stalin in April and May 1940. And these 4,000 men were only a part of the roughly 22,000 Polish prisoners the Russians murdered around the same time and buried in other, similar mass graves in Russia. As if this wasn't bad enough, like wolves around a grave, the competing nations of World War II—the Germans, Russians, British, and Americans—began to fight with each other over who was responsible. The full truth would not come out until almost fifty years later.

"A BROTHERLY HAND"

When the German army invaded Poland on September 1, 1939—touching off World War II—Poland became a battleground, one of many times in that beleaguered nation's history. Poland has the misfortune to lie in the central plain of Eastern Europe and thus it has been fought over by invading armies and subdivided by more powerful countries for centuries. Catherine the Great of Russia annexed much of eastern Poland in the late eighteenth century, claiming that these lands were traditionally Russian. At the same time Prussia annexed the western part of Poland and the Austrian Empire annexed the southern part of the country. Until the beginning of the twentieth century, these three powers controlled the divided Poland. This all changed by the end of World War I. The Russian Revolution toppled the tsars while the defeat of the Germans and Austrians caused the former Austro-Hungarian Empire to disintegrate.

The Poles recovered their statehood at the end of 1918. After soundly defeating and embarrassing the invading Red Army in the Battle of Vistula in

1920, the independent Poland was secure. It was a security that would be short-lived. On August 23, 1939, Adolf Hitler and Joseph Stalin signed the secret Nazi–Soviet Non-Aggression Pact, which called for them to invade Poland and then partition it. Germany struck first, sending five German armies across the Polish border (about 1.5 million troops) using blitzkrieg tactics that would soon become world-famous. Fast-moving panzer divisions encircled and trapped Polish armies, while screeching squadrons of Stuka dive-bombers pummeled Polish roads and rail transport.

The Poles, taken by surprise, fought bravely, but within a week their army was forced to retreat from the borders. Within two weeks, Warsaw was blazing from German bomber attacks and the Polish government had fled into exile. Then, on September 17, the Russians attacked from the east, although they claimed, with the dreadful hypocrisy that would mark all their dealings with the Poles, that they were not attacking at all. Instead, they told the Polish ambassador in Moscow, the Red Army was merely reaching out "a brotherly hand . . . to extricate the Polish people from the unfortunate war into which they were dragged by their unwise leaders."

Polish soldiers were therefore confused upon encountering Red Army units entering Poland. Some Polish units fought the Soviets, but others, whose communication with their high command had been disrupted, put down their arms, especially when the Soviets claimed they had come to Poland to fight the Fascists. Within a few weeks, the Russians, without actually declaring war, had taken a third of Poland's territory and captured about 230,000 Polish soldiers, including at least 20,000 officers and military and civilian police.

Overwhelmed by this huge haul of POWs, the Russians established temporary "transit-distribution" camps in Poland and western Russia to deal with the massive inflow of humanity. The Soviets made certain decisions right away. They released Polish enlisted men of Ukrainian and Belorussian descent. They sent other enlisted men to work on Russian highways or in Russian mines. They sent captives from so-called "German Poland" (the part of Poland newly conquered by the Nazis) to the German-occupied zone, an agreement previously reached in the Nazi–Soviet Non-Aggression Pact. These included Jewish Poles, who were almost certainly sent to their deaths.

By the end of December 1939 about 38,000 Poles were held prisoner in Soviet camps. More then half of them were officers—regular and reserve officers (among them many members of the elite of the nation, such as teachers, lawyers, and physicians). About 15,000 of these were sent to three camps in the Soviet Union: the generals and army officers to Starobelsk in Ukraine and Kozelsk in Russia and the police to Ostashkov in Russia. Perhaps because of overcrowding in these camps, another 7,000 Polish officers and police were sent to various military jails in western Belorussia and western Ukraine.

"WE WILL GIVE OUR LIVES"

The diaries found on the bodies of the dead buried in Katyń, as well as the testimony of a few survivors, provide certain details about the Polish POWs' existence in the late fall and winter of 1939–1940. The camps, all of them built on the sites of former monasteries and churches taken over by the Soviets, were extremely overcrowded and food was scarce. According to one scholar, "the standard daily fare was two servings of very thin soup, often with bits of rotten fish, rarely meat, and two small rations of soggy black bread." The Russians forbade both religious services and contact with relatives, although Poles in all three camps defied this ban by secretly praying, either by themselves or with some of the forty-five clergymen (only two of whom were to survive) also being held prisoner in the camps.

The Poles were subjected to intense attempts at political re-education by NKVD intelligence men who flooded the camps, demanding the Poles attempt to speak Russian, read Russian newspapers, and learn Communist theory. The NKVD held special indoctrination classes, which they forced the Poles to attend. Loudspeakers blared a daily diet of Soviet propaganda—how Soviet Russia was the salvation of the Poles and "the only land of true freedom."

With a few exceptions, the Polish officers ignored this (most Communist newspapers were used for rolling cigarettes or as toilet paper). The officers in these camps had an extraordinary esprit and believed in their country above everything else. Many of them had fought against the Bolsheviks in 1920, in the war that had resulted in the freedom of the Polish nation, and they would not under any circumstances bow down to the Russians. They organized secret musical groups that played Polish folk music on homemade instruments and even printed secret newspapers that they passed from hand to hand after lights out.

And they wrote heart-rending songs, one or two of which survived in the diaries found on dead men's bodies. One verse went like this:

> When we are needed,
> If fate so decrees,
> We will not think of wounds or graves,
> And for Thee, beloved country,
> We will give our lives.

OIL PORTRAIT OF LAVENTRI BERIA BY UNKNOWN ARTIST. BERIA, LOOKING ALMOST PROFESSORIAL HERE, WAS IN FACT THE RUTHLESS HEAD OF THE SOVIET NKVD WHO DRAFTED THE ORDER TO ELIMINATE THE POLISH PRISONERS.

AKG-IMAGES/RIA NOWOSTI

"THE CREAM OF THE CLASS ENEMY"

NKVD agents subjected each Polish officer to lengthy and well-detailed interrogations, whose purpose was ostensibly to discover where the officer's political sympathies lay and hence to decide his fate. It was an exhaustive process that shows how thorough, and yet how mindless and soulless, the Soviet bureaucracy was.

Each Polish officer spent hours with his assigned NKVD operative, both in formal interviews and informal conversations. Some of the Poles were amazed at the lack of sophistication of their interrogators. An NKVD questioner insisted to one Polish officer, an amateur artist who had spent time in Paris, that the Polish government must have sent him to France to sketch out a secret street-by-street map of the city. The NKVD man could simply not believe it when the Pole told him that street maps were available cheaply at every Paris news kiosk.

Yet the interrogators could be clever. One Polish officer, who was transported out of Kozelsk and thus avoided the mass executions that would shortly come, described a conversation with his interrogator, an NKVD agent named Samarin:

Samarin: Let us imagine that the public prosecutor annuls your case. Let us suppose that your request to return to German-occupied Poland is complied with, that the Germans allow you to live at liberty in Warsaw in your apartment. What would you do?

Prisoner: I would rest after my exhausting experience.

Samarin: Supposing I turned up at your apartment for one day, would you give me a cup of tea?

Prisoner: I do not know if there would be any tea there.

Samarin: And would you put me up for the night?

Prisoner: You have the large Soviet Legation in Warsaw. You would be better off and more comfortable there.

So went a typical game of cat and mouse between interrogator and interrogated. In the meantime, Soviet informers—mainly Russian guards who pretended to be friendly—took the pulse of the camp from overheard conversations and casual exchanges. Most Polish officers, they reported to their NKVD superiors, were still "anti-Soviet." Many of them believed the rumors being spread by the NKVD that the interrogations were a formality and that they would soon be released back to their homes, or even formed up to lead a special battalion against the Germans.

In fact, there was no question of letting these Polish officers go. On March 5, 1940, Lavrenti Beria, the sinister head of the NKVD, presented Joseph Stalin with a document that read, in part:

"To Comrade Stalin:

A large number of former officers of the Polish Army . . . all of them sworn enemies of Soviet authority [and] full of hatred for the Soviet system, are currently being held in prisoner-of-war camps of the USSR NKVD . . .

The military and police officers in the camps are attempting to continue their counter-revolutionary activities and are carrying out anti-Soviet agitation. Each of them is waiting only for his release in

order to enter actively into the struggle against Soviet authority . . .
In view of the fact that all of them are hardened and uncompromising
enemies of Soviet authority, the USSR NKVD considers it necessary
.˙. [to] apply to them the supreme penalty: shooting."

Stalin's signature is scrawled at the top of the first page of this document,
but this obviously constituted only the formal seal of approval. (This document
was also accepted by five other members of the Communist Party Polit buro,
among them the prime minister.) By March 5, he and Beria would have discussed
the need for the executions for some time. Scholars continue to debate the exact
reasons for the murder of so many Polish officers. The historian Norman Davies
wrote: "From the Soviet point of view, they [the Polish officers] were the cream
of the class enemy."

Most current day historians believe that Stalin wanted the Poles dead because
they could make up a military elite whose invaluable spirit and experience (much
of it gained against the Russians in 1920) could be used against the Soviet Union
in the future. Among the officers were also hundreds of doctors, lawyers, university professors, intellectuals, priests, writers, and politicians—people who were
the traditional enemies of Communism and who had, in fact, died by the thousands in Russia during the upheaval of the Bolshevik Revolution.

In a sense, it mattered little what the Poles said to their interrogators. Except
for a contingent of perhaps 400 men—who, for reasons that remain a mystery
to this day, were sent to other camps and survived—the grim future of the Polish
officers was set in stone almost the very second they were taken prisoner.

"THE ROULETTE HOUR"

Beginning on April 3, starting with the Kozelsk camp, groups of Polish officers were given special rations (quite generous by the standard of those they had
become accustomed to—800 grams [28 oz] of bread, sugar, and three herrings)
and told to gather their belongings. When they asked where they were going,
the Russians told them they were "heading west," which was the case—they
were heading toward Smolensk—and the giddy rumor flew among the Poles that
Smolensk was a way station on the journey home.

Each transport roundup of 250 or so Polish officers began with a 10:00 a.m. phone call to camp authorities from the NKVD headquarters in Moscow. These murderous bureaucrats spelled out the name of each man on the transport list to a clerk who carefully wrote down the information. Men heard from the camp grapevine that Moscow was calling and waited impatiently to see whether a guard would come and tell them to collect their belongings and line up—it was what the prisoners called, with unconscious irony, "the roulette hour."

After the prisoners queued up, the Russians took them out of the prison, placed them in vans and trucks, and drove them through the woods to a railroad station some five miles (8 km) away. Heavily armed soldiers with dogs guarded the prisoners' every move, which alarmed some of the officers—if they were being released, why was such security necessary? This impression was heightened by the fact that some of the Poles were beaten severely as they were crammed aboard windowless boxcars for their trip to Smolensk, 150 miles (241.4 km) away. They scrawled their worries across the walls of the boxcars in pencil—graffiti the NKVD, ever alert, scrubbed away after each trip.

Depending on how much train traffic there was, the trip to Smolensk could take two days, although it was usually completed in less than twenty-four hours. The train finally came to a halt eight miles (12.9 km) west of Smolensk, near a little village called Gniezdovo in the Katyń forest. Some of the men wrote on the wall: "We're getting off at Gniezdovo!" They may have felt they were going to a temporary camp, or were to be handed over to the Germans who controlled western Poland. Or perhaps they were being allowed to stretch their legs after the long, dark train trip.

Offloaded in groups of thirty, the prisoners had only a brief glimpse of the outside world, a smell of pine-scented air, before being forced aboard a large bus known as a black raven, which had a narrow passageway running down its center. Off the passageway were numerous small compartments, barely big enough for a man to crouch in, into which the NKVD guards pushed the Polish officers. Then the bus, with blacked-out windows, rumbled off.

Only one Polish POW journeyed as far as the train station at Gniezdovo and survived. His name was Stanislaw Swianiewicz, and he was a professor of economics who had joined the Polish army and was later captured by the Russians.

He was transported from Kozelsk on April 29, arriving in Gniezdovo the next day. He was standing in his boxcar along with his fellow POWs, waiting for his turn to be offloaded, when an NKVD colonel came to the door, shouted out his name, and ordered him to step outside. The colonel locked him in an empty boxcar equipped with racks for luggage. Seeing a hole on the wall near the ceiling, Swianiewicz climbed up on one of the racks and pretended to sleep while peering through the hole. He saw the POWs being gathered in "a fairly large open area, with patches of grass." The colonel who had picked him out—"a tall, stout, middle-aged man, with dark hair and a ruddy face"—was directing the operation of putting the prisoners into the black raven.

Swianiewicz couldn't quite figure out what was wrong with the picture before him. "Clearly my companions were being taken to a place in the vicinity, only a few miles away," he wrote. "It was a fine spring day and I wondered why [the POWs] were not told to march there, as had been the usual procedure on arrival at camps . . . [And] why the fixed bayonets of the escort? I could think of no reasonable explanation. But then, on that brilliant spring day, it never occurred to me that the operation might entail the execution of my companions."

The Russians took Swianiewicz shortly thereafter to an NKVD prison in Smolensk and then transferred him to the infamous Lubyanka Prison in Moscow, where he was charged with espionage for a pre-war book he had written on the Russian economy, which the Russians considered "treasonous." They sentenced him to the gulag. However, he survived, left the Soviet Union and lived in the United Kingdom until 1997, and was instrumental in bringing the horror of Katyń Forest to the attention of the world.

KATYŃ

There is no question about the fate of the Polish officers who entered the black raven that shuttled back and forth from Gniezdovo to the hidden clearing in the woods of Katyń—they were murdered by NKVD executioners. However, there is a great deal of historical speculation about how this happened. It appears that, at first, the black raven was driven to the execution site, where the Polish officers, disoriented from crouching in the darkened van, were taken out one by one. They were marched a few steps to the lip of a mass grave, one of eight found in

the forest, knocked to their knees, and dispatched with a single shot to the base of the skull with a Walther PPK pistol, a time-honored Bolshevik method of execution that killed its victims instantly, with little bloodshed. The NKVD then pushed each man into the grave and summoned the next man from the bus.

However, the flaw in this method would have been that those aboard the black raven could hear the sound of shots being fired and many—young officers, after all—would have struggled. This can be seen from the fact that many of the corpses buried in mass graves at Katyń had their overcoats thrown over their heads, their hands tied behind them, and sawdust stuffed in their mouths. It is possible some of those who fought their executioners were bayoneted to death. Those execution pits that held the corpses of the men killed at the site of the grave presented chaotic scenes, with bodies twisted this way and that.

But in other grave sites, bodies were stacked neatly one atop the other, which indicates to some researchers that the Poles were killed elsewhere and then brought to the forest pits for burial. The question becomes, where? A diary was discovered on the body of Major Adam Solski, which was dated April 9 and apparently scrawled just before his death:

> Ever since dawn it has been a peculiar day. Departure in lorries [black ravens] filled with cells: horrible. Taken to forest somewhere, something like a summer resort. Very thorough search of our belongings. They took my watch, which showed time as 6:30 . . . asked about my ring, which was taken, ruble belt, pen knife.

The reference to the "summer resort" could have been to the NKVD summer retreat in the forest, built in the 1920s, a large building the Germans later referred to as "Little Castle," or it could have been one of numerous residences of Soviet officials, hidden away in the scenic woods. There, the Polish officers would have been taken by surprise and murdered individually in sound-proof cells—as the NKVD apparently did with prisoners from Ostashkov—at which point their bodies would be carted away to be placed in the pits inside the forest. Since Katyń was a Bolshevik execution site from the days just following the Russian Revolution—in fact, the Germans discovered older mass graves containing the bodies of several hundred victims of the Bolsheviks—the modus operandi for this type of killing could have already been in place.

There is also the possibility that many of those buried in Katyń were killed in the NKVD prison in Smolensk—a former NKVD officer later testified that these men were taken to a cellar room where there was an open sewer manhole. The NKVD made them lie down with their heads over the manhole, at which point the Russians shot them in the back of the head. They then took the bodies for burial in Goats' Hills.

After all the bodies were buried in the eight deep mass graves, the Russians spread tons of sand, covered the sand with topsoil, and then planted pine and birch tree saplings.

"MAY I COME IN?"

Though the murder of all of the 22,000 Polish officers is called the Katyń Forest Massacre, the 4,000 bodies found at Katyń represented only those taken from the Kozelsk camp. The Russians took roughly another 4,000 POWs from the Starobelsk camp west to the town of Kharkov, where they murdered them in an NKVD prison. There was a horrible etiquette to the killing of the men from Starobelsk. A guard would lead them, with bound hands, to the door of a windowless room.

"May I come in?" he would ask, after knocking.

"Come in," would be the reply. Inside the room would be an NKVD prosecutor with an executioner. The prosecutor would ask the prisoner his name and date of birth. He then told the guard that he could go. Waiting outside the room, the guard heard a single shot, at which point the prosecutor called him in and told him to drag the body outside the prison through a secret entrance, where it was placed aboard a truck for transport to a park outside Kharkov to be buried in one of numerous mass graves.

The Polish police officers from Ostashkov, 6,500 strong, were transported via boxcar to the town of Kalinin (the Russian city now called Tver), where they were murdered in a local prison by a group of Moscow NKVD men led by the infamous Vasili Blokhin (See "History's Most Prolific Executioner" at right), who may have personally executed almost every man from Ostashkov. These men were then buried in a forest near the Russian village of Mednoe, off the Moscow–Leningrad highway.

The rest of the victims of what became known as the Katyń Massacre, those Polish prisoners, who were distributed to camps in Ukraine and Belorussia, were transferred to NKVD prisons within Russia. The NKVD record keepers, meticulous as always, recorded 7,305 of them shot in various jails in cities such as Kiev and Minsk. Their final burial places have never been found.

THE DEAD

The killings of the Polish officers took place over roughly a six-week period, from early April to mid- or late May 1940. A year later, in June 1941, the Germans, taking Stalin completely by surprise, abrogated the Nazi–Soviet Non-Aggression Pact and launched a massive and cataclysmic invasion of Russia, sending the Russian army reeling back, and devouring large sections of Eastern Europe, including all of Poland and most of western Russia. However, the Russian army

HISTORY'S MOST PROLIFIC EXECUTIONER

Vasili Mikhailovich Blokhin, the NKVD major in charge of executing the Polish officers from the Ostashkov camp, was a man who believed in personally doing the killing that his superiors had ordered him to supervise.

Born in 1895, he was known as the NKVD's chief executioner, having been hand-picked for this position by Joseph Stalin himself. Blokhin personally killed tens of thousands of men and women during Stalin's Great Purges of the 1930s, so it was only natural the NKVD would turn to him when it came time to dispatch the officers held in the Soviet prison camps. Along with a team of about thirty NKVD men from Moscow, mainly drivers and prison guards, Blokhin arrived at the NKVD prison in Talinin and set himself up in a sound-proofed cellar room that had a sloping floor for drainage. He then put on his special uniform, consisting of a leather cap, long leather apron, and elbow-length gloves. On a table next to him was a bricfcase filled with his own personal Walther PPK pistols, for Blokhin, a true artist at his trade, would use no one else's tools but his own.

After the prisoner's identity was verified, he was brought handcuffed into the cellar room where Blokhin awaited in his long apron, like some horrible butcher. One guard later testified: "The men held [tho priooncr'o] arms and [Dlokhin] shot him in the base of the skull . . . that's all." Blokhin worked fast and efficiently, killing an average of one person every three minutes during the course of ten-hour nights—the killings were always done at night, so that the bodies could be disposed of in darkness.

Although this has never been completely proven, historians suspect that Blokhin shot 6,000 men over a period of twenty-eight days, which would make him one of the most prolific murderers of all time. (Another, perhaps more realistic figure, however, puts his death total at "only" 1,000.) However many people he killed, Blokhin was consistently promoted by his superiors for performing "special tasks." He lost his job, however, after Stalin died. The cause of Blokhin's death, in 1955, was listed as suicide.

ANOTHER NAZI PHOTO CLEARLY
SHOWS A CORPSE IN THE UNIFORM
OF A POLISH MAJOR—ONE OF THE
MISTAKES THE NKVD MADE WAS
NOT STRIPPING THE MEN OF THEIR
UNIFORMS BEFORE SHOOTING THEM.

steadied, and won a pivotal victory against the Germans at Stalingrad in a bloody battle ending in February 1943.

The Nazis immediately recognized the propaganda value in the discovery of the Polish corpses in Katyń Forest. The Soviets were now allies with the British and the Americans, as well as with the Poles, who had formed a government and army in exile, and whose pilots had been instrumental in helping defeat the German air force during the desperate Battle for Britain in the fall of 1940. And for months, the Polish government had beseeched Joseph Stalin to give them word of the missing Polish officers, who, as far as their families were concerned, had simply vanished into thin air in the winter of 1939–1940.

At one point, Stalin told a representative of the Polish government-in-exile that 15,000 of these officers had escaped into Manchuria. This was, as the historian Allen Paul has written, a "preposterous" claim. But the Poles continued to search for leads as to what happened to the officers. While they had their suspicions about Stalin, they could not prove anything. They were also organizing an army in Russia with which to invade and liberate Poland from the Germans, and thus felt they needed to cooperate with Stalin as much as possible, although it was like making a bargain with the devil.

Then came the discovery of the Katyń Forest bodies. The Germans carefully excavated all eight graves filled with Polish officers. Though the NKVD were ruthless executioners, they did not cover their tracks very well. They stripped the Polish officers of their valuables but left many of them with personal identity papers and diaries, which gave clues as to what had happened. They also buried them in their uniforms, which allowed forensic scientists—men of the

International Medical Commission, including some of the foremost autopsy specialists in the world, brought in by the Nazis—a chance to identify not only the prisoners' units, but sometimes the individual corpses themselves.

Unlike the Russians, the Nazis, who by 1943 had engaged in mass murder on a far greater scale than that seen in the Katyń Forest (see "The Ravine of Women" on page 184), made it a point to strip bodies of all clothing and identification. (By this time, in any event, they had moved toward mass incineration as a way to dispose of their victims.) In addition to leaving the clothing intact, the Russians had been unlucky in terms of the preservation of the corpses. The weight of tons of sand upon the corpses had pressed them together. Only the top layer of corpses, more exposed to bacteria, leaked cadaverine fluid. This formed a kind of embalming seal around the corpses farther below, keeping them more or less intact.

"ST. PAUL'S CURSE"

The Nazi propaganda machine kicked into high gear after the discovery, excavation, and meticulous examination of the Katyń dead. On April 13, 1943, the Germans announced that they had discovered the "missing" Polish officers, "bestially murdered by the Bolsheviks." In fact, they had only discovered 4,000 of them, not the entire 12,000 that they claimed, but the news made a big splash across the world. A delegation of Poles from the German-occupied territory (e.g., Red Cross members and a few well-known writers) was flown to the grave sites to view the corpses and the accompanying evidence, while Nazi cameramen filmed and snapped pictures. The Nazis also invited journalists from neutral countries and international commission of physicians from German-occupied states to view the graves, and even brought in British and U.S. prisoners of war (see "An Inconvenient Truth," page 182) to witness forensic examinations.

On April 15, the Soviet Union Information Bureau reacted vehemently:

In launching this monstrous invention, the German-Fascist scoundrels did not hesitate at the most unscrupulous and base lies in their attempts to cover up the crimes that, as has now become evident, were perpetrated by themselves. The German-Fascist reports on this subject leave no doubt as to the tragic fate of the former Polish prisoners of war . . . who fell into the hands of the German-Fascist hangmen.

In other words, they accused the Germans of killing the Poles after the Soviets left them behind when they withdrew from the area in the summer of 1941. It is hard to say whose hypocrisy is greater here—that of the Nazis, who were in the midst of perpetrating the worst mass murder in history, or that of the Soviets, who had actually killed the Polish officers and then tried to cover up the crime.

Immediately, however, the Polish government-in-exile had questions. The figure of 12,000 was soon disproven—there were only 4,000 corpses at Katyń. So where were the rest? And if the Germans had captured the Polish officers when the Soviets withdrew, why had not the Soviets mentioned this previously?

There was more hypocrisy to come. Although high officials in the British and U.S. governments privately believed what the Germans were saying about the mass executions, they chose to side with the Soviets, and ignore the evidence presented by the Germans. This caused some Allied diplomats pangs of conscience. Sir Owen O'Malley, British ambassador to the Polish government-in-exile, wrote in one confidential memorandum: "We have perforce used the good name of England like the murderers used the little conifers [a reference to the saplings planted by the Soviets at Katyń] to cover up a massacre . . . May it not be that we now stand in danger of bemusing not only others but ourselves, of falling . . . under St. Paul's curse on those who can see cruelty 'and burn not'"? Even as high a personage as the U.S. president, Franklin Roosevelt, felt compelled to participate in a cover-up of the Katyń Forest massacre (see "An Inconvenient Truth").

Yet the greater goal of the Allies—to destroy Germany at all costs—came before acknowledging the true murderers of 22,000 Polish officers. As Allen Paul writes, a cold political calculation entered into the equation. Under the circumstances, the allies "could not indulge in the dubious luxury of indicting the Soviets for a crime that could not be avenged."

The tides of war eventually changed, and the Germans were forced to retreat from Smolensk after a Soviet counter-offensive in September 1943. The Red Army now reoccupied Katyń Forest and set about the greatest exercise in hypocrisy of all—the "Special Commission for Ascertaining and Investigating the Circumstances of the Shooting of Polish Officer Prisoners by the German-Fascist Invaders in Katyń Forest."

This so-called Special Commission—directed by Joseph Stalin's personal physician, N.N. Burdenko—dug up the bodies that the Nazis had reburied, briefly examined them, and reported their findings. They claimed that these men (whom the Soviets also claimed numbered 12,000) had been captured by the Nazis while working on road projects for the Soviets, murdered by Hitler's henchmen, and then dug up again three years later in an elaborate attempt to frame the Soviet Union and sow discord among the Allies.

It was a typical Stalin Alice-in-Wonderland moment, but there was nothing frivolous about it. As the Polish people continued to press Stalin for the truth, he turned the tables on them, claiming that in not accepting the Soviet claim of innocence, the Polish government-in-exile was siding with the Nazis. He then broke diplomatic relations with them and used this as an excuse to get the British and Americans to support the alternative Polish puppet government he had set up in Moscow and would soon install in Warsaw, in place of the legitimate Polish government.

"TO THE POLISH SOLDIERS"

It would take a long time for the Soviet government to admit to murdering 22,000 Polish officers. In the meantime, the Iron Curtain closed over Poland, where even mentioning the story of Katyń could be dangerous. In 1980, when the Polish trade union Solidarity put up a monument that read: "Katyń, 1940," the police tore it down and replaced it with one that read: "To the Polish soldiers—victims of Hitlerite fascism—reposing in the soil of Katyń."

For almost fifty years, the families of those who were murdered wondered about the fate of their loved ones. Poles in general understood that their nation had been robbed of the best of its leaders, men in their thirties and forties who could have guided the nation in the years to come.

AN INCONVENIENT TRUTH

Beginning in 1943, an U.S. naval officer named George Howard Earle, who was President Franklin Roosevelt's special envoy to the Balkans, decided to thoroughly investigate the Katyń massacre to bring the truth of the matter before the president. Earle had extensive, prewar contacts in Eastern Europe and spent nearly a year gathering evidence that he was convinced proved that the Soviets had murdered the Polish officers.

In May 1944, Earle brought this evidence, including photographs, in front of Roosevelt. After listening to him and looking at the pictures taken at the Katyń exhumations, Roosevelt exclaimed:

"George, this is entirely German propaganda and a German plot. I am absolutely convinced the Russians did not do this."

Earle, who had been stationed in Turkey, could not put the matter out of his mind, and in March 1945 sent Roosevelt a letter saying that he would soon publish an article detailing his beliefs about Katyń, unless Roosevelt instructed him not to. Roosevelt replied: "I have noted with concern your plan to publish your unfavorable opinion of one of our allies . . . I not only do not wish it, but I specifically forbid you to publish any information or opinion [about Katyń]."

Shortly thereafter, Earle was abruptly transferred to Samoa, where he stayed until Roosevelt's death the following month. The U.S. navy chief of personnel brought him back to Washington and apologized to him, saying that Earle's transfer had not been the decision of the navy. Obviously, Franklin Roosevelt felt that the truth about Katyń was far too explosive for the world to hear.

WHEN THIS PHOTOGRAPH WAS TAKEN IN 1938, GEORGE EARLE (SEATED, TO ROOSEVELT'S RIGHT) WAS GOVERNOR OF PENNSYLVANIA AND AN INFLUENTIAL ADVISOR. LATER, ROOSEVELT'S SPECIAL EMISSARY TO THE BALKANS, HE FAILED TO CONVINCE THE PRESIDENT OF THE TRUTH BEHIND THE KATYŃ FOREST MASSACRE.

ASSOCIATED PRESS

Finally, in 1989, as the Iron Curtain was being torn asunder, Soviet scholars were allowed to reveal that Joseph Stalin had ordered the Katyń Forest killings. The following year, Mikhail Gorbachev admitted that the NKVD had also killed the rest of the prisoners from the other camps. Finally, in 1990, the USSR officially expressed "profound regret" for the killings. Since then, more evidence has been compiled that points to exactly how the Polish officers died; however, the descendents of the Katyń victims feel that the Russians need to be more forthcoming with information and records. (There are even rumors that film of the Katyń Forest executions exists, something the Russian government denies.)

In the last decade or so, the Russian government has retreated from the Soviet stance of openness and is now demanding that the Poles take responsibility for the estimated 20,000 Russians who died in Polish POW camps after the 1920 war, but most scholars feel that the deaths of these men, caused by illness from poor camp conditions, is a very different thing than the deliberate massacre of the Polish officers at the insistence of Russia's head of state.

While real reconciliation between Russia and Poland—now an independent nation—is probably a distant hope, the fact remains that the Polish people have never forgotten the truth of what happened at Katyń Forest.

CHAPTER 11

"THE RAVINE OF WOMEN"

BABI YAR, SEPTEMBER 29–30, 1941

IN TWO DAYS, GERMAN SPECIAL EXECUTION UNITS SHOT 33,000
JEWS IN THIS PICTURESQUE UKRAINIAN RAVINE, SENDING
SHOCKWAVES OF HORROR THROUGH EASTERN EUROPE

Wild grasses rustle over Babi Yar.
The trees look sternly, as if passing judgment . . .
And I myself, like one long soundless scream
Above the thousands and thousands interred.
I am every old man executed here,
As I am every child murdered here.
—*Babi Yar*, by Yevgeni Yevtushenko

IT WAS KNOWN IN UKRAINIAN AS *BABI YAR*, "THE RAVINE OF WOMEN," and it was one of several deep erosion chasms etched into the earth on the outskirts of the ancient and beautiful city of Kiev, capital of the Ukraine. Babi Yar was huge—one Russian writer described it as "enormous, you might even say majestic: deep and wide, like a mountain gorge." Until September 29, 1941, Babi Yar was considered a peaceful place. In good weather, children came to make their way down the numerous small cuts of the gorge onto its hard-packed dirt floor, and there they chased each other and played football. Above the gorge there was a playground. The city's old Jewish cemetery also stood nearby.

However, on September 29, 1941, Babi Yar changed from a tranquil place of beauty to the scene of the worst single massacre of the entire

PART OF THE BABI YAR RAVINE ON
THE OUTSKIRTS OF KIEV. PHOTO
TAKEN BY SOVIET ARMY UNITS
THAT ARRIVED IN THE WAKE OF
THE RETREATING GERMAN ARMY
AND UNEARTHED THE BODIES OF
THOSE EXECUTED DURING THE
NAZI OCCUPATION.

ASSOCIATED PRESS

Holocaust, where German soldiers armed with machine guns killed 33,771 Jews in two days. Babi Yar became a place filled with "horrible scenes of human grief and despair," as one of the few eyewitnesses later testified, a place whose horrors, as the Holocaust historian Martin Gilbert writes, "were endless and obscene."

Babi Yar gave warning to Jews throughout Eastern Europe that the Nazis were truly bent on exterminating their culture and religion. But it also helped German officials like Heinrich Himmler understand that a more efficient way of killing and disposing of the bodies of mass numbers of Jews—such as the gas chamber and the crematoria of the concentration camps—needed to be found.

MURDER SQUADS

On June 22, 1941, the German army massed one-and-a-half million men on its eastern borders and launched Operation Barbarossa, a surprise attack on its former ally, the Soviet Union. From the Baltic to the Black Sea, German forces sent the inexperienced and often poorly armed troops of Joseph Stalin reeling back into the heartland of Russia. Hundreds of thousands surrendered as German panzer divisions raced for Moscow and the vital oilfields of the Caucasus.

Trailing after the German frontline units were four special companies, the likes of whom had never been seen before in warfare. They were unique in their bureaucratic organization and intent; special units in warfare had been organized to assassinate political or military leaders, but not to murder civilian populations. These were the *Einsatzgruppen*, or murder squads, and it was their job to carry out the extermination of entire Jewish communities in countries such as Poland, Latvia, Lithuania, Estonia, and the Ukraine. This was no mere harassment of the Jewish community, or random killing, but a systematic massacre planned by Himmler and other leaders of the *Schutzstaffel*, or SS. The *Einsatzgruppen* were broken down into smaller units known as *Sonderkommandos* to cover as much area as possible. These joined forces with local anti-Semitic thugs to begin killing almost immediately.

In the border village of Virbalis, Lithuania, only a few days after the invasion began, Jews "were placed alive in anti-tank trenches about two kilometers [1.2 miles] long and killed by machine guns," reported an eyewitness. "Lime was thereupon sprayed upon them and a second group was made to lie down. They were similarly shot . . . Only the children were not shot. They were caught by the legs, their heads hit against stones and they were thereupon buried alive."

As the German army progressed eastward, massacres happened in village after village. However, *Eisensatzgruppe* C—one of two directly responsible for killing Jews in the Ukraine—complained in a report to headquarters on September 12, 1941: "Across the lines rumors appear and are circulated among the Jews about the fate they can expect." Too many Jews were escaping with retreating Russian forces. "The solution of the Jewish problem, one of the most important ones, is proceeding, alas, slowly," wrote an officer in *Eisensatzgruppe* D. The *Sonderkommandos* were angry that they were only able to kill 4,000 Jews in the city of Kishinev, Moldavia, which—according to the SS—had a prewar Jewish population of some 60,000.

But there was still plenty of murdering to be done. From August 27 to August 29, the Germans led 11,000 Jews from a town called Kamenetz Podolski in the southwestern Ukraine to a series of bomb craters on the outskirts. One young Jewish survivor named Leslie Gordon, who had been deported from Budapest, was taken with a group of men to widen some of the holes with picks and shovels—he thought he was digging anti-tank ditches. Then:

> Shortly after this we saw the people coming up also with shovels and different tools in their hands and they had been ordered to lay down their tools. [The Germans] ordered [them] to take off all their clothes, they were put in order, and then they were all naked. They were sent to the ditches and SS men, some of them drunk, some of them sober, and some of them photographing, it seems, these people numbering about three hundred to four hundred, I don't know the exact number, were all executed and most of them only got hurt and got buried alive. Quick-lime was brought there too, four or five truckloads of quicklime.

Gordon's father, mother, four brothers, and sister all died at the hands of the Germans. In his testimony after the war, he said that the killings caused some of the SS men to "get almost hysterical," to "get close to a nervous breakdown." Others just kept a stony silence and kept on killing and killing.

THE CAPTURE OF KIEV

This whirlwind of slaughter reached the city of Kiev on September 19, 1941, when the Soviets surrendered after a battle that had lasted eighty-three days and resulted in the death or surrender of an entire Soviet army group. German aerial bombardment caused the destruction of a good deal of the city, which had largely been evacuated by civilians. About 180,000 Jews lived in the city when Hitler's invasion of Eastern Europe began, but now, to the chagrin of the Nazi killers, there were perhaps 33,000. The rest had fled east, even if it meant going farther into the Soviet Union, which had a history of pogroms and other persecutions of Jews.

At first, when the Germans marched through the streets of Kiev, some of those who had been left behind thought things would be all right. "Soldiers were looking out [from the backs of military trucks]," wrote one civilian. "They seemed very fresh, very cheerful. Others were walking along the streets. They laughed without apparent reason . . . Almost all the Germans had phrase-books in their hands and shouted to the girls in the pavement: 'Hey, girl! Bolshevik kaput! Come with us, walk—*spatzieren! Bitte!*'"

Soon, however, this show of friendliness, however heavy-handed, was replaced by the spectacle of German soldiers wandering the city looting. It appeared to the increasingly uneasy residents of Kiev that they had been given *carte blanche* to do this by their commanding officers. They stopped men and women on the street and demanded their watches, coats, and jackets. They broke into stores and private houses and took everything that wasn't nailed down. One man saw three German soldiers walking down the street with an ornate empty coffin obviously pilfered from a funeral home. Another saw a German officer carrying a children's bike he had had just stolen from an eight-year-old girl. When the child persisted in following him, crying, he turned and kicked her in the stomach. (Letters found on the bodies of German soldiers later showed that many of them were "taking orders" from their wives and children back home for shoes, toys, and other goods.)

The victims of these crimes were mostly Jews and their persecutors were not only German soldiers but Ukrainian Christians, both the thuggish militia hired by the SS to act as *Polizei*, but also civilians who had a long-term hatred of

Jews. The situation for the Jewish population of Kiev worsened considerably on September 24, when explosions started going off in the city, enormous blasts, one after another, in the buildings the Germans had commandeered for their high command to live and work in. Huge fires began to burn, leaving thousands of civilians homeless. The explosions, it was discovered after the war, were the work of the military arm of the NKVD, the Russian intelligence agency, which let officers left behind to booby-trap the buildings the Germans were most likely to take possession of. The Russians estimated the blasts killed 10,000 Germans, which was probably a great exaggeration. But certainly hundreds of important officers died in the blasts.

The Ukrainian civilians who had lost their homes believed that the explosions had been started by that age-old scapegoat, the Jews—anti-Semitism was rife in Eastern Europe at the time, which made it far easier for the Nazis to demonize and eliminate the Jews. They began to attack Jews in the street and the Jewish population of the city was terrified that Ukrainians would institute a pogrom against them, as in the past. Thus, when a German poster appeared all over the city on September 28, ordering the evacuation of the Jews, some of them were relieved—they thought they might be on their way to a safer place.

ON THE WAY TO BABI YAR

The poster read, in German, Russian, and Ukrainian: "All Zhids of Kiev and its environs must appear on Monday 29 September 1941 at 8:00 in the morning at the intersection of Melnikovskaya and Dochtourovskaya Streets . . . Take with you your documents, money, valuable articles, and also warm clothing, undergarments, etc. Whatever of the Zhids shall fail to comply and is later found elsewhere will be shot."

The wording of the text in Russian and Ukrainian was vulgar (the use of the word Zhid, or Yid, for Jew) and grammatically incorrect, which supports the assertions of most scholars that the Germans planned the Babi Yar massacre completely on their own, without even the aid of local translators. The most likely planner was Dr. Paul Blobel, an alcoholic former architect who was commander of *Einsatzgruppe* C, and who had participated in numerous massacres during the invasion of Eastern Europe and Russia. During his trial at Nuremberg

"THEY ALL TUMBLE INTO THE GRAVE"

Although in 1941 there was already experimentation with mobile vans in which small groups of Jews and Gypsies and other "undesirables" were gassed, the killings performed by the *Einsatzgruppen* in Eastern Europe were done mainly by shooting. Members of these units killed thousands of people each. They were often drunk and quickly became callous. Thirty-five-year-old Sergeant Felix Landau kept a diary, which gives a rare first-hand glimpse into the work of one such killer. It is horrifying in large part for its complete lack of affect:

July 14, 1941

Again I am roused from deep sleep. "Get up for execution!" Alright, why not?

We drive a few kilometers along the main road til we reach a wood. We go into the wood and look for a spot suitable for mass execution. We order the prisoners to dig their graves. Only two of them are crying, the others show courage. What can they be thinking? I believe each still has the hope of not being shot. I don't feel the slightest stir of pity. That's how it is and has got to be . . .

Slowly the grave gets bigger and deeper. Two are crying without letup. I let them dig so they can't think. The work really calms them. Money, watches, and valuables are collected. The two women go first to be shot. Placed at the edge of the grave they face the soldiers. They get shot . . .

The shooting goes on. Two heads have been shot off. Nearly all fall into the grave unconscious only to suffer a long while. Our revolvers don't help either. The last group has to throw the corpses into the grave; they have to stand ready for their own execution. They all tumble into the grave.

IN A TYPICAL SCENE OF HORROR, A SOVIET JEW IS EXECUTED BY A MEMBER OF A NAZI MURDER SQUAD WHILE OTHER GERMAN SOLDIERS CASUALLY CHAT AND WATCH.

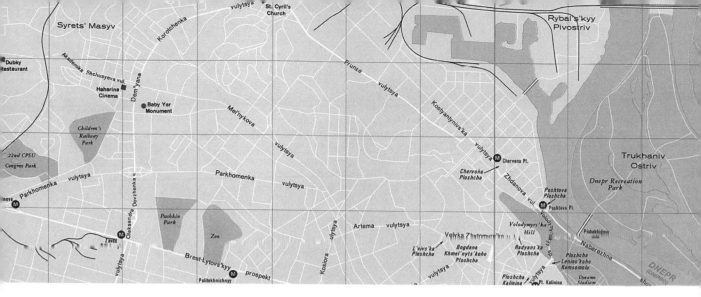

after the war (he was hanged for his crimes in 1951), Blobel claimed he was not present at the Babi Yar massacre, but this is unlikely. With other *Einsatzgruppen* actions something of a disappointment to Nazi superiors, it appears that Blobel was determined to make a grand success of the extermination of the Jews of Kiev.

He was aided by the fact that many of the Jews, despite disturbing rumors they had heard of mass killings, were reassured by the fact that they had been told to bring their belongings with them. The poster had spoken of "relocation," and some Jews convinced themselves that they would be taken on trains to a prison farm, which might be better for them than staying in Kiev with the Ukrainian population aroused against them because of the explosions. Yet the Jewish population in Kiev was either very young—perhaps 30 percent of those who died at Babi Yar were under the age of eight—or quite old. The Germans would have no use for such people on a prison farm. A twelve-year-old non-Jewish boy who witnessed the beginning of the evacuation later recalled:

> They were starting before dark in order to be early at the trains to secure seats. With crying children, old and sick, weeping and bickering, the Jews from the large truck farm next to our house were pouring onto the street . . . [There was] a hum of voices . . . "Where are they taking us?"—"How shall we go?" In one group, the word *ghetto* was repeated continually. A not-too-young excited woman cut in: "What are you talking about? This is death!" Old women started to weep and it resembled weird singing . . . There were protesting voices—what right did

they have to spread panic? But it was already known that one woman had killed herself and poisoned her children. Also, near the Opera, a young girl had thrown herself out a window and now lying on the pavement, covered with a white sheet . . .

Suddenly a commotion spread among the crowd . . . They said that further . . . along Melnika Street stood a line of soldiers . . . They were letting people in but would not let anyone out.

"THE EARTH WAS MOVING LONG AFTER"

As the Jews approached Babi Yar, in the northern suburbs of Kiev, it became clear to them that they were not being taken to relocation trains. A line of soldiers began to funnel them toward a grassy copse of woods just before the edge of the ravine. At first the soldiers were relatively polite, but as the evacuees got closer to Babi Yar they acted with increasing ferocity.

A night watchman at the Jewish cemetery, who was not Jewish, hid among the gravestones and watched. The soldiers of the *Sonderkommando*

. . . formed a corridor and drove the panic-stricken people towards the huge glade, where soldiers with sticks, swearings [*sic*], and dogs, who were tearing the people's bodies, forced the people to undress, to form columns in hundreds, and then to go in the columns in twos towards the mouth of the ravine.

The watchman continued:

. . . they found themselves on the narrow ground above the precipice, twenty to twenty-five meters [65.6 to 82 feet] in height, and on the opposite side there were the German machine guns. The killed, wounded, and half-alive people fell down and were smashed there. Then the next hundred were brought, and everything repeated again. The policemen took the children by the legs and threw them alive into the Yar.

It is possible that there were as few as fifty SS soldiers doing the actual killing at Babi Yar, with Ukrainian policemen acting as crowd control, which raises the question as to why the Jews did not attempt to overwhelm them. There was Jewish resistance in Kiev—Jewish partisans operated in the area, waging guerilla warfare against the Nazis—and just prior to the Babi Yar massacre, a young girl ran down a Kiev street with a pistol, killing two SS officers before shooting herself.

But the mostly aging and very young people, staring down the barrels of machine guns and perhaps somehow thinking they might survive (see "They All Tumble into the Grave," page 190) marched in slow procession toward their deaths. Stripped naked, they were made to stand on a narrow sand shelf cut into the cliff above a growing pile of bloody, twitching bodies, while from across the ravine the German machine guns chattered, and a new group of bodies joined those below.

The killing went on throughout September 29, until dark made it impossible to see, and then continued the morning of September 30, until the Germans had disposed of all the evacuees. The first night, the cemetery watchman later recalled, the Germans undermined the wall of the ravine with dynamite, burying the people who had fallen there. "But the earth was moving long after," the man said, "because wounded and still-alive Jews were still moving. One girl was crying: 'Mammy, why do they pour sand into my eyes?'"

DINA PRONICHEVA

Very few Jews were able to escape the horrid maw of Babi Yar. One of them was Dina Pronicheva, the mother of two young children, who was an actress with the Kiev Puppet Theater. Pronicheva saw the proclamation posted on the walls on September 28, but had a Russian name and did not look Jewish, and so decided that she would stay in Kiev with her children. But, since her parents were elderly, she thought she might escort them to the trains waiting to "relocate" them, and then return to her children.

In the 1960s, she told her story to a Russian journalist named Anatoly Kouznetsoff. When she arrived at her parent's house at about six that morning, she found the entire neighborhood awake. Those who were Jewish had packed their belongings and were giving keys to their houses to their non-Jewish neighbors, with instructions on how to water plants and feed the pets while they were away.

Pronicheva and her parents then joined a long procession of mainly elderly people through the streets of Kiev. The long line of people moved very slowly and they only reached the Jewish cemetery in late afternoon. Instead of passing by it, Pronicheva realized to her surprise they were being funneled into the cemetery through a gate. But then she heard the sound of guns, volleys fired over and over again:

The sound of firing could be clearly heard, a lonely plane was circling overhead. The atmosphere was strained and panicky.

Dina heard snatches of conversation.

"This is war—war! They are taking us to the rear."

"But why only Jews?"

Some half-witted old woman volunteered an incredible explanation: "Because we are a nation close to the Germans and they want to evacuate us first."

Pronicheva watched the Germans stop the people ahead of them; force them to place their luggage in piles; and then count them off in groups of fifteen, sending them off ahead. They were then forced to take off their warm coats (it was a chilly, windy day). A soldier came and tore Pronicheva's fur coat from her back. She suddenly realized that she had walked into an execution. Her parents realized it, too. Her father said to her, mildly, "Go away, my dear. We don't need your help any longer."

Thinking of her children, she pushed her way back through the crowd to the cemetery gate, but a soldier stopped her. "Ah, Jewess! Get back!" Pronicheva went helplessly back to join her parents. Now, as they approached the cliff of Babi Yar, the true horror began. She and the rest of those about to be killed were forced to walk a gauntlet of German soldiers who hit them with rubber truncheons and yelled *"Schnell! Schnell!"* If anyone fell, police dogs tore him or her apart. Pronicheva muttered to herself: "I must not fall! I must not fall!" Once through the gauntlet, the Jews were met by Ukrainian *polizei* shouting: "Undress! Quick! Quick!" Those who didn't move quickly enough were beaten with clubs and brass knuckles. Naked, the terrified Jews jostled forward toward the sound of shots, which grew ever louder. Dina heard her mother yell, "Baby, you don't look like one! Save yourself!"

Once again, Pronicheva tried to escape her fate. She did not undress and instead went to an official and claimed she was not Jewish. This time the man listened to her and sent her off to sit with a group of people, who claimed they had merely been seeing friends and relatives off and gotten caught in the dragnet. A soldier told them: "Sit there. Wait until they shoot the Jews. Then we'll let you go."

Pronicheva watched as naked people, bloody from beatings, were forced through a gap in an earthen wall at the lip of the ravine. She could not see what happened there, but could hear gunfire and screams. Some of the Jews began to laugh hysterically as they got near the gap. Others quite literally turned gray. Children were torn from their mothers' arms and tossed like dolls over the wall, into the ravine.

Pronicheva and the rest of her little group were forced to wait until it was nearly dark, but it appeared they were going to be let go, until a German SS officer showed up and scoffed: "Shoot them at once. If one of them gets away, we won't get a single Jew tomorrow."

And to her horror, she and those she was with were forced up and herded toward the lip of the cliff of Babi Yar.

ESCAPE FROM BABI YAR

Because it was getting so late, Pronicheva and the others were not forced to undress, but were herded through the gap in the wall and found themselves standing on the narrow path cut into the wall, facing machine guns on the other side. As Anatoly Kouznetsoff relates:

Dina looked down and her head went around—it seemed to be so deep. Below her was a sea of blood-smeared bodies . . . When the last person of [Dina's group] reached the end of the shelf, one of the soldiers got behind the machine gun, and started to fire. Dina felt, rather than saw, the bodies starting to fall from the shelf, and how the line of fire was approaching her. She thought "Now . . . now . . ." Without waiting, she clenched her fists and hurled herself down.

She seemed to be falling forever. Indeed, it must have seemed quite a distance. When she hit the bottom she felt no pain. Warm blood splashed her face, as if she had fallen into a bath of blood. She lay face up, her arms spread, her eyes closed.

There were moans, groans, and sobs around her and beneath her: many were still alive. The mass of bodies were quivering, settling down, getting packed more tightly. And now, soldiers appeared on the shelf, their torches shining down, firing their pistols spasmodically at those who appeared to still be alive . . . Then she felt men walking over the bodies. They were SS men who had come down into the ravine . . . An SS man stumbled over Dina and she must have looked suspicious. He shone his torch at her, lifted her, and started to hit her. But she hung limply, showing no signs of life. He hit her breast, stepped upon her arm so that it cracked, but did not shoot and went off.

In a few moments she heard a Ukrainian voice: "All right. Let's cover them up!"

Shovelfuls of dirt and sand began to fall on Pronicheva, covering her up. She tried not to move, but as her mouth filled with dirt she decided that being shot was better than being buried alive, and so she pulled herself, with her uninjured arm, up through the sea of bodies to the surface. Fortunately, it was now so dark that no one could see her. Using strength she did not think she had, she crawled to the nearest wall and pulled herself up, little by little. When she reached the top, she grabbed hold of a bush, pulled herself up, and lay panting on the ground. She nearly fell back into the ravine in terror when she heard a voice:

"Don't be afraid . . . I'm alive."

"IT IS THE JEWS WHO HAVE DONE THIS"

The site of the massacre at Babi Yar felt haunted to the residents of Kiev for many years. For twenty years after the war's end, Babi Yar's collapsed and serpentine canyon filled up with junk, water, and mud, so that it looked like a small lake. "It was motionless," wrote author Sarah Kyron, "and mixed up with silt, and it seemed from afar to be greenish, as if the tears of the people who had been killed there had come out of the soil."

Sometime during the 1950s, as the water in the ravine rose higher, a wall was built to protect a nearby brickyard. In 1961, this wall collapsed during a rainstorm and a massive stream of liquid clay, mixed with skeletal remains, poured out on the streets of Kiev. The flood rushed down a hill and overwhelmed a local streetcar depot, burying entire streetcars as well as passengers. Twenty-four people were killed. After the disaster, one Ukrainian woman riding on a nearby streetcar yelled: "It is the Jews who have done this. They are taking their revenge on us. They always will."

For many years after the war, the Soviet Union, which controlled the Ukraine, refused to put up memorials to the Jews who had died there, although in 1974 it did erect a monument to Soviet resistance fighters; however, this monument was about a mile (1.6 km) away from the actual site of the massacre, at the place where the Nazis burned Jewish remains to conceal the evidence. However, after the fall of the Soviet Union a memorial—a bronze menorah—was placed on the site of the massacre itself, which is now part of a large, forested park where people jog and walk their dogs.

PAUL BLOBEL AT HIS WAR CRIMES
TRIAL AFTER THE WAR. BLOBEL
WAS THE ALCOHOLIC OFFICER IN
CHARGE OF THE EIZENGRUPPEN
UNIT THAT COMMITTED THE
MASSACRE AT BABI YAR. HE WAS
EXECUTED BY HANGING IN 1951.

"THAT'S MY JEWS"

The voice belonged to a small boy named Motya, who was wearing shorts and a shirt. They stared at each other in astonishment, until Dina said: "Keep quiet. Crawl after me." They crawled through the darkness. As the sun came up, they hid in some bushes and watched Germans sorting through clothing that had belonged to the Jews and putting it on carts and trucks to be taken away.

They were not the only escapees from the pit of Babi Yar. At one point, an old woman came running by with a child chasing her, crying out: "Granny! I'm afraid!" She was trying to get rid of the boy, but the Germans saw her and shot both of them. Shortly after this, the machine-gunning started up again and lasted the whole day. She and Motya kept hidden and when the dark came, they began to crawl again. However, disoriented, hungry, and dehydrated, they apparently crawled in a circle and came back to Babi Yar. As dawn broke on the second morning, Motya crawled ahead. Suddenly he called back: "Don't come here! Germans!"

Shots rang out and Motya was killed. But the Germans did not understand what he had said, and his heroic warning saved Pronicheva, who now crawled away again. She was recaptured by the Germans, but escaped again, by jumping off the back of a moving truck, and found her way to the Polish wife of her brother, who hid her. She survived the war, the only true eyewitness to Babi Yar, and was even reunited with her children.

Other Jews also escaped from Babi Yar, but as the weather turned colder they were captured and taken back to the killing grounds. German records show that 7,000 were killed in October at Babi Yar. Eight thousand more died in November. As the Germans killed more and more people there, they would dynamite a section of the twisting ravine, close it off, and move on to the next section. Estimates vary, but there were probably 100,000 people in total killed at Babi Yar between 1941 and 1943. (Later, these people also included gypsies and mentally ill patients.) But the exact number of people killed on September 28–29, which was 33,771, according to meticulous German record keepers, would set a new record for massacring the most people in the shortest period of time.

By mid-1943, the Germans were in full retreat as the Soviet army pursued them back toward their borders. Afraid of leaving a record of their atrocities behind, the SS took 300 Jewish prisoners from a local concentration camp and forced them to do the grisly job of digging up the remains of those killed at Babi Yar and cremating them in a method invented by Paul Blobel (who, fired from active duty due to his excessive drinking, supervised this horrific task), which consisted of placing bodies on iron railway ties, then placing a layer of wood above them, then another layer of bodies, etc., after which kerosene was sprayed onto the biers and the corpses set alight. Blobel testified that it took two days for these fires to burn down. The Germans brought in special bone crushing machines to destroy the bones that would not burn. The ashes were then scattered on local farms to act as fertilizer.

Most of the 300 prisoners were executed, although fifteen escaped to tell the story. But it was evident from this frantic and unsuccessful attempt to hide the tale of slaughter at Babi Yar that the Nazis were concerned with covering their tracks. The Germans had largely discontinued *Einsatzgruppen* units because massive massacres like Babi Yar simply could not be hidden, either from Germany's enemies or the general public. Whereas efficient modern gas chambers and crematoria could dispense with Jews in a far more efficient way. In this way, the Nazis learned a valuable lesson from Babi Yar.

All that is left to relate is one more tale from the many obscene horrors of Babi Yar. In March 1942, about six months after the killings, a Gestapo officer named Albert Hartel was riding in a German staff car with Paul Blobel, head of *Einsatzgruppe* C. They were on their way to lunch at a villa on the outskirts of Kiev when they passed by a strange, desolate expanse of land, covered with hollow craters, from which small, gurgling explosions shot up geysers of black earth. Unbeknownst to Hartel, they were passing the filled-in ravine of Babi Yar, where 30,000 decomposing bodies had produced gas, which, now that spring was arriving, was rising to the surface.

Blobel smiled at Hartel and said:

"That's my Jews."

CHAPTER 12

"MACHTE ALLE KAPUT"

THE MALMEDY MASSACRE, DECEMBER 17, 1944

THE KILLING OF DOZENS OF AMERICAN PRISONERS BY GERMAN SS MEN IN A SNOWY BELGIAN FIELD HARDENED THE ATTITUDES OF AMERICAN GIS TOWARD THEIR ENEMY

T HE BELGIAN FARMER, WHOSE NAME WAS HENRI LEJOLY, WAS surprised at the nonchalance of the U.S. troops. Standing in the barren field outside of the town of Malmedy on that cold early afternoon in the winter of 1944, they smoked and joked with each other. Some of them had placed their hands on their helmets in a casual token of surrender to the Waffen-SS troops of *Kampfgruppe Peiper*—the mechanized task force commanded by the brilliant young German Colonel Joachim Peiper—as it passed by, but beyond that they seemed remarkably unconcerned.

The offhand behavior of the roughly 115 U.S. prisoners may have been because the men came from Battery B of the 285th Field Observation Battery. This was an outfit whose job was to spot enemy artillery emplacements and transmit their location to other U.S. units. It had seen relatively little frontline duty and was filled with numerous green replacements.

Most of the SS troops, including Joachim Peiper, had seen extensive duty in the grim killing fields of the Eastern Front. As *Kampfgruppe Peiper* passed by these Americans, an SS soldier suddenly stood up in the back of his halftrack, aimed his pistol, and fired it twice into a group of U.S. prisoners. One of them crumpled to the ground. Terrified U.S. soldiers in the field suddenly began to run. Then a German machine gun at

the back of another halftrack opened up and U.S. prisoners fell screaming to the ground. Within a matter of a few minutes, the field was covered with quickly coagulating pools of blood and writhing bodies. Then the SS men began to walk among the injured and the dead, pistols out.

"A GREATER RISK"

The Battle of the Bulge was the largest battle ever fought in the history of the U.S. infantry and one of the bloodiest battles of World War II, which was the most costly war in human history. The U.S. troops suffered 81,000 casualties, which included 18,000 dead, while their German opponents were hit with 70,000 casualties, including 20,000 dead. The battle lasted forty days in December and January of 1944–1945, in atrocious winter weather that was the worst seen in the Ardennes region of Belgium in twenty years, and could easily have resulted in a devastating loss for Allied forces, one that might have stalemated a war that they seemed well on their way to winning.

With all of these matters of great importance, why has so much attention been paid to the killing of eighty-four U.S. soldiers in a small field on December 17, 1944? The Germans of *Kampfgruppe Peiper*, seventy of whom were convicted in a war crimes tribunal after the war, were surprised—executing prisoners was standard fare on the Eastern Front. So, too, were many U.S. soldiers who had done battle in the Pacific, where the Japanese treated U.S. POWs with casual brutality. Perhaps one reason for the attention paid to the Malmedy Massacre is that many Americans at the time, including, possibly, those of Battery B standing in the field that day, thought that, against the Germans at least, they were fighting a "civilized" war with adversaries who shared the same racial heritage as thousands of GIs.

Another reason for the focus on Malmedy is that, as word spread like wildfire through the U.S. frontline ranks in the immediate aftermath of the killings, U.S. soldiers vowed to take no prisoners. Within a few weeks of Malmedy, one U.S. unit had machine-gunned sixty German prisoners to death in a small Belgian village called Chenogne (see "Death at Chenogne," page 203). As even the official U.S. military history of the Battle of the Bulge states: "It is probable the Germans attempting to surrender in the days immediately following [the killings at Malmedy] ran a greater risk."

DEATH AT CHENOGNE

On New Year's Day, 1945, as the Battle of the Bulge was still being fought, a unit of the U.S. 11th Armored Division engaged the SS in the Belgian village of Chenogne. After an intense firefight, the Germans housed in the village attempted to come out of the buildings, which had been set afire by shells from U.S. Sherman tanks. The first men to come out were German medics waving Red Cross flags. The Americans shot them down immediately. More and more Germans rushed out and they, too, were machine-gunned.

Finally, according to an eyewitness account by U.S. Private John Fague, the GIs took about sixty Germans prisoner. They were all lined up on a street in the village, when a U.S. sergeant walked up shouting: "Not here. The others in the woods will see. Take them over that hill."

By "the others" the sergeant meant the Germans who had not yet surrendered and would be watching from a nearby forest. Fague then said: "I knew they were going to shoot them and I hated this business. They [the GIs] marched the prisoners back over the hill to murder them with the rest of the prisoners we had secured that morning . . . There must have been 25 or 30 German boys in each group. Machine guns were being set up. These boys were to be machine-gunned and murdered."

Later, as evening was falling, Fague saw the bodies of the dead Germans lying in the snow. Just then, a jeep carrying an officer came roaring down the road. The officer shouted something to the man ahead of Fague. The man turned to Fague and said: "Did you hear that? Somebody fouled up. We're supposed to take prisoners."

By then, of course, it was too late. No one was ever prosecuted for the killing of these German prisoners. On January 4, 1945, General George S. Patton wrote in his diary: "The Eleventh Armored is very green and took unnecessary losses to no effect. There were also some unfortunate incidents in the shooting of prisoners. I hope we can conceal this."

This official military history goes on to state that "there is no evidence that American troops took advantage of orders, explicit or implicit, to kill their SS prisoners," but any GI fighting in Belgium in the days after December 17, 1944, could tell a very different story.

"THE GHOST FRONT"

In a sense, the Allied war against the Germans since the D-Day landings of June 6, 1944, had gone almost too well. After a fierce fight in Normandy, the Americans and British had broken out of their beachheads at the end of July and sent the Wehrmacht reeling backward, ceding vast areas of France and Belgium to the U.S. armored divisions of the First and Third Armies and the British Twenty-fifth Army Group. But such was the speed of the Allied advance that outfits began to outrun their supply lines. By late fall, the sixty-five Allied divisions operating in northeastern Europe were facing vital supplies shortages, especially of fuel, and their offensive had sputtered to a halt.

Digging in for the winter, the Americans and British sought to consolidate their gains and build up fuel supplies for a massive push into Germany in the early spring. The Allied lines were weakest along a 100-mile (160.9 km) stretch from southern Belgium into Luxembourg, a place where U.S. commander Omar Bradley took what he called a "calculated risk" by placing only six U.S. divisions—about 60,000 men—three of which were untried in battle and three of which were exhausted from months of heavy combat.

This area covered the rugged and desolate Ardennes Forest and was mountainous and remote. As December 1944 began, the Ardennes fell prey to the worst winter weather it had experienced in a generation, with temperatures hovering below 0°F (-18°C) for days at a time. Snow blanketed the little towns, vacation chateaus, and deep forests of the area. The area was so thinly held by GIs billeted (if they were lucky) in Belgian inns and private homes that it was called "the Ghost Front." The GIs knew that their German enemies were out there in the snow and fog, but believed that they would never attempt a serious attack in such conditions.

But that is exactly what the Germans did, in a massive counteroffensive personally planned by Adolf Hitler. His goal was to punch through this weakly held

part of the Allied line and send his armored divisions streaking toward Antwerp. Once he captured this vital port, he could force the Allies to sue for peace. With the greatest of secrecy, aided by winter weather that kept Allied planes on the ground, he assembled a force of 250,000 men, 1,400 tanks, and 2,000 artillery guns on the eastern edge of the Ardennes. And, at 5:30 a.m. on December 16, this blitzkrieg struck the unsuspecting Americans.

JOACHIM PEIPER

Up and down an 85-mile (136.8 km) front, mortars, rockets, and heavy artillery shells literally blasted American troops out of bed or shook the ground around their frigid foxholes. After an hour, the barrage stopped and then, in numerous strategic places along the front, giant searchlights were turned on, blinding the Americans and turning the foggy morning a glowing white. German infantry—wearing winter camouflage clothing that most of the Americans did not possess—attacked out of the ethereal mist, firing burp guns from the hip. Behind them came the grumbling roar of massive Tiger and Panther tanks.

Many of the astonished and terrified Americans—a large number of them cooks and clerks—picked up rifles and fought back, while some threw away their arms and immediately ran away. Massive confusion was the order of the day. Even at the headquarters of the Supreme Allied Command, it was at first thought that this German attack was a feint, a prelude to another main attack somewhere else along the Allied lines. With the skies filled with clouds, Allied scout planes could not get a clear picture of just how enormous the attack was, and frantic reports from infantry units in the area were confused and fragmented.

In fact, the Battle of the Bulge, as it would become known for the deep indentation the attacking German forces pushed into the U.S. lines, quickly became a series of confused small actions, with isolated units engaging each other in fierce battles. Communications were terrible and no one quite knew

THE DASHING YOUNG COLONEL JOACHIM PEIPER, COMMANDER OF THE LEADING BATTLE FORMATION OF THE GERMAN FIRST PANZER DIVISION. IT WAS MEN IN HIS UNIT WHO KILLED THE AMERICAN GIS AT MALMEDY.

where the Germans were. In some instances, U.S. outfits were completely sur-rounded by the attacking Germans while, a few miles (kilometers) away, the GIs wiped out entire German companies. However, in the beginning of the attack, the Germans possessed the element of surprise and a sense of purpose and direc-tion—they knew what they were there for and where they were heading.

Spearheading the German attack was a remarkable twenty-nine-year-old SS colonel named Joachim Peiper. Peiper was the commander of *Kampfgruppe Peiper*, the leading battle formation of the First Panzer Division—he had been personally picked by Adolf Hitler to be the point person on the Sixth Panzer Army's drive to seize the bridges of the Meuse River and capture Antwerp. Holder of the Knight's Cross with Oak Leaves, Germany's highest military dec-oration; an ardent Nazi; and a hardened veteran of fighting in France, Italy, and on the Eastern Front; Peiper was admired by his soldiers, but known as a brutal fighter. He had probably ordered an attack by his unit, which caused the deaths of forty-three Italian civilians in the village of Boves, Italy, in 1943, and in numer-ous actions against partisans in Russia, his unit deliberately burned villages and killed Russian civilians.

And on the morning of December 17, the second day of the German attack, he was a frustrated man. Because of a heroic and determined resistance by ele-ments of the U.S. 99th Infantry Division, his task force, which consisted of 117 tanks, 149 halftracks, and 24 artillery pieces, was already 12 hours behind schedule. Time is always important in military operations, but in the Ardennes in December 1944, it was the most crucial factor that Peiper, and by extension the entire Wehrmacht, faced. They must reach the bridges on the Meuse River before the sky cleared and the Allied planes, which enjoyed almost total air supe-riority, could turn their tanks into smoldering wrecks blocking the narrow roads and halting Germany's last chance at saving itself from total defeat.

"YOU KNOW WHAT TO DO WITH THE PRISONERS"

At around 8:00 a.m. on December 17, a convoy carrying Battery B, 285th Field Observation Battery, set out from Schevehutte, on the border of Germany and Belgium, on its way to St. Vith, Belgium, which was about to become a focal point of one of the great clashes in the Battle of the Bulge. The convoy consisted of about 130 men, thirty jeeps, weapons carriers, and trucks and was led by Captain Roger Mills, and Lieutenants Virgil Lary and Perry Reardon.

The day was clear, with temperatures well below freezing, and a light dusting of snow on the ground. Battery B reached the Belgian town of Malmedy around noon. After passing through the town, the convoy was stopped on its eastern edge by Lt. Colonel David Pergrin, in charge of a company of combat engineers who were all that were left to defend Malmedy. Pergrin warned Mills and Lary that a German armored column had been seen approaching from the southeast. He advised them to go to St. Vith by another route, but Mills and Lary refused, perhaps because ahead of them were several members of Battery B who had been laying down road markers, and they did not wish to abandon them, or perhaps simply because the route they were to take was stated in their orders.

For whatever reason, Battery B proceeded along its designated route until it came to a crossroads about 2.5 miles (4 km) east of Malmedy, which the Belgians called Baugnez but the Americans referred to as Five Points, because five roads intersected here. There was a café there, as well as three small farms. Shortly after it passed this crossroads, the column began to receive fire from two German tanks that were 1,000 yards (914.4 m) down the road. These tanks were the spearhead of *Kampfgruffe Peiper*, led by Lieutenant Werner Sternebeck, and their 88-mm guns and machine guns easily tore up the U.S. column. Sternebeck and his tanks proceeded down the road, pushing burning and wrecked U.S. jeeps and trucks out of the way and firing their machine guns at U.S. soldiers who cowered in ditches—something Sternebeck later told historian Michael Reynolds that he did to get the Americans to surrender, which most of them did, since they were armed only with rifles and pistols, weapons that could not possibly fight off tanks.

Sternebeck then sent the Americans, numbering about 115 in all, marching with their hands held high back to the crossroads at Five Points. (Perhaps eleven men of Battery B had been killed in the initial attack.) He assembled the prisoners in a field there and waited with his tanks and halftracks for further orders. The delay upset Peiper. Racing to the front of the German column, he upbraided Sternebeck for engaging Battery B—because the noise might alert more powerful U.S. combat units nearby—and told him to keep moving. Sternebeck moved

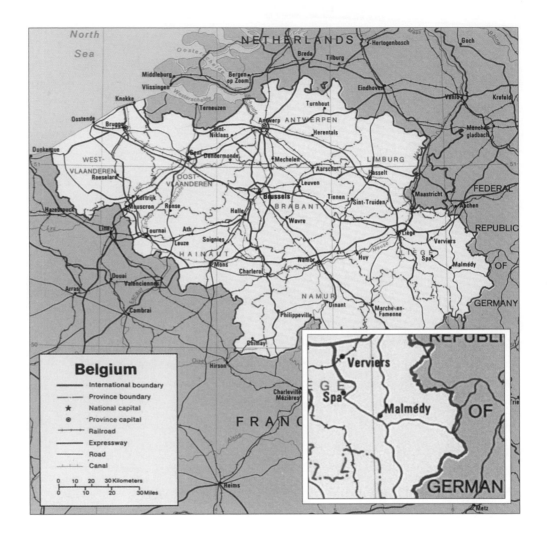

out, followed closely by Peiper, and the long line of *Kampfgruffe Peiper* began to pass the Americans standing in the field, some of whom had begun to relax, put their hands down, and light cigarettes.

After an hour or so, it must have seemed to them that the worst danger was over, perhaps the Germans were even going to leave them there as they continued on. Peiper left an SS major named Werner Poetschke in charge of the prisoners, but the men guarding them seem to have changed as unit after unit of Germans passed by on the road. However, at around 4:00 that afternoon, soldiers from the SS 3rd Pioneer company were detailed to permanently guard the prisoners. According to testimony at the war crimes trial, Major Poetschke was heard by a U.S. soldier who understood German telling a Sergeant Beutner: "You know what to do with the prisoners."

"THE GERMANS KILLED EVERYBODY!"

Sergeant Beutner then stopped a halftrack that held a 75-mm cannon and attempted to depress its barrel low enough to aim at the prisoners in the field. When the gun crew was unable to do this, Beutner gave up in disgust and waved the halftrack on, much to the relief of the now edgy and nervous Americans in the field. But then another German unit came by and those Americans who could speak German heard a lieutenant in this unit give the order: *Machte alle Kaput!* "Kill the Americans." At first, the Germans present merely stared at the officer, but then Pfc. George Fleps, an ethnic German from Romania, stood up in his halftrack and fired twice at the crowd of Americans.

The Americans in the rear of the group began to run away, even as an officer yelled "Stand fast!" thinking that the Germans would shoot them if they saw them escaping. In fact, this is what happened. Seeing Americans fleeing, a machine gun on the back of a halftrack opened up, cutting down those who stood in the field and those trying to escape. The farmer, Henri Lejoly, watched in horror as the Americans screamed and cowered as the machine gun bullets tore them apart.

To this day it is uncertain if the Germans would have shot the Americans had they not tried to run—many German soldiers present later claimed they were merely killing escaping prisoners. However, surviving Americans distinctly remember the German order to kill coming before any of the POWs tried to escape. However, what the Germans did next reinforces the belief that they intended to kill the Americans from the beginning. As the GIs lay moaning on the ground, SS men walked among them, kicking men in the testicles or in the head. If they moved, the SS men would casually lean over and shoot them in the head. Some survivors later testified that the Germans were laughing as they did this.

THE FIRST GUANTANAMO

The controversy over U.S. treatment of alleged Al-Qaeda terrorists—treatment that included torture—was not the only instance of sanctioned torture in U.S. history.

In 1946, shortly before the trial of Joachim Peiper and his seventy men was to begin on the site of the former Dachau concentration camp, Lt. Colonel Willis Everett, who had been appointed to defense attorney for the SS men, interviewed a number of them. Despite the fact that they were separated from each other and in solitary confinement (and thus had no way of tailoring their stories) each had a similar tale to tell. They said that U.S. interrogators had forced false confessions out of them through numerous means. The accused were surprised to hear they were going to trial—they said they had already had a trial, which was conducted in a room with black curtains, lit with only two candles. They said that the judge was a U.S. officer who sat at a table covered with a black cloth, which had a white cross embroidered on it. Witnesses testified against them and each prisoner was sentenced to death. Before they died, they were told, they must write out a confession to their crimes. When the men refused, one was dictated to them, which they were forced to sign under threat of violence.

In Everett's investigation, the prosecution admitted that these mock trials had taken place ("How else would we get these birds to talk?" said one U.S. prosecutor.) The prisoners also said that they had been beaten by interrogators and that one of their number, eighteen-year-old Private Arvid Freimuth, had hung himself in his cell after repeated beatings. (A statement supposedly from Freimuth, although parts of it were not signed by him, was introduced in evidence against the other SS men and helped to convict them.) According to the prisoners, U.S. interrogators placed black hoods over their heads and beat them with brass knuckles, kicked them repeatedly in the testicles, in some cases causing permanent damage, and also posed as priests to get the Catholics among them to make admissions during confession.

Everett fought a lonely and heroic fight to save these SS men after their convictions and was actually able to get the Secretary of the Army to stay the sentences of all but six of those facing death. Everett, now a civilian lawyer, took the case before a Senate subcommittee in 1949. He hoped to get a new trial for the Malmedy SS men, but the Senate refused to hold hearings on the case, claiming that Everett was an anti-Semite, since he was pointed in his criticism of the fact that the U.S. army had allowed only Jewish interrogators to interview the SS prisoners—men who might naturally have had a reason to be harsh on the Germans.

Even though the Senate report was negative from Everett's point of view, the Army commuted the death sentences of those remaining on death row, including Peiper, to life imprisonment in 1951, citing confusion raised by the flawed interrogations.

Lejoly, who was a German sympathizer, nevertheless could not believe his eyes as he watched one SS man allow a U.S. medic to bandage a wounded soldier, after which the German shot both men dead. Eleven Americans fled to the café nearby, but the Germans set it on fire and then gunned down the men as they ran out. As this killing was going on, the German column continued to pass through Five Points, and soldiers on halftracks chatted and pointed. Some fired into already dead Americans, as if to practice their aim.

Amazingly enough, some sixty Americans were still alive in the field after the machine-gunning. As the SS massacred the survivors, they realized they had no choice but to try to escape, and they rose and ran as fast as they could to the back of the field, heading for a nearby woods. The Germans swept them with rifle and machine gun fire, but made little attempt to chase after them. Perhaps forty made good their escape into the deepening dusk. Most of them attempted to make their way back to Malmedy, some wandering for days before they returned. However, early that evening, three escapees did encounter a patrol led by Colonel Pergrin, who had heard the shooting and was coming to investigate. The men, covered with blood, were hysterical.

"The Germans killed everybody!" they shouted at Pergrin.

AFTERMATH OF THE MASSACRE

That evening, Pergrin sent back word to 1st Army Headquarters that there had been a massacre of some type at Malmedy. The area around Five Points was so hotly contested that it was not until nearly a month after the massacre, on January 14, that the U.S. army was able to recover the bodies of the eighty-four men who had been killed in that field. Autopsies conducted on the frozen corpses showed that forty-one men had been shot in the head at close range and another ten had had their heads bashed in with rifle butts. Nine still had their arms raised above their heads.

However, immediately after the massacre occurred and well before the bodies were recovered, the news quickly spread through the GIs fighting for their lives in the Ardennes. As one historian has written, tales of the shootings "enraged the Americans and inspired them to fight with conviction and with little compassion, especially towards the SS . . . ." Although official U.S. military histories deny this, there is strong evidence that U.S. commanders gave orders for the killing of prisoners. Before an attack against the Germans on December 21, four days after the massacre, the headquarters of the 328th Infantry sent out an order that read, in part: "No SS troops or paratroopers will be taken prisoner but will be shot on sight."

Many of the Americans fighting in the Battle of the Bulge were green replacements who had never seen combat before, let alone this kind of vicious and bloody fighting. Many of them had run away at the first sign of the German attack. But some of these same GIs later recalled that the story of the Malmedy Massacre so angered them that they decided they would now stand and fight with everything they had. And they did.

By the time the Battle of the Bulge wound down in late January 1945, fresh Allied replacements, the tenacious stand of the battered GIs, and clearing weather (which allowed Allied airborne operations) combined to halt the German advance. Joachim Peiper never reached the Meuse, his much-sought-after goal. Of his 5,000-man force, only 800 survived to return to Germany.

By the time the war ended, the U.S. public knew all about the Malmedy massacre and clamored for revenge. On May 16, 1946, a year after the end of hostilities in Europe, Peiper and seventy of his men (almost one in ten of the surviving members of *Kampfgruppe Peiper*) were placed on trial for war crimes connected with the massacre. The trials were deliberately held on the site of the Dachau concentration camp, to garner maximum symbolism from the event.

Not all of the presumed guilty could be punished—both Major Poetschke and Sergeant Beutner died in action during the war. But at the end of the proceedings, all seventy of the SS men, as well as Peiper, had been convicted of war crimes by a six-man panel of U.S. officers. Forty-three of them, including Peiper, were sentenced to die by hanging, twenty-two to life imprisonment, and the rest to ten- to twenty-year sentences.

However, the trials were tainted by later testimony that the SS men had been tortured by U.S. interrogators (see "The First Guantanamo," page 210) before their trials. All of the death sentences were commuted to imprisonment and, in 1956, Joachim Peiper became the last member of the group to walk out of jail. Peiper, who was murdered in France in 1976 by a shadow group of anti-Nazi terrorists who called themselves "the Avengers," always claimed that he did not give express orders to kill the prisoners at Malmedy, and he probably did not.

He did testify that "after the battle of Normandy, my unit was composed of mainly young, fanatical soldiers. A good many of them had lost their parents, their sisters and brothers, during the [Allied] bombing [of German cities]. They had seen for themselves thousands of mangled corpses . . . after a terror raid had passed. Their hatred of the enemy was such, I swear, I could not always keep it under control."

This may have been true, but Peiper also had a reputation for brutality to prisoners that his men certainly knew about. There were other instances of SS men under his control killing GI prisoners during his dash through Belgium, and Peiper did nothing to stop these. Though we may never completely know the truth surrounding the Malmedy massacre—who ordered it, and whether it was at least partly an attempt to stop escaping prisoners—there is no doubt that, in the end, the deaths there stiffened U.S. resolve to destroy the Nazis, and the hated SS, wherever they found them.

CHAPTER 13

"THE GREATEST STILLNESS"

MASSACRE AT SHARPEVILLE, SOUTH AFRICA, MARCH 21, 1960

WHEN SOUTH AFRICAN POLICE FIRED POINT-BLANK
INTO A CROWD OF THOUSANDS OF BLACK PROTESTORS,
WITH PREDICTABLY BLOODY RESULTS, THE FUTURE
OF THE COUNTRY CHANGED FOREVER

ARMED SOUTH AFRICAN POLICE SURVEY THE KILLING FIELD AT SHARPEVILLE IN THE WAKE OF THE MASSACRE. THE POLICE FIRING ON AFRICAN BLACKS LASTED ONLY SECONDS, BUT IN THE END, 69 PEOPLE DIED AND 180 WERE WOUNDED.

"**W**E DID NOT KILL THEM BECAUSE THEY WERE BLACK," ONE SOUTH African policeman later avowed. "It was because they acted like wild animals." Another remembered, much later: "We were terrified by . . . the natives, by their howls against us." Yet another, shortly after the massacre: "If they do these things, they must learn the hard way."

The "natives" who "howled" and acted like "wild animals" were the black Africans of the township of Sharpeville, fifty miles (80.5 km) south of Johannesburg. They had gathered by the thousands in front of the Sharpeville police station on Monday morning, March 21, 1960, to protest a particularly insidious and brutal form of repression by the white authorities: the passbook or reference book, an identity card, which every black African was forced to carry under penalty of imprisonment. For hours, men, women, and children had shouted, danced, and taunted the increasing nervous members of the South African Police (SAP) who stood behind a wire mesh fence. Despite the fact that the police had four Saracen armored cars that could deliver sustained bursts of automatic weapons, the crowd pressed closer and closer.

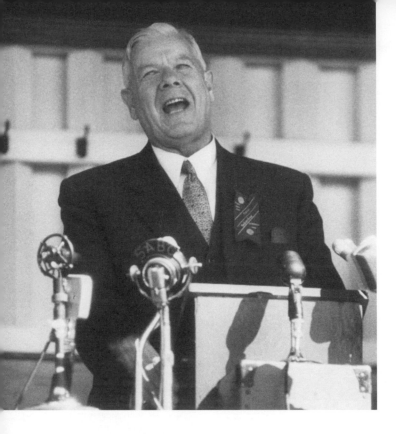

And then, somehow, the volatile situation exploded, and the police opened fire directly into the mass of people with Sten submachine guns, pistols, and .303 rifles that may have been loaded with the hollow-point bullets known as dum-dums, which inflict great damage on human flesh. The firing lasted a matter of seconds and after it was over, both killers and victims remembered, "a great stillness" fell on the open field in front of the police station, which was now littered with dead and wounded. No one present knew it, but in that stillness, the future of South Africa had changed forever.

As historian Philip Frankel writes in *An Ordinary Atrocity*, his seminal study of Sharpeville, "The Sharpeville massacre . . . represents a moment or occurrence after whose appearance on the historic landscape of South Africa nothing was quite what it had been, and nothing could quite be anticipated."

SOUTH AFRICAN PRIME MINISTER HENDRIK VERWOERD, SPEAKING SHORTLY AFTER THE INCIDENT AT SHARPEVILLE. VERWOERD WAS ONE OF APARTHEID'S ARCHITECTS AND CALLED FOR TOTAL SEPARATION OF WHITES AND BLACKS.

TIME & LIFE PICTURES/GETTY IMAGES

"THERE IS NO PLACE FOR HIM"

Formed in 1910 after the bloody Anglo-Boer War of 1899–1902, the Union of South Africa combined the colonies of the Afrikaner majority of South Africa with those of the British minority, in a move that ushered in a new era of cooperation between the two groups, which were sometimes bitter enemies. Of course, the rights of the black majority of South Africa—the *kaffirs*, as the Afrikaners called them—were never considered, unless it was to come to new ways to censor and control this burgeoning population.

In 1923, so-called passbook laws were put into effect, forcing any black African male over the age of sixteen to constantly carry identity books. These laws were expanded under the repressive National Party, which came into power in 1948 and made racial segregation, long a part of life in South Africa, an official policy known as apartheid—or "apartness." Under apartheid, black Africans were stripped of their South African citizenship, becoming citizens of ten tribally oriented homelands (or *bantustans*), and provided with greatly inferior education, medical care, and public services. When Hendrik Verwoerd, one of the architects of apartheid, was elected prime minister in 1958, he said his goal was "total territorial separation for whites and blacks." Verwoerd wrote: "There is no place for him [the black African] in the European community above the level of certain forms of labour."

Passbooks became a way to carefully monitor the movement of any black man (and, after a new law passed in 1956, woman) who ventured out of his homeland. Men and women were forced to carry their passbooks at all times to prove that they were "entitled to be, remain, work, or reside" in a "white" area. Each passbook contained the black African's picture, tribe, identity number, tax stamp, and employer's signature (the latter had to be renewed each month to prove the bearer was still employed). If a black African ventured out without his passbook, he could and often would be sent to prison, even if he had merely forgotten it or lost it—which makes it understandable why, in 1959, two black African workers died trying to rescue their passbooks from their burning factory.

A JOHANNESBURG POLICEMAN USES A CANE AND WHIP TO DRIVE A BLACK SPECTATOR FROM A COURTHOUSE DURING THE 1958 TRIAL OF 130 SOUTH AFRICAN BLACK WOMEN ARRESTED FOR PROTESTING THE PASSBOOK LAWS.

The passbook system was no mere nuisance. It meant that no black African was ever safe from being questioned or harassed by the police, and it also meant that husbands, wives, and families were often separated.

"A GOVERNMENT OF THE AFRICANS"

The policies of Verwoerd and his government naturally met with opposition among South African blacks, and particularly from two political organizations that had arisen to protest the racial inequities in South Africa. One was the African National Congress (ANC), which had formed in 1912, in response to the creation of the Union of South Africa, which had entrenched white minority rule. The

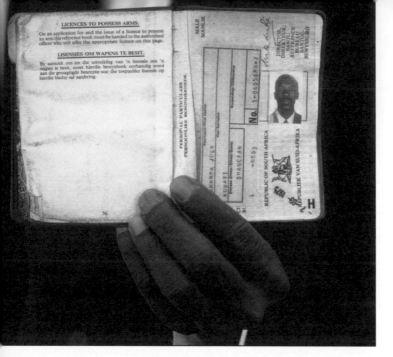

leadership of the ANC was filled with middle-class black professionals who believed in liberal principles, nonviolent tactics, and embraced the plight of other ethnic groups who were racially oppressed, like South Africa's large Indian population.

Although young members of the ANC, like Nelson Mandela and Oliver Tambo, pushed for more radical forms of action, the ANC's numerous nonviolent protests had little impact on South African life, where segregation and apartheid policies grew worse almost daily. In 1959, a more radical splinter group had broken off from the ANC. Calling itself the Pan-Africanist Congress (PAC) and led by thirty-five-year-old Robert Sobukwe, it sought a "government of the Africans, by Africans, for Africans." It wanted to enlist the growing number of restless young Africans buried under the policies of apartheid for whom the protests of the ANC were far too tame. As 1960 dawned, the times were changing, with other countries in Africa achieving their independence. It was time to end the repressive rule that had so long held black South Africa back. In December 1959, Sobukwe declared that South Africa would be free within four years.

Sobukwe decided first to strike at the heart of what one writer has called "the greatest daily burden of life under apartheid": the passbook system. He called for a national series of demonstrations in homelands across South Africa to take place on March 21, 1960. On this day, African demonstrators would leave their passbooks at home, refuse to go to work, and present themselves at their local police station demanding to be arrested. It was the hope of Sobukwe and other PAC leaders that the protest would swamp the South African system of justice and make enforcing passbook laws impossible.

Despite the aggressive nature of the protest, Sobukwe cautioned his community organizers to make sure the demonstrations remained peaceful. He even went so far as to write the police commissioner, Major General C.I. Rademeyer, emphasizing that PAC members were nonviolent, would submit peacefully to arrest, and would also comply with police orders to disperse. If there was going to be a source of trouble, Sobukwe told the police commander, it would be from "trigger-happy, African-hating" police.

"IZWE LETHU"

March 21 dawned sunny in Sharpeville, South Africa, with the promise of another hot day ahead. A black suburb of the steel manufacturing center of Vereeniging, where many of the residents of Sharpeville were employed, it was a relatively enlightened township with decent housing and sanitation. Although by 1960, when economic conditions within South Africa were on the downturn and unemployment was rising, it was beginning to have problems associated with poverty, substance abuse, and gangs.

The PAC had made far-reaching efforts to organize the protest that day in Sharpeville. PAC organizers arrived early in the morning telling people to leave their passbooks at home and not go to work (they also turned bus drivers away from the township, so most citizens were unable to get to work even if they tried). Beginning around 10:00 a.m., a crowd of 5,000 Africans—which would expand to 7,000 or so—began to gather outside the police station. The crowd was filled with women and children as well as men. Many of the demonstrators were giving the thumbs up "Afrika" salute and shouting the PAC slogan *Izwe Lethu*, or "Our Land."

Around the country there were other demonstrations—Sobukwe led one in Johannesburg itself—where crowds sometimes reached as many as 20,000. These were

ROBERT SOBUKWE, HEAD OF THE PAC, WAS SENTENCED TO PRISON FOR THREE YEARS FOR INCITING BLACKS TO RESIST THE PASS LAWS IN THE DEMONSTRATION THAT LED TO THE KILLINGS AT SHARPEVILLE.
AFRICANPICTURES/ AKG-IMAGES

dispersed by tear gas and baton charges. One black man was shot and killed by police during a demonstration in Vanderbijlpark, claiming that he had thrown rocks at them.

The crowd at Sharpeville ebbed and flowed, with many people assuming they were going to hear a statement read out by the PAC, after which they would disperse (the police were refusing to arrest anyone on passbook violations). There is a good deal of controversy about how hostile the crowd actually was, whether they were throwing rocks, and whether they were armed. Though PAC organizers later said that the crowd was good-natured, nonviolent, and filled with women who sang and danced, the SAP claimed that the crowd was continually threatening, at times "hailing" stones down upon them, and pressing in on the 4-foot (1.2 m)-tall wire fence that surrounded the police compound. The dancing women, police said, were actually, "undulating" around their men, a traditional Bantu way to goad warriors into action. The police also said that there were guns in the crowd, and that many of the men carried knobkerries, or traditional African clubs.

The truth probably falls somewhere in between. There was no hail of stones falling upon the police, but there were men in the crowd with clubs, and there were also men with pistols, particularly some of the local gang members present, who were distinguishable from most of the population of Sharpeville by their colorful dress. The twelve policemen who originally manned the station called for more and more reinforcements, until, by 1:00 p.m., almost 300 police officers manned the police compound (156 of the officers were white, 138 were black, and only about 35 actually worked in and around Sharpeville—the rest had been bused in). They also had four Saracen armored cars.

What was not stated in press reports at the time, but what can be considered as a reason for the extreme nervousness of the police, was that only a few weeks earlier, a thousand rioters, protesting a police raid on a bar selling illegal liquor, had broken into a police station at a black township called Cato Manor, and killed nine policemen. Some of them had been stoned to death; others were disemboweled.

One of the black protestors at Sharpeville later said: "We took great delight in shouting 'Cato Manor' . . . because we knew it would disturb the boers [the police.]" And indeed, as Philip Frankel writes, "there was a deep sense of dread among the police, a veritable psychosis of fear" as the crowd chanted slogans in Sesotho, a language the white policemen could not understand, except for the single phrase: "Cato Manor." Their commander, Colonel J. Pienaar, ordered his men to set up a defensive line along the west side of the fence. At around the same time, the police officers who had been inside the Saracen armored cars came out and climbed to the top of the vehicles, holding Sten guns.

THE SHOT

While the police claimed that they ordered the crowd repeatedly to disperse, there is little evidence that this was the case. They did employ the tactic of having low-flying planes buzz the crowd, apparently in an attempt to frighten protestors into thinking they might be bombed or tear-gassed, but, according to one of the few reporters present, people in the mob threw their hats at the planes and laughed. By the time the planes flew away, it was about 1:30 in the afternoon.

As the crowd pressed against the fence, several of the police officers standing just behind it were scratched, either by the fence itself or possibly, as some police claimed, by knives in the hands of the protestors. Many of those standing right up against the fence were African women who goaded the police by lifting their skirts at them and jeeringly reaching through the fence to try to touch them. The white police did not quite understand this gesture, but it enraged the black officers, who understood it as a sexual taunt against their male potency.

Then, as fate would have it, into this volatile mix came a black gang member named Geelbooi, who had been roughly interrogated by the police some months earlier. Still angry over his treatment, and apparently either monumentally hungover from a weekend of drinking, or possibly still drunk, he thought he spotted one of his police interrogators standing with the SAP forces behind the fence. Pulling a small caliber pistol, he said: "I will shoot that pig!" and started to aim the gun, but a friend with him tried to wrestle it away. Geelbooi pulled the trigger twice, the shots going harmlessly straight up into the air, but that was all it took.

SOWETO, 1976

On June 16, 1976, some 30,000 high school students in Soweto, a group of townships southwest of Johannesburg, took to the streets to protest a government decision on an old law that stated that half of the classes in South African schools were to be taught in Afrikaans, the language of the white minority rulers of South Africa, and the other half of the classes in English. Since most of the teachers in black schools had little familiarity with Afrikaans, they preferred to teach in English, but the government remained adamant and protests began to develop.

The South African Students' Movement (SASM) organized long columns of students to march through Soweto on June 16, carrying placards and chanting slogans, aiming to converge on a local junior high school. The mood, according to witnesses, was calm, but then a South African policeman inexplicably drew his revolver and fired into the crowd, killing Hector Petersen, a thirteen-year-old schoolboy. The students picked up bricks and stones and fought back, forcing the police to withdraw. Students then rioted, overturning buses and other vehicles, attacking government buildings, and killing two white people.

Clashes with police spread through South Africa and the rioting lasted for ten days. According to the police, 176 blacks were killed (although black organizations have long pegged the figure as being much higher). A picture of Hector Petersen lying dead in a friend's arms was published in newspapers around the world, and became an iconic image of the rioting. The following month, the government ruled that it would not attempt to enforce the law saying classes needed to be taught in Afrikaans, but as with the massacre at Sharpeville, the Soweto riots became a turning point in the struggle of Africans to free themselves from apartheid.

The police already on edge, with loaded guns and fingers on their triggers, reacted automatically and began spraying the crowd with submachine gun, pistol, and rifle fire. In the space of perhaps 30 seconds comprising two separate volleys, they unleashed perhaps 400 rounds—the "volume and intensity of the police fire was cataclysmic," as Frankel writes, especially directed at a close-packed group. Aiming was not necessary. One reporter present wrote: "One of the policemen was standing on top of a Saracen, and it looked as though he was firing his gun into the crowd. He was swinging it around in a wide arc from his hip as though he were panning a movie camera."

At first, even as people in the front ranks of the protestors began to fall, no one could believe it. They were sure the police were firing blanks to scare people—the same reporter saw women running away laughing and shouting, as if it were a game. But then a bullet hit one of the women perhaps ten yards (9.1 m) from where the reporter crouched. "Her companion, a young man, went back when she fell. He thought she had stumbled. Then he turned her over and saw that her chest had been shot away. He looked at the blood on his hand and said, 'My God, she's gone!'"

Even those shot—in the moments before they died—could not believe it. Medical personnel later reported the "dumbfounded" looks on the faces of the corpses they saw. One policeman shouted to his friends: "Look at how they are dead!" But still they killed. One young black man raced at the police lines, begging them to stop, shouting: "You've shot enough!"

And he, too, was gunned down.

The crowd, finally understanding what was happening, wheeled away from the police compound, racing to get away from the field of fire, but this brought them in a parallel line in front of the police, and many were shot as the fusillade ended. Then came "a crystal and almost palpable silence" as both the police and the crowd, a wide distance now between them, surveyed the field were hundreds of bodies lay.

"ON THE DYING SIDE"

The first move came from the police, who sent one constable through the fence gate to move cautiously among the bodies, prodding them with a toe to see whether any were still alive. He began picking up stones, examining them, and then tossing them over the fence into the compound, which many feel was an attempt to foster a claim that the blacks had stoned the police before the SAP opened fire.

Then more police began to venture forth, poking at bodies. While some policemen did begin to help those who were wounded, others acted in more macabre ways. Medical help would arrive in a half an hour, but in the meantime, some of the white police decided to appoint themselves mercy killers, putting bullets into the heads of people whom one officer later described as being "on the dying side."

The black policemen were worse—especially those who did not live in Sharpeville or neighboring townships. Some researchers think that it was these police who singled out black women to kill (eight died in the massacre) after they were taunted. There is testimony that one five-man group of black officers went out into the field after the slaughter and used assegais (a native spear) to slash the throats of the wounded. Some of the dead bore bullet wounds, but were also beaten with police batons. Women lying wounded on the field were often sexually mutilated—doctors noted that the corpses of women had a much higher proportion of stab wounds to the upper thighs and the abdomen. When one white officer saw this was happening he told the black officers to stop ("because we are in enough trouble already," he reportedly said), but this was only after ten minutes of such carnage.

There was also a heavy presence of children in the crowd. One reporter saw children leaping through the grass, running away "like rabbits" and a photographer found himself fleeing beside a boy "with his coat pulled over his head, as if to protect himself from bullets." Ten children died in the fusillade.

Medical personnel finally arrived and began loading the wounded onto ambulances, without the help of the police, who almost to a man refused to touch wounded blacks. Finally, some of the protestors themselves bravely began searching the tall grass of the field for the wounded—"for those dogs who were still chewing," as one police officer said at the time—and loading them into cars or trucks, whatever vehicles were available, to take them to the hospital.

ROBBEN ISLAND: PLACE OF EXILE

Robben Island has long been home to outcasts, prisoners, and exiles. Located in Table Bay, about four miles (6.4 km) off the coast of Cape Town, South Africa, it was used in the seventeenth century as a prison—the British colonial government sentenced rebel Xhosa chief Makanda Nxele to life imprisonment there in 1819 (Nxele drowned trying to escape).

From 1836 to 1931, Robben Island was a leper colony, and a place where animals were placed under quarantine. It achieved notoriety from the mid-twentieth century onward, when the South African government turned it into a harsh maximum-security prison. Between 1961 and 1991, it held up to 3,000 political prisoners, most famous of all future South African President Nelson Mandela, who spent more than a quarter of a century there. Conditions were cruel. Families were allowed a visit only once every six months, for thirty closely supervised minutes, and the only reading material allowed was the Bible.

Security on the island was so tough that no one ever escaped and few people, aside from prisoners and their immediate families, even set foot on the island prior to 1980, when political prisoners began to be removed. The island is now a museum, an ineffable symbol of both the racism of the South African regime and the heroism of those who strove to overcome it. Visiting Robben Island when he became president of South Africa, Nelson Mandela said: "Today when I look at Robben Island, I see it as a celebration of the struggle and a symbol of the finest qualities of the human spirit, rather than as a monument to the brutal tyranny and oppression of apartheid."

NELSON MANDELA SPENT MORE THEN A QUARTER OF A CENTURY AT ROBBEN ISLAND, WHICH HELD UP TO 3,000 POLITICAL PRISONERS BETWEEN 1961–1991.

ASSOCIATED PRESS

The pain and indignities of the massacre did not end on the field in front of the Sharpeville SAP compound, either. At the hospital in Vereeniging, where the dead and wounded were taken, plainclothes South African security police relentlessly questioned the injured. Other plainclothes police supposedly took away at least a dozen bodies, possibly those who had been either injured by dum-dum bullets or cut apart by the assegais, to hide this evidence from medical examiners. Or perhaps it was simply to lower the body count, which was placed officially at 69 dead (with 180 wounded) but which the PAC claimed was much higher.

Many of the dead were buried in the Sharpeville Native Cemetery, but even there they could not lie in peace. For years after the massacre, white thugs would arrive in cars, shouting "Afrika!" and throwing rocks and bottles. Wooden crosses and other grave markers were desecrated with graffiti like "Kaffir" or "Sobukwe." Many families decided to simply stop marking graves, to protect them from such blasphemies, and relied on their memories to bring them to the shallow depressions in the earth beneath which their loved ones lay.

"THE SHOOTING OF A FEW KAFFIRS"

After the shooting, one police officer who was present at Sharpeville said that, while the police knew there would be an outcry against the massacre, "the enemies of South Africa would soon forget the shooting of a few Kaffirs." This proved, fortunately, not to be the case. In the wake of the shooting, photographs and reports of the killings circulated around the world, as did the predictable crackdowns by the South African government after the massacre. A state of emergency was declared, and the ANC and PAC were outlawed. Robert Sobukwe was sent to prison for three years, to be followed by hundreds of other activists, including the likes of Nelson Mandela, who spent a quarter of a century in prison, and Steve Biko, who died at the hands of South African police.

The atrocity at Sharpeville forced the world to see the real nature of South African apartheid and racism. It was, as Philip Frankel writes, "a nefariously malignant event which instantly transformed the body politic of South Africa." Within Africa itself, the response of many developing countries to the Sharpeville massacre was to use it as a rallying cry to warn their people against white repression.

Outside of Africa, the international community began to gradually turn away from the Verwoerd government. A month after the massacre, the United Nations condemned South Africa's racial policies, as did Great Britain and the United States, both of which had previously stated that South Africa's internal racial policies were its own business. Perhaps even more potently for South Africa, foreign investors, sensing trouble, began pulling capital out of South African business ventures, which helped lower the value of the country's currency and which would eventually contribute to an economic downturn. South Africa was, as Martin Meredith has written, "propelled into an era of isolation from which there was to be no escape."

Most importantly, as a result of both the massacre and the ensuing repressive acts of the South African government, armed struggle began in South Africa, a struggle that would end, after many long and painful years, with the elimination of apartheid in 1990, followed by the country's first democratic elections in 1994.

CHAPTER 14

"THIS NAZI KIND OF THING"

MASSACRE AT MY LAI, MARCH 16, 1968

AFTER YOUNG GIS SLAUGHTERED 500 UNARMED VIETNAM MEN, WOMEN, AND CHILDREN, THE MAJORITY OF AMERICANS TURNED AGAINST THE VIETNAM WAR FOR THE FIRST TIME

THERE WERE 120 OF THEM AND THEY WERE FROM ALL OVER THE United States—Pennsylvania, West Virginia, California, Florida, Texas, New York. An army report later called them "a typical cross section of American youth." Their average age was twenty. Some were black, some were white, and some were Mexican American. They liked beer, rock and roll, a little grass every now and then, girls, and fast cars. They had trained together at Fort Benning, Georgia, which is where they first received their identity as Charlie Company of the 1st Battalion, 20th Infantry Regiment, 11th Brigade, 23rd Infantry Division (known as the Americal Division). They were remembered at Fort Benning as a stellar company, one of the best in the battalion, high-spirited but disciplined.

When they first got to Vietnam in December 1967, one of the young soldiers of Charlie Company later recalled, "we were supposed to be the good guys in white hats." For their first weeks, the company was stationed in a rear area where the soldiers played with the young children, giving them candy and soft drinks. But then the men of Charlie Company were moved to Quang Ngai Province on the eastern coast of the country, where beautiful pastoral villages nestled between waving rice paddies and the sand dunes abutting the South China Sea. But once there, bad things began to happen to Charlie

A PHOTO TAKEN BY ARMY PHOTOGRAPHER RONALD HAEBERLE—ONE OF MANY THAT SHOCKED THE AMERICAN PUBLIC— SHOWS CORPSES OF VIETNAM CIVILIANS MURDERED BY AMERICAN GIS AT THE VIETNAMESE HAMLET OF MY LAI.

TIME & LIFE PICTURES/GETTY IMAGES

Company. Quang Ngai was known to MACV, the U.S. high command in Vietnam, as a stronghold of the Viet Cong (VC), a place where this elusive enemy operated with impunity and, importantly in the events to come, was supported by the local population. After the Tet Offensive at the end of January 1968—in which the North Vietnamese Army (NVA) and Viet Cong units attacked U.S. and South Vietnamese forces throughout South Vietnam—the MACV believed that the crack Viet Cong 48th Battalion had retreated to Quang Ngai and, in particular, to an area called Son My, a group of villages known to the GIs as "Pinkville." The area was known as Pinkville because it was colored red on army maps, which signified a heavy local population.

In the case of Pinkville, however, red came to signify the blood of innocent people—perhaps 500 in all—who were slaughtered by these young Americans in a massacre that, for the first time, caused a majority of the United States' public to turn against the war.

TASK FORCE BARKER

As it operated in the Pinkville area in early 1968, Charlie Company was part of three companies belonging to Task Force Barker, named after its commanding officer, Lt. Colonel Frank Barker Jr. Task Force Barker's job was to root out the Viet Cong wherever it could find them. But Charlie Company and the other U.S. units had a difficult time locating the VC, who moved at night and lived in underground tunnels. What the GIs did find were booby traps and land mines, which took a heavy toll on the Task Force during February and the beginning of March. In six weeks, twenty-eight of Charlie Company's men were wounded and four died, almost all of them because of booby traps or hidden snipers. The men quickly became frustrated. They were fighting a dangerous war against an enemy they could rarely see, who nonetheless inflicted serious damage. The trip wires that set off land mines had been placed across paths and in rice paddies near villages that almost certainly supported the guerilla fighters who snuck out in the night to do this. And yet, as young Americans lost their arms and legs and lives, these villagers went about their daily existence as if it were none of their concern.

The frustration of the GIs of Task Force Baker turned into rage—a rage they began to vent against the citizens of Quang Ngai Province. Higher-ups

A MAP OF SOUTHEAST ASIA IN 1968. THE MASSACRE TOOK PLACE IN A VILLAGE IN THE QUANG NGAI PROVINCE IN THE EASTERN COAST OF VIETNAM IN A SMALL VILLAGE DUBBED MY LAI 4.

COURTESY OF THE UNIVERSITY OF TEXAS LIBRARIES, THE UNIVERSITY OF TEXAS AT AUSTIN

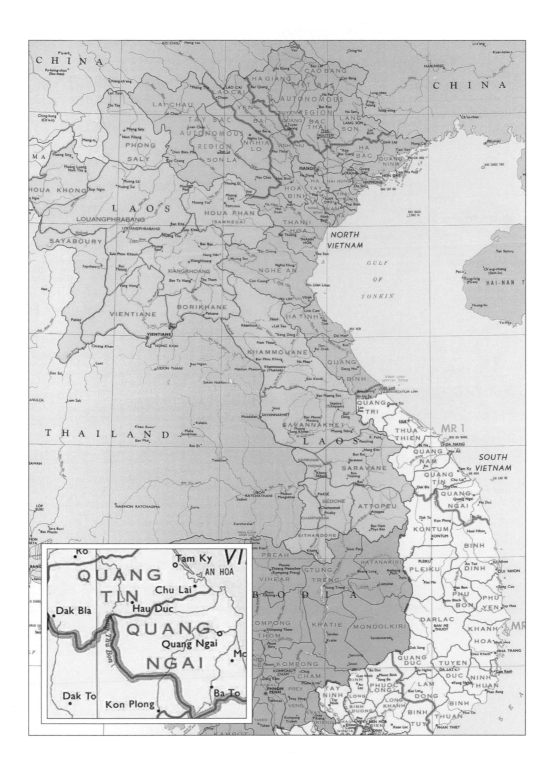

A PHOTO OF LIEUTENANT WILLIAM CALLEY, TAKEN IN 1971 AT HIS COURT-MARTIAL AT FORT BENNING, GEORGIA, FOR CRIMES CONNECTED WITH THE MASSACRE AT MY LAI. TO THIS DAY, CALLEY HAS SAID THE KILLINGS DID NOT DISTURB HIM.

ASSOCIATED PRESS

clamored for a body count to show the success of the unit's operations in the area. The men of Charlie Company joked that "anything that's dead and isn't white is a VC"—in other words, there was no difference between civilians and the enemy when it came to counting the dead.

The leader of the company's first platoon was a twenty-four-year-old lieutenant named William Calley, a bland-faced young man, born in Florida, who had begun his military career as a clerk-typist. He stood 5 feet, 4 inches (1.6 m) tall and spent much of his early days with Charlie Company convincing the men not to hand out candy and other treats to Vietnamese children, who, he said, frightened him. His men had little respect for him. One thought him a "nervous, excitable person who yelled a lot." Others said that he could barely read a military map. It probably didn't help matters any that Captain Ernest Medina, the thirty-three-year-old commander of Charlie Company, routinely referred to Calley in front of his men as "young thing," "sweetheart," and "Lieutenant Shithead."

At the same time, Calley's blatant hostility toward the Vietnamese civilians whom Charlie Company encountered started to rub off on his men. One soldier later said: "If [the company] wanted to do something wrong, it was okay with Calley." By March 1968, the men of Charlie Company had begun to fall into what Seymour Hersh, the first journalist to report on the My Lai massacre, referred to in his book *Cover-Up* as "an easy pattern of violence." Civilians were beaten and abused. At the beginning of March, a first platoon radio operator grew frustrated when an old Vietnamese man got in his way. He picked him up and threw him down a well. Lt. Calley leaned over the well and shot the man to death. The second platoon gained a reputation as a team of roving rapists. One second platoon GI, testifying against William Calley at his court-martial, had this rather casual exchange with Calley's defense attorney.

> **Q.** Didn't you carry a woman half-nude on your shoulders and throw her down and say that she was too dirty to rape? You did do that, didn't you?
>
> **A.** Oh yeah, but it wasn't at My Lai . . .

"THEY WERE GOING TO LEVEL PINKVILLE"

On March 14, while out on patrol, a Charlie Company squad tripped a booby trap, which killed one of the most popular sergeants in the company, blinded another soldier, and wounded several others. The next night, during a memorial service for the sergeant, the men of the company angrily talked of seeking revenge for his death.

Captain Medina rose to speak at the service. He told the men that their mission, the next morning, would be to attack a small village known as My Lai 4. Intelligence information revealed that elements of the 48th Viet Cong Battalion were located there. (Other companies in Task Force Barker would attack villages nearby—see "The Forgotten Massacre at My Khe 4," page 241.) Medina told them that all the villagers of My Lai 4 would have left the hamlet to go to a nearby marketplace by 7:00 a.m. Thus, anyone remaining in the village would be Viet Cong. The soldiers were to kill any Viet Cong, shoot livestock, poison wells, burn crops, set fire to thatched homes, and explode brick ones with dynamite.

Medina claimed later that his impassioned speech at the memorial service was merely a means to "fire up" the men, that he did not give "any instructions as to what to do with the women and children in the village." Many of the soldiers heard something different, saying Medina had told them to kill any Vietnamese who moved. A South Vietnamese Army interpreter came upon a group of Charlie Company men about two hours after Medina had spoken with them. He later testified that a large number of the men were drunk. The interpreter also related: "One of the soldiers told me that tomorrow they would go on an operation and they would kill women, children, cattle, and everything . . . 'I'm not joking, that's the truth,' the man said." Because the man was drunk, the interpreter discounted what he said. But another GI later told an interviewer:

"My understanding was, we were going in, it was going to be one helluva fight, we were gonna kick some ass, and there wasn't going to be anyone left when we got done."

No one, now, will ever know what Medina actually said to his men on the night of March 15. There was testimony at Medina's court-martial that he was under extreme pressure from Lt. Colonel Frank Barker to produce significant body counts out of Pinkville. An army chaplain who attended a briefing given by Barker about the attack earlier on the 15th testified that he had heard Barker and another officer say they were going to "level Pinkville." The priest went on: "You could cut the hostility with a knife. Nothing was said about resettlement [of the civilian population]." The chaplain told Barker: "I didn't think we made war like that." Barker replied: "It's a tough war."

The priest was surprised at the level of emotion to be found even at battalion level. It was not, he thought, a good sign.

"FIRING AND CRYING"

Around 7:30 a.m. on March 16, 1968, the 700 inhabitants of the village of My Lai 4 were peacefully going about their business. Far from being at the marketplace, most of them were squatting outside their homes preparing their morning meals when artillery shells began landing around the village. The first helicopter gunships swept in, strafing the hamlet and the surrounding rice paddies with machine gun fire and rockets. The gunships reported that they killed several Viet Cong with weapons, but no weapons were ever recovered, nor were any bodies of guerillas.

After the gunships dispersed, nine helicopters carrying members of Charlie Company landed near the village. According to the plan worked out the day before, Lt. Calley's first platoon assaulted the village along with the second platoon, led by Lt. Stephen Brooks. The third platoon and Captain Medina waited in reserve outside the village, while overhead in a circling command helicopter was Lt. Col. Barker.

There was no resistance as Calley's platoon ran into the village. They immediately shot an old man who had jumped out of a hiding place waving his hands in surrender. They then began going into homes and pulling people out to interrogate them about possible VC activity in the region. This was standard operating procedure on "search and destroy" missions such as this one, but what happened next was not standard. One soldier stabbed a village man in the back with a bayonet as he stood with his hands up. Another civilian who did not answer quickly enough was thrown into a well and had a hand grenade dropped in after him.

About twenty elderly women raced to a nearby temple and fell outside it on their knees, praying. Members of the first platoon executed each one with a shot to the back of the head. They herded about eighty Vietnamese men, women, and children to a plaza area just south of the village, a place used for town meetings. They were screaming: "No VC! No VC!" but it did them little good. Calley told a sergeant named Paul Meadlo: "You know what to do with them, Meadlo."

Meadlo later testified as a witness for the prosecution (under grant of immunity) at Calley's trial for murdering 109 Vietnamese civilians. Calley's remark meant, as far as Meadlo was concerned, that "he wanted me to guard them."

But ten minutes later Calley came back and said: "How come they're not dead?" Meadlo continued in his testimony:

> I said, "I didn't know we were supposed to kill them." He said, "I want them dead." He backed off twenty or thirty feet [6.1 or 9.1 m] and started shooting into the people—the Viet Cong—shooting automatic. He was beside me. He burned four or five magazines. I burned off a few, about there, I helped shoot them.

The prosecuting attorney then asked Meadlo:

> **Q.** What were the people doing after you shot them?
>
> **A.** They were lying down.
>
> **Q.** Why were they lying down?
>
> **A.** They were mortally wounded.
>
> **Q.** How were you feeling at that time?
>
> **A.** I was mortally upset, scared, because of the briefing we had the day before.

Another soldier named Robert Maples testified that he saw Meadlo weeping during the incident. Calley's defense attorney probed further.

> **Q.** Well, tell me, what was so remarkable about Meadlo that made you remember him?
>
> **A.** He was firing and crying.
>
> **Q.** He was pointing his weapon away from you and you saw tears in his eyes?
>
> **A.** Yes.

Two days after the My Lai massacre, Paul Meadlo had his foot blown off by a land mine. He believed God was punishing him for his actions at My Lai, which was why he agreed to testify against Calley.

THE DITCH

By 9:00, the GIs of Charlie Company had killed about ninety men, women, and children, and the third platoon, with Captain Medina, had moved into the village. There is some dispute as to when Medina entered My Lai. He said he was not in the hamlet until 10 a.m., but others, including Meadlo, put him there as early as 9 a.m. Meadlo also claimed Medina was a witness to the murders going on, which Medina denied. It is almost impossible to believe that Medina could have missed the chaos and bloody insanity going on around him.

Army photographer Ronald Haeberle had come along with the platoon to document the attack on the Viet Cong. Instead, he was an eyewitness to slaughter. He saw thirty different GIs kill about 100 civilians. He tried to take a picture of a young child, but before he could snap the shot, the child was killed in front of his eyes. Haeberle watched as GIs fondled teenage Vietnamese girls, and then took them away to rape.

The soldiers would stop what they were doing around him, saying, "Hey, here comes the photographer," but when he turned his back they would continue killing. Finally, Haeberle put away his official army camera and took out his own personal one, and began taking pictures of the dead bodies that lay sprawled everywhere.

Probably the worst place that horrific day was a drainage ditch that ran along the eastern side of My Lai. Around 10 a.m., Calley ordered about a dozen members of his platoon, including Paul Meadlo, to herd eighty to ninety old men, women, and children to this ditch. He then ordered the men to push the civilians into the ditch. Some of them refused this command, but others obeyed it. One man who was there, Paul Conti, testified:

They—Calley and Meadlo—got on line and fired directly into the people. There were bursts and single shots for two minutes. It was automatic. The people screamed and yelled and fell. I guess they tried to get up, too. They couldn't. That was it. The people were pretty well messed up. Lots of heads were shot off, pieces of heads and pieces of flesh flew off the sides and arms. They were all messed up.

THE RESURRECTION OF WILLIAM CALLEY

Known as Lieutenant Shithead to his commanding officer, despised by his own troops (who often discussed whether they should "frag," or deliberately kill, him), Lieutenant William Calley was, as one historian has written, "the worst officer in the worst company in the army."

And when he was convicted of murdering Vietnamese civilians in 1971, it appeared that he was going to get what he deserved—life imprisonment at hard labor. But then powerful forces came to his aid. Many Americans, especially in the South, did not want to see him punished, thinking he was, at most, a pawn in the hands of superior officers. A pop song called "The Battle Hymn of Lieutenant Calley" sold 200,000 copies in three days and Calley was suddenly a folk hero.

As Calley's appeals worked their way through the courts, President Richard Nixon allowed Calley to spend his time not in the stockade, but under house arrest at Fort Leavenworth, Kansas. After three and a half years, he was paroled. Calley then dropped his long-time girlfriend, and began dating and finally married Penny Vick, the daughter of a wealthy jeweler in Columbus, Georgia. Calley's wedding in Georgia was a society event, attended by the mayor and the local sheriff. He then took over management of his father-in-law's business, until 2005, at which point he and his wife were divorced and he moved in with his son, a Ph.D. student living in Atlanta. When a British newspaper tried to contact him for an interview, he demanded $25,000 and then walked away when the reporter did not show up with the money.

Calley, sixty-seven years old in 2009, has always claimed that the killings at My Lai did not disturb him. "We weren't in My Lai to kill human beings, really," he said in a book he wrote called *Body Count.* "We were there to kill ideology that is carried by—I don't know—Pawns. Blobs. Pieces of flesh. And I wasn't in My Lai to destroy intelligent men. I was there to destroy an intangible. To destroy communism."

The attorney for William Calley tried to shake Conti's story.

Q. Did you see any dead bodies at My Lai—how many?

A. Quite a few.

Q. Were they sleeping or did they appear to be dead?

A. Well, they had holes in 'em so I assumed they were dead.

"HOW IS IT THAT THEY WOULD COME AND DO THIS TO US?"

Conspicuous in their absence at the trials of Medina and Calley were the voices of those who survived the massacre—the people of My Lai. There were few of them, and those who did survive were lost in the chaos of Vietnam at the time. In the early 1990s, Michael Bilton and Kevin Sim interviewed a few of those who had been there for their book *Four Hours in My Lai*. Most of them were alive to tell the tale because they had hidden beneath the bodies of their families or deep in holes in the ground.

The survivors expressed astonishment that the GIs had attacked them in this manner. Truong Moi, an eighteen-year-old fisherman, was checking his nets when the Americans attacked. He hid in a bush during the entire attack, then approached his village that afternoon, after the Americans had left. He found a scene of horror. His brother, his sister, and her two young children were dead. His elderly mother's charred corpse lay behind her home. Twenty-four members of his family were dead. Some of the children had their throats cut; others were disemboweled. Moi's only contact with the GIs prior to this had been in January, when they had come to My Lai, treated the sick, and given candy to the children.

"How is it that they would come and do this to us, when we have done nothing to them?" he asked himself.

A thirty-year-old widow named Pham Thi Thuam was one of those pushed into the ditch by Calley and his men. She had her six-year-old daughter with her. When the M-16s began to cut them down, she fell on top of her daughter and held her hand over the child's mouth to keep her from crying out. Corpses of her friends and neighbors fell on top of them. When she thought it was safe, she pushed the bodies away from her and ran with her daughter toward the treeline.

The GI's fired at her, but she and her daughter managed to escape. Thuam later discovered that pieces of the brains of those who had been killed around her had stuck into her hair like bits of clay.

A ten-year-old girl named Pham Thi Trinh hid inside her house while the Americans took away her family. Peering through a window, she watched her fifteen-year-old sister being raped by a GI. When he was done, he pulled up his pants, took his rifle, and shot her. Trinh crawled outside and found her mother on the back veranda, with a huge bullet hole in her, lying on her back and holding Trinh's seven-month-old brother in her arms. Her mother whispered to her: "Run and hide so you can live . . . as for me, I think I am going to die."

"EVERYWHERE WE'D LOOK WE'D SEE BODIES"

Shortly after 11 a.m., the massacre was over. Charlie Company had killed about 400 people in roughly four hours. And not just killed, but mutilated. As one historian has written, the people of My Lai died in "astonishingly violent, painful and terrifying ways." People were blown apart by hand grenades. One person was beheaded. Several women and girls had their vaginas slit open with bayonets. Many people had their throats cut. Some were scalped.

There was only one GI hurt. He shot himself in the foot when he was trying to clear the breech of his jammed .45 pistol. He had given it to another member of his platoon who wanted to use it to shoot a small boy who was crawling around on a pile of corpses. That platoonmate had shot the boy in the neck, but the boy had still not died, and when he tried to shoot him again, the pistol jammed. He returned it in disgust to its original owner who, trying to clear the jam, shot himself.

While all of this was going on, black smoke from the burning village of My Lai rose high into the sky. There were numerous helicopters in the sky—the one containing Colonel Frank Barker and members of his command staff, but also one flown by Warrant Officer Hugh Thompson, whose job that day was to provide air reconnaissance for the operations going on around Pinkville. As Thompson and his crew flew back and forth over the area during the morning hours, looking for possible counterattacks, Thompson became concerned about the number of dead he was seeing. "Everywhere we'd look we'd see bodies.

THE FORGOTTEN MASSACRE AT MY KHE 4

On March 16, 1968, while Charlie Company was assaulting the village of My Lai 4, another U.S. attack was taking place about 1.5 miles (2.4 km) away. This was an assault by Bravo Company, one of the two other companies in Task Force Barker, on a village known as My Lai 1.

The GIs of Bravo Company leaped from their helicopters into the rice paddies outside of My Lai 1 at around 8:15 a.m., almost an hour after Charlie Company had made its attack. Bullets buzzed around their ears and Bravo Company at first thought it was under attack, until commanding officers realized that the fire was "friendly"—that is, from Charlie Company at My Lai. The GIs then moved out against My Lai 1, which was surrounded by a thick hedge that the Viet Cong had booby-trapped. One such device exploded, killing a lieutenant and seriously injuring four other GIs. After the wounded were flown away by helicopter, another attempt at penetrating the hedge was made. This time, three more soldiers were wounded by an explosion.

Enraged, but unwilling to make another attempt to get through the deadly hedgerow, elements of Bravo Company decided instead to attack a small village known as My Khe 4, which was across a nearby wooden bridge. It was inhabited by about 100 to 200 old men, women, and children, who could be seen walking around the village, working and doing chores. A lieutenant named Willingham ordered his men to set two machine guns on the outskirts of the hamlet, but did not order them to open fire. However, a rumor spread through U.S. ranks that a grenade had been thrown (some said a sniper had opened fire), and the U.S. machine gunners began spraying the village with bullets and then, as one GI recalled, "everybody was shooting and [Vietnamese] people were on top of this hill and running around like crazy people."

One GI later told journalist Seymour Hersh that "we were having a good time . . . it was sort of like being in a shooting gallery." The village was dotted with trees and shrubbery and the GIs made a game of shooting at people when they popped up from hiding. Another GI described how the soldiers laughed when another soldier tried to kill a crawling infant from close range with a .45 pistol, but kept missing. The firing kept on until about noon, with the soldiers dynamiting bunkers underneath houses—if any Vietnamese ran out, they were shot.

It is generally accepted that the death toll at My Khe 4 was about 100 civilians, bringing the number of noncombatants killed in the area that morning to about 500. At the time of the My Lai investigation, the Army charged Lieutenant Willingham with the deaths of twenty civilians, but never prosecuted him and eventually dropped the charges.

There were infants, two-, three-, four-, five-year-olds, women, very old men, no draft-age people whatsoever."

As the helicopter circled lower, its crew began to see shocking things: a woman kneeling by the side of the road, with her hat beside her, and her brains blown out onto the dirt. They saw another woman who was wounded and radioed for help, and even marked her position with smoke. "A few minutes later," Thompson reported, "up walks a captain, steps up to her, nudges her with his foot, steps back, and blows her away."

Then Thompson saw the bodies piled high in the drainage ditch, U.S. soldiers standing around them with their weapons, and he couldn't understand how so many civilians had come to die there. "Every house in Vietnam," he later said, "had a bunker under it," and that is where villagers would have hidden from artillery fire. It finally dawned on him that these people had been massacred by Americans. One of the few heroes of the day, Thompson landed his helicopter between the GIs of Charlie Company and the ditch, and told his gunner to fire on the Americans if they interfered. Then he rescued those Vietnamese left alive—about twelve—and took them to safety.

Aside from the actions of Thompson and a few others in Charlie Company who refused to fire on civilians, there was little nobility on the ground that day. A cover-up started almost immediately. Captain Medina reported 128 dead, with 100 of them being Viet Cong and 28 civilians killed by mistake. Hugh Thompson filed a complaint with his commanding officer alleging war crimes and Medina was told to return to My Lai and count the bodies there (they had been buried by the Vietnamese in three mass graves). But before he could do so, another officer countermanded the order, and simply asked Medina how many civilian dead there were. "Twenty-eight," Medina replied, and the investigation went no further.

"THIS NAZI KIND OF THING"

Although a few members of Charlie Company began to regret their actions and those of their fellow soldiers and spoke of contacting the press or public about the atrocities, nothing happened for an entire year. It is possible the story of My Lai would have remained a dirty military secret but for the actions of an ex-GI and Vietnam vet named Ron Ridenhour, who was not at My Lai, but heard about what happened there before he left the service in December 1968. A soldier who had been with Charlie Company at My Lai told him: "We just went in there and killed everybody. It was this Nazi kind of thing."

This disturbed Ridenhour so much that in March 1969, he sent a letter about what he called the "Pinkville Massacre" to President Richard Nixon, the Joint Chiefs of Staff, and various members of Congress. This caused enough of a stir to prompt an investigation by the Army's Inspector General's Office, which interviewed dozens of people who had been there and eventually sent the matter to the Criminal Investigation Division. On September 5, 1969, William Calley was charged with six counts of premeditated murder. But shortly thereafter, the U.S. public learned about the massacre at My Lai through articles written by Seymour Hersh as well as an interview with Paul Meadlo on the CBS news show "Sixty Minutes."

With increasing pressure from the public, the army eventually decided to bring charges against twenty-five military personnel involved in the massacre or charged with covering it up. These include 102 counts of murder brought against Captain Ernest Medina, who was theoretically responsible for the murders committed by his men. However, a jury acquitted Medina of all charges, unable to directly link him to the murders. The other cases were never brought to trial, mainly because most of those involved were no longer in the military, which made military prosecution difficult.

The one man who was convicted of murder in the case was Calley. Though he claimed that "I was just carrying out my orders" (from Medina), Calley was found guilty of premeditated murder and sentenced to life imprisonment. However, President Richard Nixon ordered him placed under house arrest after Calley had spent only a weekend in jail. Calley was to spend three-and-a-half years under house arrest, only to be paroled without serving further jail time.

AMERICAN GI RON RIDENHOUR
WALKS ALONG A SAIGON STREET
IN 1971. RIDENHOUR HEARD ABOUT
THE "PINKVILLE" MASSACRE
AFTER RETURNING TO THE
UNITED STATES AND WROTE A
LETTER THAT PROMPTED AN
INVESTIGATION BY THE ARMY'S
INSPECTOR GENERAL'S OFFICE.

ASSOCIATED PRESS

The My Lai massacre had an enormous effect on a United States radically divided about the right and wrong of the Vietnam War. Though most Americans did not want to see Calley and his fellow soldiers prosecuted, the pictures and stories of the massacre disseminated by the mass media horrified them. Two weeks after Calley was convicted, a Harris Poll showed that, for the first time, a majority of the American public disapproved of the Vietnam War. With the exception of a few incidents in American history—the Sand Creek Massacre (see page 92), as well as the torture of Moro rebels in the Philippines by U.S. marines at the turn of the century—America had never considered its young men capable of such atrocities. Now Americans could see, in living color before their very eyes, what such wanton killing looked like. And they wanted nothing to do with it, or the war that produced it.

The My Lai massacre had the further effect of forcing thoughtful commanders in the U.S. military to find different ways of doing things—to understand that placing a high premium on "body counts" and "kill ratios" made such events as My Lai likely to occur again. After the Vietnam War, the military went through a long period of refocusing its efforts on a better-trained and educated volunteer army. The results would be seen in the brilliantly successful Desert Storm operations of the First Gulf War, where, before troops went into battle, their commanders cautioned them: "No My Lais—understand?"

Of course, the Iraq War—the most controversial U.S. war since Vietnam, and one that divided the country in a similar, if not quite as dramatic, way—would eventually produce more My Lais. U.S. citizens would learn about the brutality against Iraqi prisoners at Abu Ghraib prison and the killing of twenty-four civilians by U.S. Marines in Haditha in western Iraq. And, in April 2009, the Justice Department released shocking "torture memos" that detailed brutal interrogation methods used by the CIA against suspected Al-Qaeda terrorists, methods approved by the Bush White House. But it can be said that America's innocence about her young men was forever shattered by what occurred that March day in My Lai in 1968.

CHAPTER 15

TERROR IN THE YEAR ZERO

THE CAMBODIAN GENOCIDE, 1975–1979

POL POT AND HIS KHMER ROUGE COMMITTED GENOCIDE
ON AN EPIC SCALE, DESTROYING WAR-TORN CAMBODIA'S
INFRASTRUCTURE AND SLAUGHTERING ITS CITIZENS

O N THE MORNING OF APRIL 17, 1975, STREAMS OF YOUNG MEN, ALL heavily armed and wearing either black pajamas or olive green camouflage uniforms, poured into the ancient Cambodian capital city of Phnom Penh. The young men were silent, almost solemn, without any of the glee and unruliness of a conquering army, although that is what they were.

Those city dwellers who dared to come out onto the street to greet them were struck by the fact that so many of these soldiers seemed to be under fifteen years of age. One citizen who watched them said they seemed "alert and distrustful, like soldiers on patrol." The soldiers looked at foreigners as if "they were creatures from another planet," said one American reporter observing them. The same reporter watched one of the young men attempting to start a captured motorcycle. When he could not do so, he pulled out a pistol and shot it.

The inhabitants of Phnom Penh, and the whole of Cambodia, had just undergone five years of bloody civil war beginning in 1970. The war was between the Khmer Rouge—these young peasant boys who now trod the city streets suspiciously, fingering their AK-47s—and the government forces of the ruler Lon Nol, who the United States had installed in a right-wing military coup. Lon Nol had now fled and the Khmer Rouge, 700,000 strong and directed by their shadowy leader Pol Pot, was in control.

YOUNG KHMER ROUGE SOLDIERS
ENTERING PHNOM PENH ON APRIL
17, 1975, AS THE CITY FELL TO THE
FORCES OF POL POT AND THE
CAMBODIAN GENOCIDE BEGAN.

AFP/GETTY IMAGES

Phnom Penh was a city ready for peace. Half a million Cambodians had died in the civil war, at least 150,000 of them civilians. Khmer forces had shelled and fired rockets at Phnom Penh for at least a year now. The city was filled with refugees, basic services like water and electricity were sporadic, and there was little food. Lon Nol was a corrupt and unloved leader; perhaps, some Cambodians felt, these Khmer Rouge were at least willing to deal with people fairly.

These fond hopes evaporated almost immediately. By the afternoon of April 17, the Khmer began a massive evacuation of Phnom Penh, with soldiers going door to door, firing shots in the air, and telling people they had ten minutes to leave their homes. The rebels told some citizens that the Americans were going to bomb the city. But they simply ordered the majority out onto the roads leading north, west, and east of the city. There this vast procession was joined by city-dwellers from other Cambodian towns. Within two weeks, Phnom Penh was a ghost town. Indeed, in the next four years, Cambodia itself would become the victim of a cruel and unrelenting genocide that would turn it into a country of ghosts and leave permanent scars.

SALOTH SAR'S REVOLUTION

Cambodia, in ancient times, was Kampuchea, home to the Khmer kingdom, whose capital was the fabled Angkor, famous for its twelfth-century temples. The French colonized it in the mid-nineteenth century, and in 1953, it won its independence under King Norodom Sihanouk, who ruled the country until 1970. Sihanouk spent much of his time during this period attempting to keep his 7 million–strong nation out of the war that was intensifying in neighboring Vietnam, between the United States and South Vietnam and the North Vietnamese and Viet Cong guerillas.

Sihanouk was a charismatic and clever man, but keeping neutral in such a situation was difficult. He gave tacit approval for North Vietnam to use Cambodian borderlands as sanctuaries, but then the United States pressured him into allowing the U.S. Air Force to secretly bomb his own country to try and destroy North Vietnamese safe havens. The bombing that began in the mid-1960s continued for four years, and may have taken as many as

750,000 Cambodian lives. The horror of the bombing drew new recruits to the small, Vietnamese-backed Khmer Rouge guerilla movement, which opposed Sihanouk for years.

The Khmer were led by a man named Saloth Sar, who would become known to the world as Pol Pot (see "Brother Number One," page 250). Sar was born to a well-to do family of Cambodian peasant stock in 1928, was educated (and radicalized) in Paris, and then came back to Cambodia to foment a people's revolution against Sihanouk. Leading small groups of young Khmer (or peasant people), Sar had little success until the chaos of the Vietnam War. The U.S. bombing caused the ranks of the Khmer Rouge—the Red, or Communist, Khmer, as the French called them—to swell.

When Lon Nol overthrew King Sihanouk in 1970, the wily Sihanouk fled to Beijing, where he announced his support for none other than his old enemy, Saloth Sar and his Khmer Rouge. With Lon Nol's corrupt government in place and increased bombing by the Americans, hundreds of thousands of young Cambodians joined the forces of the Khmer Rouge. When the U.S.-backed government of South Vietnam collapsed in 1975 and the Americans abandoned the country, Lon Nol's puppet government collapsed as well. The Khmer swept into Cambodia's cities and took control of the reins of government, led by Sar, who styled himself Brother Number One of a socialist government where all were equals.

Soon, however, Sar announced to the world that his new name would be Pol Pot. It was not uncommon for famous revolutionaries to take pseudonyms; the odd thing about Pol Pot was that he took his name *after* his revolution was successful, not while he was underground. And while Stalin means "steel" and Ho Chi Minh means "the enlightened one," "Pol Pot" has no meaning at all. It is simply a common Cambodian name.

A 1979 PHOTOGRAPH OF POL POT. THE MURDEROUS KHMER LEADER LIKED TO POSE AS A HUMBLE PEASANT AND BE CALLED BROTHER NUMBER ONE, BUT HIS RUTHLESS PROGRAM OF "PURIFICATION" KILLED HUNDREDS OF THOUSANDS OF CAMBODIANS.

BROTHER NUMBER ONE

Saloth Sar, who would become known as the fearsome Pol Pot, was a cipher even to his fellow Communists. The first journalists to interview him after his takeover of Cambodia came from behind the Iron Curtain in Yugoslavia, and the first thing they asked him was: "Who are you, Comrade Pol Pot?"

A question people are still asking themselves. Pol Pot was born in rural Cambodia in 1928, the youngest in a family of seven. His parents were fairly well-off peasants who owned land, water buffalo, and had a family connection to the Cambodian royal court. After high school, Pol Pot received a scholarship to study radio electricity in Paris and while there he learned about Marxist theory and began to dream of liberating his country from the Cambodian royal family.

Pol Pot arrived back home in 1953 to find that King Sihanouk had declared martial law to suppress the Cambodian independence movement. This angered thousands of young Cambodians, including Pol Pot and his brother, who went to Vietnam to receive training from the Vietnamese, already deeply engaged in their revolution against the French. Returning to Cambodia, he spent the next decade and a half consolidating his position in what became known as the Kampuchean Communist Party, which began the Khmer Rouge. He launched his rebellion against Sihanouk in the late 1960s and, with the help of China, Vietnam, and the United States, successfully took over the country in 1975.

And then he instituted a mass genocide. The question, almost thirty-five years later, is why? His ruthless program of "purification" was an attempt to brutally sever ties with a capitalist past and begin Cambodia anew. But unlike Mao, upon whose Great Leap Forward Pol Pot modeled a large part of his massive agrarian work farm policy, Pol Pot kept himself hidden. He assumed a meaningless nom de plume and liked to be known as Brother Number One. He kept his decision-making process deeply secret and was little known to the Cambodian public. It is likely that the process of genocide began as a way to purge possible enemies and allow the Khmer Rouge to take revenge on those they considered their repressors, but Pol Pot's actions in continuing to destroy the country's intellectuals and those who ran its infrastructure were ultimately self-defeating.

Quite possibly, he was mad with power and paranoia. Before he died in the jungle in 1998, he gave one interview, to Nate Thayer, a journalist for the *Far East Economic Review*. In it he said: "Look at me now. Do you think . . . I am a violent person? No. So far as my conscience and my mission is concerned, there was no problem."

"TO DESTROY YOU IS NO LOSS"

There is nothing common about what Pol Pot decided to do next. He embarked on a radical experiment to create an agrarian utopia, modeled after Chairman Mao Zedong's Great Leap Forward program in China, which also included forced evacuations of Chinese cities. Within a short time after April 17, 1975, Pol Pot declared a "Super Great Leap Forward" for Cambodia, which he renamed the Democratic Republic of Kampuchea. He banned all education, religion, money, businesses, private ownership, literature, culture, and even family groups.

"This is the Year Zero," he announced. It was the end of 2,000 years of Cambodian history, the beginning of the country as a massive work farm where all labored for the good of the people. Cities, rife with French and U.S. influences, were considered evil places (Phnom Penh was called "the great whore of the Mekong"). People living in cities were henceforth known as "new people" or "April 17th people." New people were considered to have been corrupted, probably hopelessly, by capitalism, compared with the peasants, or "old people" of the countryside, who possessed an ideological purity.

Those being evacuated from the cities to the vast rural areas found out very quickly what being a "new person" meant. As they reached the country, the evacuees from Phnom Penh were met by special squads of Khmer soldiers asking them their names and occupations. They led away those who served in the military or were teachers, engineers, scientists, or government workers. The others were allowed to proceed, but soon heard shots fired in the distance. To their horror, it became apparent that the Khmer Rouge was killing anyone with an education or even tentative connections to the military or government.

One woman named Bouchan Sameth, interviewed by the genocide historian Ben Kiernan, said that the Khmer Rouge told members of her family to return to Phnom Penh, where they could help rebuild the city, using their experience in education and local industry. But a few weeks later, when she was still on her forced march through the countryside, she met a man who told her he had been lined up near a ditch with her cousin and others, at which point they were all shot—the man had played dead and then ran off into the countryside. He advised Sameth to change her name, because all names were being recorded by officials of *Angkar Loeu*, the secretive "high organization" that governed Cambodia and whose pronouncements were followed to the letter by the Khmer Rouge cadre.

Some new people traveled for only a few days to reach the detention centers/farming cooperatives they were to be placed in; others were on the road for longer than a month. The young Khmer soldiers began to openly execute people. They shot people for climbing coconut trees to gather fruit or begging food from local peasants. It soon became apparent that almost anything could get a new person killed. Wearing glasses could do it, as could knowing a foreign language, laughing, or listening to music. The Khmer were indifferent. They had a favorite saying: "To spare you is no profit," they repeated to the horror of the city dwellers they were guarding. "To destroy you is no loss."

This was driven home to a Cambodian named Ngoy Taing Heng who witnessed a later deportation of citizens from Phnom Penh. He said that as 3,000 of them crossed the Mekong River on ferry boats, the Khmer Rouge blew them up. "The Mekong flowed blood-red," he said.

"A GIANT WORKSHOP"

Under Pol Pot, Cambodia was divided into geographical districts run by separate groups of Khmer who answered to the dictates of Angkar. After years of war, the Cambodian people were starving, and so Pol Pot's answer to this was to develop a "four-year plan" in which all Cambodians were to work together to produce an average national rice yield of 1.4 tons (1.2 metric tons) per acre. The fact that, even at optimum conditions, Cambodians had never produced more than a third of this amount did not seem to disturb Pol Pot.

The Khmer took the new people—who at this point probably made up 30 percent of Cambodia's population—to the countryside and distributed them among various camps. These camps were also home to the peasants of the area; that is, the "old people" or "base people," who received better treatment and more food, at least at first. The country was now becoming what the author William Shawcross called "a giant workshop." The Khmer separated families upon arrival at their labor farms. They lived in barracks or thatched huts—some of the new people were even forced to inhabit crawl spaces underneath barracks.

A daily ration of rice before the war might be almost 2 cups (400 g) of rice per person; the Khmer Rouge now brought it down to less than 1 cup (100 g), per person per day.

People who had never worked the fields before were now forced to dig irrigation ditches, plant and harvest rice, and build earthen dams twelve to fourteen hours a day. Sometimes, after work, they were allowed to forage for food; at other times, they were not. People dropped dead of starvation on a regular basis. In the meantime, executions continued. You could be killed if your work was "weak" or if you were disrespectful. Women might be executed if they wore their shirts unbuttoned or their hair too long. Ordinary emotions could get you killed—as one survivor wrote: "Sadness was a sign of spiritual confusion, joy a sign of individualism, [while] an indecisive point of view indicated a petty bourgeois intellectualism."

The killers kept fairly regular hours, murdering people between 6:00 and 11:00 a.m., breaking for lunch, resuming from 2:00 to 6:00 p.m., stopping for supper, then finishing off with a stint of executions from 7:00 to 9:00 p.m. Often they forced those to be killed to dig their own graves. The favorite methods of killing were hacking at victims' necks with a hoe or ax, beating them to

DESPAIR CAN BE READILY SEEN ON THE FACES OF THIS YOUNG TRIO CAPTURED BY THE KHMER ROUGE. THE GENOCIDE RESULTED IN THE DESTRUCTION OF AN ENTIRE GENERATION. TODAY, MORE THAN 50 PERCENT OF CAMBODIANS ARE YOUNGER THAN TWENTY-ONE AND DO NOT REMEMBER THE DAYS OF POL POT.

death with a club, or stabbing them with a sharpened bamboo stick. Execution became so regular and human life so cheap that the killers became extremely casual. One Cambodian doctor, marked for death because he had been unable to cure a sick Khmer soldier, was taken out one summer evening to be killed, but it began to rain so steadily that his executioners decided conditions were too inclement for killing. By the next morning, they had forgotten about him.

After coming home from a back-breaking day in the fields, people in work camps were subjected to so-called "livelihood meetings" in which workers were lectured on Communist theory and encouraged to confess to bourgeois sins they may have committed in the past. The Khmer cadres in attendance embraced them for this but sooner or later they would be asked to "come help us pick some fruit" or "come with us for further study," and they would be taken to the woods and killed.

As perhaps an even greater sorrow, people in the work camps were constantly spied upon by children (sometimes their own) who had been taken away by the Khmer Rouge and reeducated to believe in nothing but Angkar. These children snuck among the huts at night, waiting for adults to say something, even in a whisper, against the organization. Then they would report them.

TUOL SLENG

Even though the "killing fields" surrounding the work camps (the phrase was coined by Cambodian photojournalist Dith Pran, who survived four years in the labor camps) were horrible places, they at least offered some faint hope of survival, if new people hid their identity and submerged themselves in Khmer doctrine. This was not the case with the infamous Phnom Penh prison Tuol Sleng. An estimated 20,000 people were imprisoned at Security Prison 21 (S-21), as it was known to the Pol Pot regime, from 1976 to 1979. Ben Kiernan writes: "Archival evidence suggests that with perhaps six exceptions, no one who entered S-21 came out alive."

The Khmer converted Tuol Sleng, a former private high school housed in a five-building complex, to a prison in late 1975, its classrooms turned into tiny cells and torture chambers. The commandant of the prison was Kaing Geuk Eav, known as Duch (see "No Answer Could Avoid Death," page 260) who became

notorious for his cruelty. The prison held only about 1,500 people at any given time. At first, those brought in were former Lon Nol officials or "new people" (lawyers, doctors, Buddhist monks, teachers, engineers, and the like). These were tortured and killed simply because of their occupations, or on the chance they might know anyone plotting against the Pol Pot regime. Many of them, however, as evidenced by prison photos left behind, were children, or women with infants.

Later, Angkar turned its paranoia toward the ranks of its own party, purging those politicians whom Pol Pot thought might be undermining his policies or perhaps coop-erating with the Vietnamese, who had become his sworn enemies. The party described these people as "pests buried within." They were subject to brutal tortures, including enduring battery-powered electric shocks, having their fin-gernails torn out and rubbing alcohol poured over the wounds, being burned with hot metal, and waterboarding. Those ready for execution were either hung on a gallows—a wooden frame students had formerly used for gymnastics—or taken to be killed outside Phnom Penh near the village of Choeung Ek. Before they died, they invariably named other conspirators, who were sometimes fam-ily members, simply to get the torture over. The Khmer arrested the people named, blindfolded them, and threw them in the prison, starting the cycle all over again. The victims were almost invariably innocent. When a former Khmer official named Hu Nin was tortured, he confessed to being in the CIA, and then ended his confession: "I am not a human being, I am an animal."

Anyone could fall victim to S-21, not just Cambodians. Several Englishmen died there when their yacht floated too close to the Cambodian shore (their fate was not discovered until much later) as did at least four Americans who may have been smuggling marijuana within Cambodian territorial waters. In their confessions, the Americans fabricated stories about working for the CIA—one

THE PHOTOGRAPHER VANN NATH STANDS IN FRONT OF THE PHOTOS HE TOOK OF PRISONERS AT THE INFAMOUS TUOL SLENG PRISON. OUT OF 20,000 PEOPLE IMPRISONED THERE, PERHAPS SIX SURVIVED.

Western prisoner said he had been recruited at age twelve—simply to keep from further torture. They were treated like the other Cambodian prisoners, and strangled or shot to death, except that their bodies were placed inside tires and burned so as to erase all trace of them.

Few inmates of Tuol Sleng survived the prison. The Khmer kept some of them, like the artist Vann Nath, alive because their skills were useful—in Nath's case, he painted portraits of Pol Pot. The young photographer Nhem En took pictures of every prisoner who came in—the photographs, gathered at the site of the prison, which is now a museum (also available online at www.tuolsleng. com), show people of all ages and sexes staring at the camera in shock and dismay. The pictures are haunted. En, who has testified against former Khmer Rouge officials, including Comrade Duch, at their genocide trials, knew that all of these inmates would be tortured and killed, but there was nothing he could do about it.

"I am just a photographer, I don't know anything," he would say when anxious prisoners asked him why they had been arrested.

THE INVASION OF THE VIETNAMESE

Although the Khmer Rouge and the Vietnamese had made joint cause against the Americans, they were traditional enemies and their relationship soon deteriorated. This was partly because the Khmer Rouge seized several small islands in the Gulf of Siam that belonged to South Vietnam in 1975, as North Vietnam was busy consolidating its conquest of the country, and partly because the new Republic of Vietnam soon signed a nonaggression pact with Laos, Cambodia's neighbor on the north, thus making Pol Pot fearful that Vietnam was attempting to surround and strangle him.

His response was the persecution of Cambodia's sizeable Vietnamese minority, murdering about 100,000 Cambodians who were ethnic Vietnamese and lived mainly along the eastern borders of the country. At the end of 1977, the Vietnamese made an armed incursion about twenty miles (32 km) inside Cambodia before deciding to pull back, which Pol Pot and the Khmer celebrated as a Vietnamese defeat. In reality, however, the Vietnamese were merely

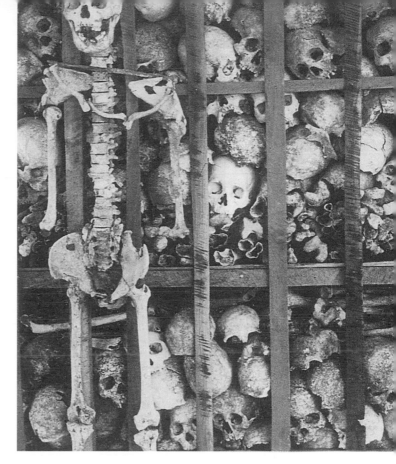

probing. To their surprise, when they pulled back, 100,000 Khmers decided to escape with them. These new men formed a sizeable anti–Pol Pot army; they told the Vietnamese that the Angkar was being torn apart by internal dissension as Pol Pot purged any dissent, real or imagined.

For most of 1978, Vietnam built up its forces along the Cambodian border, and, increasingly, there were skirmishes between the two countries. These clashes led to the evacuation of many of the "new people" who had been brought to the so-called Eastern Zone along Cambodia's border with Vietnam. Many of these people were Cambodians of ethnic Vietnamese descent, and when they were removed to other work camps in different parts of the country, it was to execute them. In September 1978, about 1,000 such people were taken to the southwestern part of the country and beaten to death with bamboo sticks and axes. Those in work camps nearby could hear them screaming. Children were put in cages meant to hold pigs, and murdered after their parents died. The dead were buried in huge pits.

This was just one part of the slaughter—genocide experts have estimated that perhaps 100,000 to 200,000 people from the Eastern Zone were killed in this way and buried in large pits. Those from the Eastern Zone were forced to wear blue scarves, which marked them, one Khmer official said, as people with "Khmer bodies but Vietnamese minds." After they were killed, Khmer cadres ripped the bloody scarves from their corpses, to be reused in the future. One witness saw Easterners being led to execution in the fall of 1977. The Khmer Rouge, he said, "tied up sometimes five people, sometimes ten people . . . I saw it three or four times. The Khmer Rouge were riding ponies, and [the Easterners] were tied up and being dragged, having to run along behind."

SKULLS OF VICTIMS OF POL POT ON DISPLAY AT A MUSEUM. IN ALL, BETWEEN 1.5 AND 2 MILLION CAMBODIANS WERE KILLED— ALMOST ONE-FOURTH OF THE COUNTRY'S POPULATION—DURING THE KHMER ROUGE GENOCIDE.

Another witness said that a month after the Khmer brought the Easterners to her zone, they began killing them. "They killed men, women, and even little babies. I saw them call families to take them away; every night they took three to five families." Newborn babies and pregnant women were also killed. The woman said that some of the Easterners were evacuees from Phnom Penh, but that many were simply Eastern peasants—the Khmer had begun killing the people who were supposedly "pure" of heart.

When the Vietnamese launched their attack, sending 100,000 troops across the Cambodian border in December 1978, ordinary Cambodians could not help but see them as liberators. The Vietnamese had expected a tough battle, but the Khmer simply collapsed. The Khmer were weakened by famine and also lacked ammunition and fuel for the military, because Pol Pot's policy of isolating the country from foreign markets kept imports at a minimum. However, Pol Pot's increasingly paranoid regime, which had now turned to murdering its own functionaries, inspired little loyalty. On January 7, 1979, two weeks after the attack had begun, the Vietnamese captured Phnom Penh. There is a final irony in the fact that Pol Pot escaped by helicopter, much as Lon Nol had on that April day four years before.

THE ECHO OF GENOCIDE

After the Vietnamese installed a puppet government in Phnom Penh, the Khmer Rouge retreated into the jungle (aided by the U.S. government, which in the years immediately after the Vietnam War was extremely hostile to the Hanoi-based Vietnamese government). The Khmer and Pol Pot waged a guerilla war against the new Cambodian government, where it was once again legal to own land, where religion was once again allowed, and where democratic elections were finally held in 1993. The Khmer Rouge became what they had started out as—a ragged guerilla force in the jungle. Pol Pot died of natural causes in his bunker in 1998, still a cipher to most people, just as the Khmer Rouge had agreed to turn him over to an international tribunal to be tried for crimes against humanity.

After Pol Pot was ousted, the world discovered the horrifying extent of his genocide. Cambodia was, literally, covered with graves, small individual

MAP OF CAMBODIA DURING THE REIGN OF POL POT. AFTER HE WAS OUSTED, THE WORLD DISCOVERED THE EXTENT OF THE GENOCIDE; THE COUNTRY WAS COVERED WITH BODIES IN BOTH SHALLOW AND MASS GRAVES.

LIBRARY OF CONGRESS

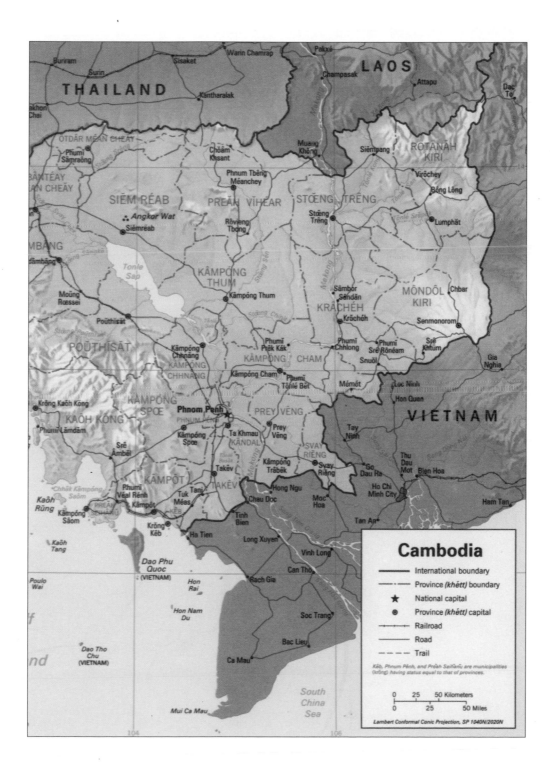

"NO ANSWER COULD AVOID DEATH"

In 2001, the newly formed Documentation Center of Cambodia, which studied and recorded the extent of the Cambodian genocide, accused seven former Khmer Rouge leaders of crimes against humanity. By 2009, only four of them had survived to be tried by a tribunal in Phnom Penh. One of them was Kaing Geuk Eav, commandant of the Tuol Sleng prison, the man known as Duch (pronounced Doik). Surprisingly, unlike other Khmer leaders, who while admitting that "mistakes" had been made, denied responsibility in the holocaust and even denied the extent of the holocaust, Duch did not shirk his role.

In 2008, he told a reporter: "I and everyone else who worked in that place (Tuol Sleng) knew that everyone who entered had to be psychologically demolished, eliminated by steady work, given no way out. No answer could avoid death. Nobody who came to us had any chance of saving himself . . . We saw enemies, enemies, enemies everywhere . . . I was cornered, like everyone else in that machine. I had no alternative. Pol Pot, the No. I Brother, said you always had to be suspicious, to fear something. And thus the usual request came: interrogate them, interrogate them better."

In March 2009, Duch, sixty-six years old, and a convert to Christianity, became the first member of the Pol Pot regime to go on trial for crimes against humanity. He was accused not only of running the prison, but of personally taking part in using torture to extract a confession from a young woman.

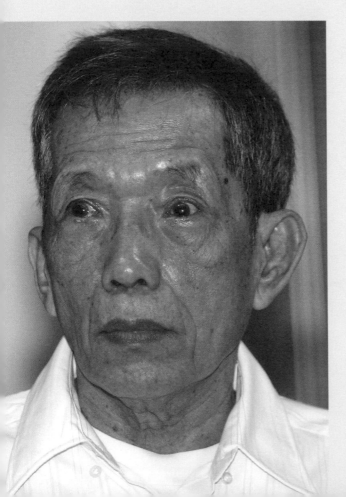

KAING GEUK EAV, THE KHMER PRISON COMMANDER KNOWN AS DUCH, WAS THE FIRST OF THE POL POT REGIME TO GO ON TRIAL FOR CRIMES AGAINST HUMANITY. HE RAN THE INFAMOUS TUOL SLENG PRISON. "NOBODY WHO CAME TO US HAD ANY CHANCE OF SAVING HIMSELF," HE SAID.

AFP/GETTY IMAGES

depressions in the ground as well as huge pits holding thousands of skeletons. Historians are still trying to understand how many new people, as well as how many peasants and members of Cambodia's twenty or so minority ethnic groups (for Pol Pot engaged in ethnic cleansing as well as political murder) the Khmer Rouge killed. In all, the total number of dead in four years of Angkar reign is probably between 1.5 and 2 million—almost one-fourth of the country's total population. In terms of sheer numbers, the Cambodian genocide, along with the Holocaust and the Armenian genocide, is one of the worst genocides of the twentieth century. An entire generation of Cambodians was lost to death or exile; thousands in future generations were maimed or killed by land mines left behind by the Khmer Rouge.

In the 1980s, the Cambodian government struggled to restore the country's crippled economy and fight off the Khmer Rouge. It was ultimately successful by 2008, the economy was growing at the rate of 10 percent a year and tourism had returned, although rural areas remained impoverished, and the country's infrastructure still had not grown appreciably since the 1970s.

More than 50 percent of the Cambodian population is under the age of twenty-one, and does not remember the days of Pol Pot and the Khmer Rouge. However, an entire generation was uprooted and destroyed by the genocide. Survivors who fled to countries like the United States suffered a high rate of suicide and psychosomatic illnesses like hysterical blindness. *The Journal of the American Medical Association* wrote in the early 1990s that 62 percent of Cambodian refugees in the United States suffered from severe post-traumatic stress disorder. They lived in poverty and their children were more often gang members. Those who remained in Cambodia suffered similar problems, as did their children, so that the genocide echoed down through the next generation. For those who survived, as much victims as the millions of dead, life continues to be stuck in the Year Zero.

CHAPTER 16

THE BLOODY GATE OF HEAVENLY PEACE

MASSACRE AT TIANANMEN SQUARE, JUNE 3–4, 1989

IN A CHINA THAT SEEMED TO BE MOVING TOWARD MODERATION, THE SLAUGHTER OF HUNDREDS OF PROTESTING STUDENTS IN TIANANMEN SQUARE SHOWED THE TRUE FACE OF THE HARD-LINE REGIME

A T THE HEART OF CHINA'S CAPITAL CITY OF BEIJING, IS TIANANMEN Square, which, at 100 acres (0.4 km²), is the largest open urban space in the world. *Tiananmen* means "Gate of Heavenly Peace" and refers to the enormous archway built in the fifteenth century, which sits on the north side of the square. The square has been called by one historian "a virtual monument to People Power." On its western side is the Great Hall of the People, on the east is the Museum of the Chinese Revolution, and on the south is the massive Mao Zedong mausoleum, built in 1977.

Despite its status as a symbol of the Chinese Revolution and the triumph of socialism, Tiananmen Square is not a welcoming place. There are no trees or benches; the vast vista is broken only by huge lampposts that feature constantly swiveling video cameras. However, Tiananmen Square has been home to some of the most important public events in recent Chinese history. Students demonstrated there in 1919 in support of the Russian Revolution. Mao Zedong stood in Tiananmen Square in 1949 and declared that China was now a "People's Republic." Military parades were held there throughout the Cold War, showing China's burgeoning power and might.

PEOPLE'S LIBERATION ARMY TANKS GUARD AN INTERSECTION LEADING TO TIANANMEN SQUARE IN JUNE 1989. THEY WERE A FAMILIAR SYMBOL OF THE REGIME'S POWER.

MANUEL CENETA/AFP/GETTY IMAGES

More famous than any of these gatherings, however, were the student protests in Tiananmen beginning in April 1989 and culminating on a hot summer night two months later. More than any other gathering there, these demonstrations were an extraordinary example of "People Power," an assembly of hundreds of thousands of students who sought to express their feelings about the future of their country. Yet these same students, in the predawn darkness of June 4, faced down tanks and soldiers, sent by socialist leaders bent on destroying them. The students who weren't massacred were dispersed and Tiananmen went back to its former sterility as a dead symbol of what is, increasingly, an outmoded political system.

In some ways, the student protestors who died at Tiananmen changed little—China, while increasingly turning to capitalism, is still a closed, repressive society that does not tolerate dissent. But the images of what happened at Tiananmen remain indelibly imprinted on the world.

"THE WRONG MAN DIED"

The events that sparked China's largest demonstration and the bloody purge that followed began on April 15, 1989, when former Communist Party General Secretary Hu Yaobang died suddenly of a heart attack at the age of seventy-three—a relatively young man, compared with the octogenarian hardliners, led by Deng Xiaoping, who had forced Hu out of his position. While possessed of certain eccentricities—he suggested that the Chinese switch from chopsticks to knives and forks—Hu was a more moderate figure and a symbol of possible hope and change to the thousands of Chinese who had begun to tire of their lack of opportunities under the current regime. Hu's death also came during a period of change, as Communist countries in Eastern Europe began to fall one by one. Chinese students and intellectual leaders were hoping this new wave of freedom would strike China, as well.

Within hours after the death of Hu, *dazi bao*, or huge posters, began to appear at Beijing University. One read: "The wrong man died, while those who should die live on." Another contained a poem:

> The sincere man died.
> The hypocrites live on.
> The compassionate man died,
> Buried by the cold-blooded . . .
> Reform lies dead in the heart.

Guided by graduate students and their professors, students began to gather in small groups to discuss Hu Yaobang and what he meant to China. There was a good deal of talk about democratic change, by which most students meant not necessarily a democracy of the type seen in the United States or Great Britain, but a "social democracy" in which the Chinese government would be more willing to open itself up to consultation with the public about important issues. They also wanted a more tolerant intellectual climate, in which people with views different from those of the regime could be heard and not punished. The issue of corruption also weighed heavily on the students. In a state that supposedly existed for the people, there was an extraordinary amount of privateering among middle- and high-level officials responsible for ration booklets, housing, jobs within government, and the like.

The death of Hu Yaobang was a touchstone for all the anger and powerlessness, the new generation of Chinese youth felt as they watched their government being run by men in their eighties. On April 16, 1989, 300 or so students went to Tiananmen Square to place wreaths at the Monument to the People's Heroes. April 18 saw 6,000 students march from Beijing University to Tiananmen Square and stage a sit-in in front of the Great Hall of the People. Other students began to clash with security guards outside the residential compound where many Chinese leaders lived.

Government officials, taken by surprise, pondered what to do. A majority faction led by Premier Li Peng thought the students were being manipulated by "bourgeois liberal elements" who sought to undermine the regime. A small group, represented by Party General Secretary Zhao Ziyang, took a more tolerant view of the students and did not want to take any repressive measures that might mar Hu Yaobang's official memorial service on April 22. However, to forestall demonstrations, the government announced it would close Tiananmen Square on April 22. But students outmaneuvered the regime by the simple expedient of showing up on April 21, 100,000 strong. The unprepared security forces could not move them.

"PLEASE HEAR OUR VOICES!"

After the memorial service, three student leaders knelt down on the steps of the Great Hall, holding over their heads a petition they wished Li Peng to read. But he did not respond. Within a few days, students began to boycott classes and organize student unions, which was illegal under Chinese law. Then, while Zhao Ziyang, a moderating influence, went to North Korea for a visit, Deng Xiaoping called a secret meeting of the Politburo, which decided to publish a strong editorial in the *People's Daily*, the Communist Party newspaper, denouncing the students.

"This is a well-planned plot . . . to confuse the people and throw the country into turmoil," it read. "[The student protests'] real aim is to reject the Chinese Communist Party and the socialist system at the most fundamental level." The government decided at this meeting to use whatever level of force necessary to crack down on the demonstrators.

The day after the editorial appeared, an extraordinary 500,000 demonstrators—which, according to one observer, included "doctors and nurses and scientists" as well as students—marched on Tiananmen Square, breaking down police barriers. They demanded and received a dialogue with some government officials, but little changed in the government position and talks broke down. High-ranking Chinese officials kept claiming that "the black hands" of agitators were at work; however, Zhao Ziyang, the General Party Secretary, continued to make moderate public statements, telling reporters that "there is no risk for the

press to open up a bit by reporting the student demonstrations." Zhao also told visiting Turkish dignitaries that China would "not only persistently carry out economic reform, but also further push forward political reform."

Student leaders—and the foreign reporters who increasingly covered the unrest in China—saw new hope in Zhao's statements, particularly after 20,000 students marched on Tiananmen on May 4 (in remembrance of the May 4, 1919, student march) and Zhao told a group of foreigners visiting China that he supported the students' "patriotism." Zhao, almost alone among the Chinese hierarchy, seems to have understood that the students were acting in a long Chinese tradition of a loyal minority seeking change, rather than as a destabilizing force for the government.

On May 13, hundreds of students began a hunger strike in Tiananmen Square, supported by thousands of others. They declared that they would end it only when the government retracted the editorial in the *People's Daily* and agreed to a televised discussion of grievances. Published student manifestos cried out: "Ours is a nation in crisis . . . Please hear our voices."

For a time, it seemed as if the Chinese government was listening. On May 18, Li Peng, Zhao Ziyang, and others went to local hospitals to visit the students who had collapsed while on hunger strike. Li Peng even met with student leaders

COMMUNIST PARTY CHIEFS DENG XIAOPING, LEFT, AND ZHAO ZIYANG. ZHAO, THE COMMUNIST PARTY CHIEF, MADE MODERATE STATEMENTS BUT IN THE END WAS POWERLESS TO STOP THE ULTRA-CONSERVATIVE FORCES LEAD BY DENG.

live on nationally broadcast television, as they requested. But it was apparent from the tense exchange between Li and the student leaders that there would be no meeting of the minds. Li Peng was angry that the student hunger strikers (whose ranks had swollen to 3,000) embarrassed him in front of visiting Soviet General Party Secretary Mikhail Gorbachev, who arrived for the first Sino-Soviet summit since 1959.

On the evening of May 18, a group of party elders, led by Li Peng and Deng Xiaoping, decide to declare martial law.

"FIRM AND ABSOLUTE MEASURES"

On May 19, students, having learned of the plan to institute martial law, called off their hunger strike and substituted for it a massive sit-down strike in Tiananmen Square, which drew 1.2 million people. Zhao Ziyang, perhaps knowing what lay ahead, spoke to the students, begging them to call things off, apologizing tearfully for having "come too late" (he was shortly thereafter ousted and replaced as party secretary).

That night, Li Peng went on television and declared martial law, saying: "We must adopt firm and resolute measures to end the turmoil swiftly." Immediately, the government sent People's Liberation Army (PLA) troops to Beijing to clear out the protestors in Tiananmen, but Beijing students and other dissidents moved by the hundreds of thousands to block intersections and keep the troops away.

By 11:00 a.m. on May 20, the government had stopped satellite transmissions to foreign countries. By May 23, more than one million people had taken to the streets of the capital city to protest martial law. Unwilling—yet—to risk a bloodbath, the government withdrew the PLA from Beijing, a humiliating failure. The students in Tiananmen celebrated. They built a 30-foot (9.1 m)-high statue they called "The Goddess of Democracy," a Statue of Liberty look-alike constructed from foam and papier mâché and clustered around it, singing the "Internationale." Tiananmen Square had by now lost its impersonal feel.

There were small tent cities, a so-called "broadcast tent," where student reporters put out the news over loudspeakers in the square, a daily newspaper, and a "conference hall," which was actually a Kentucky Fried Chicken outlet on

TANK MAN

If there is one iconic symbol of the Tiananmen Square massacre that the entire world recognizes, it is that of the lone Chinese protestor known simply as "Tank Man."

Tank Man's act of extraordinary courage took place on June 5, the day after the Chinese army had retaken Tiananmen Square. A column of seventeen tanks was driving east on Cangan Boulevard, outside the Square, when the man, in his twenties, was dressed in a white shirt and black pants, walked out in the middle of the boulevard. He was carrying shopping bags and it seemed as if he were simply coming back from a routine errand when he saw the tanks and decided to deliver his own moment of protest.

In any event, he stopped in front of the lead tank and put his hands out. The driver of the tank tried to go left, around the man, but the man moved in front of the tank. The tank then tried to go the other direction, with the same result. Finally, the tank driver stopped and turned off his engine. When he did so, the Tank Man climbed on top of the tank and attempted to have a conversation with the driver. The man is supposed to have said: "Why are you here? My city is in chaos because of you."

After a few minutes, the man got down off the tank, but when the tank started up again, he stood in front of it one more time. At that moment, onlookers rushed out and hustled him away. Because the incident took place in front of a hotel filled with Western journalists, there are numerous reports of it and pictures that the photographer Jeff Widener smuggled out of China.

Tank Man's move was extraordinarily brave for any number of reasons, not the least of which was that these same tanks had crushed people under their treads only a day before. And yet, despite worldwide attention focused on him, no one is sure who he was (or is). Reports surfaced at the time that he was a nineteen-year-old student named Wang Weilin, but these reports have since been discredited.

IN A GESTURE MADE FAMOUS AROUND THE WORLD BY PRESS PHOTOGRAPHERS SNAPPING FROM A NEARBY HOTEL, THE UNARMED "TANK MAN" STOPS A COLUMN OF PEOPLE'S LIBERATION ARMY TANKS NEAR TIANANMEN SQUARE ON JUNE 5, 1989. HIS IDENTITY HAS NEVER BEEN ESTABLISHED.
CNN VIA GETTY IMAGES

the southwest corner of the square. Thousands of students, and some foreign reporters, either stayed there twenty-four hours at a time, or rode their bicycles there to share the latest news.

But behind the scenes, tragedy was beginning. On June 2, party leaders approved the use of military force to clear the protestors from Tiananmen Square. The Chinese 27th and 38th Armies were pitted against each other in a race to reach the capital city first. An officer in the 27th told his men: "Comrades! The present circumstances are extremely dangerous and the student movement in the capital has already degenerated into turmoil and counterrevolutionary rebellion." (The 27th would win the race to the capitol, with some troops moving toward the city through the vast network of underground tunnels dug during the 1960s, when there was fear of a nuclear war with Russia.)

That evening, around 10:45, something strange happened. A column of PLA troops raced in jeeps, trucks, and armored personnel carriers through the city about 4 miles (6.4 km) west of Tiananmen Square. One of them veered off the street and crashed into a crowd of people on the sidewalk, killing three. The crowd pulled the driver from his vehicle and beat him up even though he claimed it was an accident. No one knows what caused the incident, but it enraged protestors, who marched around Tiananmen shouting, "Blood must be paid with blood!" and "Down with Li Peng!"

By the morning of June 3, soldiers of the 27th Army had moved deep into Beijing, heading down all the major intersections that led to Tiananmen Square. Tens of thousands of people blocked their way. On the afternoon of June 3, police and soldiers began clubbing and tear-gassing protestors, while the government broadcast warnings to disperse under the rule of martial law over television and radio. Still the citizens of Beijing refused to allow the PLA to pass, setting up blockades and lining up in front of the troops. At 10:30 that night, soldiers of the 27th Army began firing automatic weapons at protestors who blocked their path as they advanced on Tiananmen Square from the west.

Most of the protestors were shocked. They expected the army would use rubber bullets to disperse them (it turned out later that the Chinese police and army had pitifully little in the way of nonlethal riot-fighting weaponry). One protestor thought the bullets were rubber until he saw the sparks they made ricocheting off the pavement. Terrified, people began running away, although many stayed to risk their lives by hauling the wounded on bicycles and pull-carts to local hospitals, which immediately become overwhelmed by the number of bloodied men and women.

Soldiers sprayed machine gun fire indiscriminately at citizens cowering on the sidewalks as they broke through roadblocks and continued marching toward Tiananmen Square down the Avenue of Eternal Peace, which the protestors renamed the Road of Blood. Every time the PLA came to a major intersection, they would be met by protestors, and each time they would clear these crowds with machine gun bullets. They also sprayed gun fire at apartment buildings overhead, killing people who were merely looking out their windows. More soldiers came in from the east, also blasting their way through the roadblocks of protestors.

As June 3 turned into June 4, the protestors in Tiananmen Square could hear the sound of gunfire coming closer and closer.

"TELL THE WORLD!"

Around midnight on June 4, reporter Nicholas Kristof, of the *New York Times'*
Beijing bureau, rode a bicycle to Tiananmen Square, having read an Associated
Press teletype that said: "Chinese troops opened fire on crowds as tens of thousands of people swarmed into Beijing streets to block their way." When he
reached the square, he found himself, "on the front lines . . . about 500 feet [152.4
m] from the line of gray-green uniformed [PLA] troops" who had lately arrived
at the square. He saw two armored personnel carriers burning from Molotov
cocktails thrown by the crowd. The troops began firing. People fell to the ground
around him, and he and the Chinese students sprinted away. But gradually, the
students crept back, throwing rocks at the soldiers, who responded with more
automatic weapons fire, killing and wounding more protestors. Extraordinarily
brave rickshaw drivers, under fire, picked up the dead and wounded and drove
them from the square, "tears running silently down their cheeks."

Kristof also saw a dozen students commandeer a bus, arm themselves with
iron bars and Molotov cocktails, and drive it straight for the troops. It was pul-
verized by thousands of bullets, killing everyone aboard but one student, who
leaped out the rear door and ran away. In the meantime, Kristof later wrote,
"the Chinese in the crowd were hysterical with grief and rage . . . the protestors
grabbed at me, pulling me this way and that. They wanted me to see the bleeding
bodies as they were carted by rickshaw to the hospitals. They knew the gunfire
would be followed by enforced silence and that they would be unable to describe
what happened . . .

"'Tell the world!' a twenty-year-old art student with shaggy hair shouted
at me. Nearly incoherent with fury, he gripped my shoulder and screamed.
'You've got to tell the world what is happening, because otherwise this counts
for nothing.'"

In the meantime, word reached the students deep in Tiananmen that the
army had orders to clear the square by 6:00 a.m. By about 2:00 a.m., thousands
of students had already left the square, but thousands remained, under the light
of the lampposts, in the muggy June night. Hou Dejian, a well-known pop singer
who was in the square taking part in the hunger strike, later wrote that the square
at this hour "was ruled by a strong atmosphere of death and sacrifice."

BODY COUNT

As with so many massacres, there is a wide gulf between the casualty count given by the authorities and that provided by those who were attacked. The Chinese government has claimed that 241 people died and that perhaps 3,000 were wounded. It also claims that 6,000 People's Liberation Army troops were wounded and anywhere from "several dozen" to "hundreds" of troops were killed.

However, immediately after the massacre, the Chinese Red Cross confirmed a total of 2,600 students dead, but the organization soon retracted this figure—according to activists, because of pressure from the Chinese government. On June 4, Radio Beijing reported that "thousands" of people were killed by Chinese troops and tanks, but they, too, retracted this figure, and the anchor who made the statement was relieved of his post, to be replaced by another who gave the Chinese government's figures for the dead.

Students placed the number of dead at 6,000 killed and up to 20,000 wounded, figures that are almost universally considered to be a great exaggeration. Compounding the problem in trying to count the dead is that many students and activists were killed at separate locations around the city as the Chinese army invaded Beijing. There were also numerous activists killed after June 4 in the subsequent government crackdown.

For June 3–4 itself, Amnesty International gives figures of 1,000 Chinese students dead. *New York Times* reporter Nicholas Kristof, who was in Beijing at the time and who, along with his wife and fellow correspondent Sheryl WuDunn, won a Pulitzer Prize for reporting on the massacre, says that his best estimate is "400 to 800 people killed and several thousand wounded," most of it done in the streets around Tiananmen and not in the square itself.

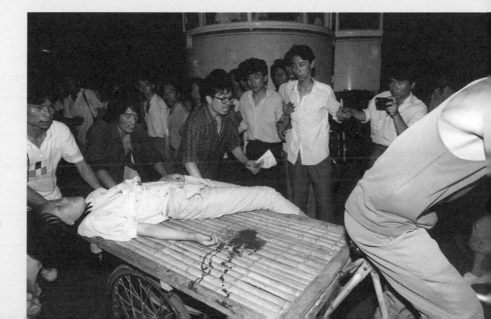

A GIRL WOUNDED DURING A CLASH BETWEEN THE PLA AND CHINESE STUDENTS IS CARRIED FROM TIANANMEN SQUARE ON A WOODEN CART.

MANUEL CENETA/AFP/GETTY IMAGES

Around 4:00 a.m., student leaders, knowing that they faced a massacre of even greater proportions, took a vote to decide whether they should stay. A journalist who was present recalled, "It was clear to me that the stay votes were much, much stronger. But . . . the student leader at the time said, 'The go's have it.'"

The students left the square watched by thousands of soldiers. As soon as they were gone, tanks entered and began running over tents while soldiers tossed pamphlets and other student papers into a huge bonfire. A tank knocked down the statue of the Goddess of Democracy and soon the announcement blared over Beijing radio: "Martial law enforcement troops have won a great victory in quelling the counterrevolutionary rebellion."

AFTERSHOCKS

At least, this is one version of what happened. Other eyewitnesses—especially students in the immediate aftermath of the event—claimed that Chinese troops slaughtered a good many more students in Tiananmen Square itself before any were able to escape, that tanks crushed dozens of students in their tents. It is probably impossible to know which version is correct, and it is also possible that students exiting from one side of the massive square would not have known what was happening at another. Even the number of those who died is still in dispute (see "Body Count," page 273).

Another massacre took place on June 5. It was little remarked upon, but was witnessed by foreign press and Chinese citizens alike. That morning, a number of Chinese attempted to re-enter Tiananmen Square, now firmly in the hands of the PLA. It is thought that many of these people were the parents of protestors, searching for signs of their children. Soldiers ordered them to halt, but they simply ignored them and kept on coming, so the soldiers fired on them.

According to one reporter, "it was as if the citizens could not believe that the army was firing on them with real ammunition." Forty minutes after being shot at, they came back and started screaming at the soldiers, and the soldiers shot them down again. According to the eyewitness, this happened "more than half a dozen times" during the day. The soldiers even shot medical workers who came to aid the wounded.

During the weeks that followed the Tiananmen Square massacre, the Chinese government arrested tens of thousands of intellectuals and activists, imprisoning some and executing an unknown number. The government was at pains to call these people "counterrevolutionaries." In September 1989, it set up an exhibit at Beijing's military museum, displaying thousands of pictures of burned armored cars and soldiers supposedly executed by protestors, to show that the regime had only been protecting itself from agitators. Even as late as 2004, the government produced a five-hour-long documentary on the Tiananmen Square protests, calling them "counterrevolutionary rebellions" and forcing officials around the country to view it.

And yet, the "counterrevolutionary" title never stuck to the protestors of Tiananmen Square, for they were obviously people who loved their country so dearly that they would walk into automatic weapons fire believing that no Chinese government could possibly intend to shoot them down. The government has never been able to erase the brutality of that June night in 1989, even as it tries to get rid of or distort the memory of it, and offers its people an opportunity to forge ahead economically. The government has turned toward capitalism, emphasizing personal initiative and personal income, and increasingly opened up Chinese markets to the West.

The bloodletting at Tiananmen Square continues to cause the international community to distrust the Chinese government. Even as fireworks exploded over Tiananmen in August 2008, celebrating the opening of the Beijing Olympics, candlelight protest vigils were held around the world to remember the nineteenth anniversary of the massacre.

But the real impact of Tiananmen is on the Chinese people themselves. As Robin Munro of Human Rights Watch has said: "What [the Chinese people] experienced in May '89 was, for the first time, a sense of civic pride, civic responsibility, and a feeling that their efforts would contribute to a better China . . . [The massacre] has induced deep cynicism among those same people who were active participants in the May '89 movement. They have been beaten back . . . and all that is left is what the Party is offering them, which is the chance to make more money, if they're lucky."

CHAPTER 17

ONE HUNDRED DAYS OF HELL

THE RWANDAN GENOCIDE, APRIL–JULY, 1994

HUTU RADICALS KILLED 800,000 TUTSI MEN, WOMEN, AND
CHILDREN IN JUST OVER THREE MONTHS IN A GENOCIDE
THAT STILL HAUNTS AFRICA AND THE WORLD

D URING THE RWANDAN GENOCIDE, PERHAPS 60,000 TUTSIS FLED
their Hutu killers, many hiding in the Nyamwiza marshes in the southeastern part of the country, near the community of Nyamata, where many
of the Tutsis had formerly lived. The Hutus who hunted them were often
their neighbors. They turned killing Tutsis into a kind of day job. Every day
for four weeks in April and May 1994, they left their huts on neighboring
hillsides, had breakfast, joined the rest of their gangs, and then waded into
the marshes with their machetes at about 9:30 a.m. They hunted and killed
Tutsis until about 4:00 p.m., when they knocked off for dinner and a night in
the local cantina. The next morning, the whole thing started up again. The
Hutus were industrious killers seven days a week.

One of the Tutsis being hunted was Evergiste Habihirwe, star of a local
soccer team. On April 11, he was herding his cattle when he found out that
the Hutus had begun to slaughter Tutsis. At first he decided to take refuge
with a close friend and former teammate, even though the man was a Hutu,
but when Evergiste arrived at his house he saw the man had already killed
two children and was holding a machete dripping with blood. Evergiste was
not seen and ran to his own house, but it was too late — the Hutus had murdered his entire family. He then raced into the marshes.

THE SKULLS OF TUTSI VICTIMS
OF THE RWANDAN GENOCIDE
OF 1994 REMAINED LINED UP IN
THE GENOCIDE MEMORIAL SITE
CHURCH IN NTARAMA, SITE OF A
PARTICULARLY BRUTAL MASSACRE.

GIANLUIGI GUERCIA/AFP/GETTY IMAGES

He later related:

My runner's legs carried me full tilt through the forest. During the day I kept my head down in the sorghum; at night I scrounged in the dirt for cassava. I would hear my teammates hunting around my house. It was the same guys who used to pass the ball back and forth to me . . . They would yell "Evergiste, we sorted through the piles of bodies, we have not yet seen your cockroach face. We are going to sniff you out, we shall work at night if we have to, but we shall get you!" . . . The players were the most dogged in cutting other players. They had that ferocity of the ball in their hearts.

Of the 60,000 or so Tutsis taking refuge in or near the marshes, 50,000 were hacked to death by mid-May. Their deaths

were a part of a fratricidal genocide that did not stop until 100 days had passed and 800,000 men, women, and children—75 percent of Rwanda's Tutsi population—had been killed, mainly with farm implements and machetes. United Nations Secretary-General Ban Ki-moon, remembering the fifteenth anniversary of the slaughter in the spring of 2009, said the Rwandan genocide "haunts our collective conscience." It was a slaughter the world could, and should, have stopped, but did not.

TUTSIS AND HUTUS

Rwanda is a tiny country in the Great Lakes region of Central Africa, bordered by Uganda on the north, Burundi on the south, the Democratic Republic of

Congo (formerly Zaire) to the west, and Tanzania to the east. It is one of the smallest countries in the world, just 26,000 square miles (41,843 km²), yet its population density is the heaviest in Africa, with roughly 300 people per square mile (1.6 km²). It's a fertile country of grasslands and rolling hills, with an average daily temperature of 73°F (23°C). Its chief crop is coffee, introduced by German missionaries in 1910, which amounts to 75 percent of the country's exports, although shipments have been frequently interrupted in the past sixty years by civil war and mass killings.

Rwanda's first inhabitants were hunter-gatherer pygmies known as Twa, but they were overwhelmed by successive migrations of two other tribes, the Tutsis and the Hutus. The Tutsis were primarily cattle-herders while the Hutus, who made up by far the greater portion of the population, were farmers. Despite this disparity, the Tutsis managed to dominate the region, mainly through their superior wealth. However, there was a good deal of intermarriage between the two groups and, by the nineteenth century, they shared a common language and cultural heritage. It is important to note that the distinctions between the two tribes were often a matter of wealth and social status—Hutus married into Tutsi families and became rich, while Tutsis often fell in status and became poor.

However, when Europeans arrived—the Germans in the late nineteenth century and, after World War I, the Belgians—they made very clear, and very racist, distinctions between Tutsis and Hutus. The Tutsi minority, who were sometimes (but not always) taller and more aquiline-featured than the Hutus, were considered "proto-European": possessing a "distant, reserved, courteous and elegant manner," as one Belgian writer put it. It was thought they must have migrated from Ethiopia, home of ancient civilizations.

The Hutus, on the other hand, were the obvious peasants, said the same Belgian writer, "childish in nature, both timid and lazy and, as often as not, extremely dirty."

Naturally, when it came time for the Germans or Belgians to create colonial administrations, they chose the Tutsis for the task of running them. Tutsi monarchs ruled the country, as they always had, and Tutsi bureaucrats collected taxes, controlled the schools, and owned most businesses. The Belgians reinforced the perceived racial differences between the two groups in 1933 by creating a mandatory identity card that stated the citizen's name and ethnic identity—Hutu, Tutsi, or Twa. Now, unlike in the past, it was not possible to change one's status by increasing one's herd of cattle. The identity card locked in racial divisions and hatred between the Tutsis and the Hutus, divisions that had been present, to some extent, in the past, but now came bloodily to the forefront of relations between the two groups.

"THE WIND OF DESTRUCTION"

In 1959, the Tutsi monarch Mwaami Rudahigwa died and the smoldering resentment of the Hutus against the Tutsis exploded. Rampaging against the Tutsis with knives, clubs, and farm implements, the Hutus killed anywhere from 10,000 to 100,000 Tutsis (estimates vary wildly) in a slaughter that the Tutsis referred to as "the wind of destruction." Bertram Russell called it "the most horrible and systematic human massacre we have had occasion to witness since the extermination of the Jews by the Nazis." Perhaps as many as 200,000 Tutsis fled to Uganda, where they plotted revenge against the Hutus. The Belgians, who knew that a day was coming soon when they would need to grant independence to Rwanda, did not stop the slaughter. They had already made the cynical calculation that in any free vote, the Hutu majority would win easily.

In 1962, Belgium granted independence to both Rwanda and neighboring Burundi. Rwanda was ruled by the political party The Party for the Emancipation of the Hutus (PARMEHUTU) and the new republic rapidly devolved into corrupt, one-party rule. In Burundi, the Tutsis held onto their minority rule after independence because they controlled the army.

The history between the two groups became bloodier and bloodier. Tutsis in Uganda and Burundi staged guerilla attacks against Rwanda, which resulted in bloody reprisals against Tutsis in that country. And when Hutu guerillas attacked Burundi in 1972, the Tutsi-controlled army staged what has been classified as a genocide, killing up to 150,000 Hutus (see "'A Grim Laboratory of Killing': The Burundi Genocide," page 288). In 1973, Juvenal Habyarimana, army chief of staff in Rwanda and a Hutu, staged a coup and took over the country, replacing PARMEHUTU with his own party, the *Mouvement Révolutionnaire National pour le Développement* (MRND), which consisted mainly of close friends and family

from northern Rwanda. While raiding Rwanda's economic resources and filling foreign bank accounts, MRND members systematically purged Rwandan
Tutsis—both teachers and students—from universities and the civil service.

By 1990, the economy of Rwanda was a wreck, the country's resources
depleted by Habyarimana, his family, and his cronies. To make matters worse, a
significant rebel force of Tutsis, known as the Rwandan Patriotic Front (RPF),
had formed in Uganda, led by Paul Kagame, a Tutsi who had been head of intelligence in the Ugandan army. Many of the members of the RPF were the children
of those Tutsis who had been forced into exile in 1959, and they wanted their
revenge. In 1990, the RPF staged a serious offensive against Hutu forces in
Rwanda, and a new civil war began.

HUTU POWER

Needing to rally the Hutus behind him at this crucial moment (as well as divert
the focus away from the poverty Rwandans had fallen into) Juvenal Habyarimana
and his inner circle—his wife, three brothers-in-law, and various generals, a

A 1994 PHOTO OF PAUL KAGAME, CURRENT PRESIDENT OF RWANDA, WHO LED THE TUTSI RWANDAN PATRIOTIC FRONT FORCES THAT INVADED RWANDA AND FINALLY STOPPED THE KILLING OF TUTSIS.

ALEXANDER JOE/AFP/GETTY IMAGES

group known as *Akazu*, or "little hut"—began to actively foment hatred against the Tutsis. They did this in a number of different ways. The state newspaper *Kangura*, as well as the two state media organs, Radio Rwanda and Radio Mille Collines, began referring to Tutsi as *inyenzi* (cockroaches). In December 1990, Kangura published a list of the "Ten Hutu Commandments," which stated that "any Hutu who married a Tutsi woman, befriends a Tutsi woman, or employs a Tutsi woman" was a traitor and that "every Tutsi is dishonest in business." Chillingly, "Commandment 8" read: "The Hutu should stop having mercy on the Tutsi."

The *Akazu* went further, forming a civilian militia called the *interahamwe*, which meant "those who stand together." Their ostensible purpose was to protect the populace from the RPF, but they were really a paramilitary group answering only to the Akazu. The interahamwe, combined with the army, the special palace guard, the police, another paramilitary group called *impunza mugambi* (the single-minded ones), and a fanatical anti-Tutsi political party, *le Coalition pour la*

Défense de la République (CDR) formed a force of perhaps 50,000. The intera-hamwe became the ground-level Hutu killing units and they were drawn from a wide range of society—there were government officials, teachers, scientists, and writers present, as well as street thugs and uneducated peasants. This group, a Physicians for Human Rights report later wrote, were "1 to 2 percent of the population; they killed out of conviction; they were trained to kill, often smoked hashish and are thought to have killed between 200 and 300 people each."

With thousands of killers being bombarded with "Hutu Power" propaganda every day, it was only a matter of time before violence broke out in Rwanda. But the catalyst for the conflagration in Rwanda was probably something Juvenal Habyarimana did not expect: his own death. The increasing military success of Paul Kagame and the RPF against Habyarimana's armed forces, combined with international pressure to put and end to the war, eventually forced the Rwandan president into signing a peace treaty with the RPF in August 1993, in Arusha, Tanzania. The so-called Arusha Accords called for the inclusion of mod-erate Hutus in the Rwandan government and for integrating the RPF into the Rwandan armed forces so that it made up 40 to 50 percent of the army.

Habyarimana's signature on this document proved to be fatal. On April 6, 1994, he returned to Rwanda in his private jet after another conference at Arusha. Just as the plane was landing at Kigali International Airport, it was hit by two surface-to-air missiles fired from nearby. The plane crashed in a ball of flames, landing on the grounds of the presidential palace and killing everyone aboard. Who ordered Habyarimana's assassination remains a mystery (see "The Death of Juvenal Habyarimana," page 284). It may have been Paul Kagame, but was more likely Hutu extremists within Habyarimana's own party. However it happened, an unprecedented slaughter was about to be unleashed on the Tutsis of Rwanda.

"THE GRAVES ARE ONLY HALF-FULL"

A well-organized plan for genocide was put into place only a few hours after Juvenal Habyarimana died. The army placed roadblocks on all roads leading out of the capital city of Kigali. The palace guard, armed with rifles, sub-machine guns, and hand grenades, spread out through Kigali, murdering

THE DEATH OF JUVENAL HABYARIMANA

The plane was a fast Dassault Falcon 50 private jet given to Juvenal Habyarimana by his contacts in the French government, and it swooped down low and fast over the airfield at Kigali. One of the soldiers guarding the nearby presidential palace remembered that he and his fellows could always tell when the president's plane was coming because it sounded so much different than the lumbering cargo planes that usually landed there.

On April 6, 1994, however, another sound was added to that of the Falcon 50's high-pitched jet engines—the whoosh of rockets. The rockets, which had been fired quite close to the airport, hit the plane in the wing and tail. It cartwheeled, burst into flames, landed in the garden of the presidential palace, and blew up. Everyone on board the plane was killed, including Juvenal Habyarimana and Cyprien Ntaryamira, the president of Burundi, who had hitched a ride back from a conference with the Rwandan president because the Falcon 50 was so fast.

The assassination of Juvenal Habyarimana launched Africa's bloodiest genocide, but to this day the person or persons responsible for it remain, as one journalist has written, "one of the great mysteries of the late twentieth century." Suspicion has been cast on radical Hutu elements in Rwanda, especially those in the military, who would have to share power with the RPF under an agreement signed by Habyarimana. In light of what happened next—Hutu killing squads taking the assassination as a signal to attack Tutsis—this makes sense.

However, in 2004, a French anti-terrorist magistrate stated that the killing had been carried out on the orders of RPF head Paul Kagame, who is now president of Rwanda. This was based on the testimony of Abdul Ruzibiza, formerly an officer in the RPF, who claimed that he was part of a group who shot down the plane using shoulder-fired surface-to-air missiles. This report, and the fact that the same magistrate has issued arrest warrants for nine of Kagame's aides, caused Kagame to break off diplomatic relations with France. However, the evidence on which the judge based his findings, particularly the testimony of Ruzibiza, has been discredited by a number of sources.

RWANDAN PRESIDENT JUVENAL HABYARIMANA, IN A PHOTO TAKEN FOUR YEARS BEFORE HIS DEATH. HIS STILL-UNSOLVED ASSASSINATION IN JUNE 1994 TOUCHED OFF THE RWANDAN GENOCIDE.

CHARLYN ZLOTNIK/GETTY IMAGES

opposition leaders, both Tutsis and moderate Hutus. The interahamwe units throughout the country rose up on orders from their commanders within forty-eight hours after the plane crash and began seeking out Tutsis. They carried machetes, *massues* (metal-studded clubs), knives, fragmentation grenades, and, in some cases, guns.

Radio announcers urged the killers on with hysterical messages, like: "The enemy is out there—go, kill him!" and "You cockroaches must know you are made of flesh. We won't let you kill! We will kill you!" Targets were easy to find. As Philip Gourevitch writes in his book *We Wish to Inform You that Tomorrow We Will Be Killed with Our Families*: "Neighbors hacked neighbors to death in their own homes, and colleagues hacked colleagues to death in their workplaces. Doctors killed their patients. Within days, the Tutsi population of many villages was all but eliminated."

Gangs of interahamwe, drunk on banana beer or high on hashish or prescription drugs looted from pharmacies, roamed the towns and countryside looking for new targets while gangs of laborers cleared corpses from the roads. People offered bounties for severed Tutsi heads. When the killing started, Tutsis (and moderate Hutus, who would make up about 20 percent of the victims) sought refuge in places they traditionally considered safe. Churches were among such places, but they were death traps.

One fifteen-year-old schoolgirl later testified that she had gone for protection to the Catholic church in the town of Ntamara, along with hundreds of others, within a week after the assassination of Habyarimana. Then the interahamwe attacked:

When we saw them coming, we closed the doors. They broke down the doors and tore some of the bricks in the back wall. They threw a few grenades through the holes where the bricks had been. But most of the people who died were killed by machetes. When they came in they were obviously furious that we had closed the doors. So they really macheted the refugees . . . People could not leave. But it was intolerable to remain in one's position as the macheting continued. So like mad, people ran up and down inside the church. All around you, people were

being killed and wounded. Eventually I decided to drop down among the dead. I raised my head slightly; an interhamwe hurled a brick at me. It hit me just on top of my eye. My face became covered with blood, which was useful in making them think I was even more dead . . .

[After the killers left] I tried to get up but it was in vain. I was so weak from my injuries and there were so many bodies everywhere you couldn't move. A few children, perhaps because they were unaware of the danger, stood up. I called one of the children to help me. She replied that she could not help me because they had cut off her arms . . . Finally, I saw another young woman I knew, a neighbor. I called out to her [but] when I looked closely I saw that she had had her arms cut off, too.

By now I don't know if what I am feeling and seeing is real life or a nightmare. I asked her if it was real life [but she did not reply] . . .

SOME OF THE VICTIMS OF THE RWANDAN GENOCIDE, IN A PHOTO TAKEN AT THE END OF MAY 1994, AT THE HEIGHT OF THE KILLING. IN ALL, ABOUT 800,000 PEOPLE WERE SLAUGHTERED.

A month went by, then two, and still the radio was goading the killers on: "The graves are only half-full! You have work to do!"

"THE EYES OF THE KILLED"

There are numerous eyewitness accounts from the victims of the Rwandan genocide, but in a stunning book called *Machete Season*, published in 2003, the French journalist Jean Hatfzfeld interviewed a group of eight or nine men who had been members of the interahamwe. Their descriptions of the killing they took part in are distant, as if it happened to someone else—as if it was not quite real life.

One man remembered:

> That morning we were roaming around, looking to rout out Tutsis who might be hidden on plots of land . . . I came upon two children sitting in the corner of a house. They were keeping quiet as mice. I asked them to come out; they stood up, they were being good. I had them walk at the head of our group. As a leader, I had recently been given a gun, besides the grenades. Walking along, without thinking, I decided to try it out. I put the two children side by side twenty meters [65.5 feet] away, I stood still, I shot twice at their backs . . . For me it was strange to see the children drop without a sound. It was almost pleasantly easy. I walked on without bending over to check that they were really dead. I don't even know if they were moved to a more suitable place and covered up. Now, too often, I am seized by the memory of those children shot straight out, like a joke.

The interahamwe were brainwashed, to some extent, by the incessant urgings of their government and were "organized for and directed to the task of slaughter," as the late Susan Sontag has written, and they did horrendous things for which they bear responsibility. Yet many of the men depicted in *Machete Season* are haunted in a way that also haunts the reader. One of them related the first time he had ever killed a person who looked him in the eyes as he did so:

> The eyes of someone you kill are immortal, if they face you at the fatal instant. They have a terrible black color. They shake you more than the streams of blood and the death rattles, even in a great turmoil of dying. The eyes of the killed, for the killer, are his great calamity, if he looks into them. They are the blame of the person he killed.

"A GRIM LABORATORY OF KILLING": THE BURUNDI GENOCIDE

"With the exception of Rwanda," writes historian René Lemarchand, "nowhere else in Africa has so much violence killed so many people in so small a space as in Burundi in the spring and summer of 1972."

Burundi, just to the south of Rwanda, was another Belgian colony that received its independence in the early 1960s and whose population encompassed a Hutu majority and a Tutsi minority. The difference was that in Burundi, the Tutsis hung onto power after independence, mainly by controlling the country's powerful armed forces. On April 29, 1972, a Hutu insurrection rose up in southern Burundi. The rebels seized control of a government armory and set about slaughtering Tutsi civilians, any they could find—perhaps 3,000 died in the first week of the rebellion alone.

Within a few weeks, the rebels had declared a "People's Republic of Burundi," but this was short-lived. The Burundi army moved in force into the countryside, slaughtering Hutus wherever they could find them. What makes this a genocide as well as a massacre is the intent of the Tutsis. It is widely believed that the powerful Tutsi Minister of Foreign Affairs, Arthemon Simbananiye, used the rebellion to carry out a pre-existing plan to exterminate the Hutu population of Burundi, especially the intellectuals, civil servants, university students, even school children, so that the Hutus could never pose a threat to the Tutsis of Burundi again. As was the case in the Rwandan genocide more than twenty years later, government radio urged Tutsis to hunt down and kill Hutus. Schoolchildren even turned in lists of their Hutu classmates, who were then hunted down and dispatched via clubs and rifle butts.

This "grim laboratory of killing" as Lemarchand calls it, had the long-term effect of radicalizing the Hutus even more, increasing their sense of themselves as victims of the Tutsis. The hatred they felt would find expression in the 1994 genocide in Rwanda.

"RAPE WAS THE RULE"

In 1998, four years after the slaughter in Rwanda, the International Criminal Tribunal for Rwanda, an international court set up by the United Nations, made the decision that so-called war rape during the genocide was an element of the genocide itself and could be charged accordingly. Rape is common during massacres, as is sexual mutilation of women, but sexual violence during the Rwandan genocide reached unprecedented proportions. An estimated 250,000 to 500,000 Tutsi women were raped; indeed, a report from the UN indicated that almost every single woman or girl who survived the genocide was a victim of sexual violence. The same report stated that "rape was the rule and its absence the exception." Many of the women were raped by men who were HIV positive; thousands became ill with AIDS, had unwanted children, or were forced to undergo abortions.

A horrific, but all-typical case involved a seventeen-year-old Tutsi girl named Louise, who was captured by a group of interahamwe who casually discussed in front of her how they were going to kill her:

> Then one of them suggested that they should rape me instead. The three of them raped me in turns. Each having finished, he walked away. As the last one finished a new group of interhamwe arrived. They ordered the man who had raped me last to rape me again. He refused. Then they threatened to burn us both alive unless he raped me again. So he raped me again. When he was through, the new group of interhamwe beat me up. Then they said, "Okay, let's go. We want to show you where you are going to go." They threw me down the pit latrine . . . I fell upright, on top of [the body of] my aunt. I could still hear the thugs talking. One of them said I might still be alive and suggested throwing a grenade in. Another commented: "Don't waste your grenade. A kid thrown that deep cannot be alive." They left. I tried to climb out. But I had bled so much I was feeling dizzy. I kept falling down. Finally I collapsed . . . When someone came to take me out of the pit, I didn't know who it was. I realized I was out of the pit when I regained consciousness. I saw a soldier standing next to me . . . .

"AGAIN AND AGAIN"

The soldier Louise saw was a member of the Tutsi RPF, whose invasion of the country and capture of Kigali, about 100 days after the killing began, finally put an end to the genocide. The failure of the international community to intervene much sooner, as it could have, is one of the great human tragedies of the war. Other countries knew what was occurring. General Romeo Dallaire, commander of the UN peacekeeping force stationed in Rwanda, sent a telegram to his superiors on January 11, 1994, warning them that a massive slaughter was being prepared, but the UN never acted on his information.

Secret reports of the U.S. Central Intelligence Agency also indicated well ahead of time that a bloodletting was about to occur—intelligence agencies in France and Belgium, two countries with close ties to Rwanda, also knew this— but nothing was done to avert the violence. During the 100 days of killing, the United States, under the administration of President Bill Clinton, cautioned its officials in writing to avoid the word "genocide." Instead, the government used words like "chaos," "confusing," and "anarchy" to describe the situation. (A word like genocide is so fraught with power that if any government official were to use it, that government would have to actually do something to stop the killing. And the UN's mandate forbids it to become involved in the internal politics of any country unless a genocide is declared.)

There are myriad reasons why the international community did not want to get involved. The United States did not want to find itself in another Somalia-type situation—U.S. forces had gotten bogged down in a civil war there in the early 1990s when they attempted to provide humanitarian relief. The United Nations regularly attempted to get parties in a war to stop fighting, but it did not understand, or perhaps did not want to understand, that the killing of so many thousands of Tutsis was not merely "collateral damage" from the war, but an actual planned ethnic cleansing, thus requiring a swifter and more radical military response.

In 1997, U.S. Secretary of State Madeline Albright gave a speech to the Organization of African Unity where she said: "We, the international community, should have been more active in the early stages of the atrocities in Rwanda in 1994, and called them what they were—genocide." Several months later, in

March 1998, Bill Clinton visited Rwanda and, although he still did not use the word genocide, he said that "it is important for the world to know that the killings were not spontaneous or accidental . . . these events grew from a policy aimed at the systematic destruction of a people"—words that lie at the heart of the definition of genocide.

It remains to be seen whether the international community will respond forcefully if another genocide on the level of the one in Rwanda occurs again. The sad fact is that politics usually trumps altruism. Samantha Power, director of the Human Rights Initiative at the Kennedy School of Government, writes: "Genocide has occurred so often and so uncontested in the last fifty years that an epithet more apt in describing recent events than the oft-changed 'Never Again' is in fact 'Again and Again.' The gap between the promise and practice of the last fifty years is dispiriting indeed."

Whether or not that gap is closed, the Rwandan genocide will remain one of the most tragic massacres in the history of the twentieth century.

CHAPTER 18

"ALLAH CAN'T HELP YOU NOW"

MASSACRE AT SREBRENICA, JULY 1995

THE UNITED NATIONS, NATO, AND THE UNITED STATES STOOD BY AS CHRISTIAN SERBS MURDERED THOUSANDS OF BOSNIAN MUSLIMS

S REBRENICA—PRONOUNCED "SREBRENEETSA"—IS AN ELONGATED stretch of houses and small buildings located in a valley in the mountains of eastern Bosnia. The name comes from the Bosnian word for silver, *srebro*; and silver has been mined in the area since the time of the Romans. In the twentieth century, Srebrenica, population about 9,000, was more famous for its spa. An infomercial produced by the government tourist agency bragged of the life-giving waters of a local natural spring, and showed visitors in gym outfits receiving massages and doing mild exercises.

It is doubtful that Srebrenica will ever be associated with the phrase "life-giving" again, however. In July 1995, the town and the green, pleasantly hilly landscape surrounding it became notorious as the site of Europe's worst massacre since World War II. The International Court of Justice has classified the massacre as a genocide because a specific ethnic group, the Bosnian Muslims, were "targeted for extinction" by the Serbian army and irregular forces. Even in a war where the term "ethnic cleansing" was coined, the beating, shooting, stabbing, burning, and clubbing deaths of 8,500 defenseless Muslim prisoners, almost all of them men, stood out.

The killings stood out for other reasons beside their wanton brutality. Like the far larger genocide in Rwanda the previous year (see page 276), the

A MAP OF BOSNIA-HERZEGOVINA. THE AREA IS CONSIDERED ONE OF THE WORLD'S "GREAT CROSSROADS" BECAUSE OF ITS HISTORY OF INVADING ARMIES, BUT ALSO NUMEROUS RELIGIOUS FAITHS.

COURTESY OF THE UNIVERSITY OF TEXAS LIBRARIES, THE UNIVERSITY OF TEXAS AT AUSTIN

international powers—the United Nations, the United States, and the powerful European countries—were aware of what was going on, but did nothing to stop it. Unlike the genocide in Rwanda, however, the United Nations was already present in Bosnia in force, had declared Srebrenica a "safe area," and had Dutch peacekeeping troops on the ground three miles (4.8 km) outside the town. Yet not only did the United Nations do nothing to deter the massacre, but it can be said that it aided and abetted it. This important debate still rages about Srebrenica. With the ability to crush the Serbs via airpower—which NATO forces in fact did just a month later—why did the UN not act at Srebrenica? Did it not care? Were Muslims worth less than Christian Serbs? Or did the major power diplomats, like many other people, think: *In Africa, yes, perhaps, but it can't happen here, in Europe, not again.*

CIVIL WAR BREAKS OUT

One historian called Bosnia "one of the world's great crossroads," not only of invading armies, but also of religious faiths, as indeed is the case with the entire Balkan Peninsula. Here three faiths collided—Roman Catholicism, Eastern Orthodox Christianity, and Islam. Bosnian Croats are those who converted to Catholicism; Bosnian Serbs became members of the Orthodox Church; and Bosnian Muslims converted to Islam after the Ottoman Turks took over the region in the fifteenth century. To a stranger, these religious differences are not immediately apparent. Ethnically, Bosnians, Croats, and Serbs are Eastern European Slavs who speak the same language. Aside from certain idiosyncrasies of dress, in fact, the only way any of the three groups can tell each other apart is by their names.

From 1945 to 1980, Slovenia and Croatia to the north, Bosnia-Herzegovina in the center, and Serbia in the south were part of the state of Yugoslavia (the name means "Land of the Southern Slavs"). Sectarian tension during these years was kept at a minimum by Yugoslavia's founder, the former World War II partisan leader Josip Tito, who ruled the country with an iron fist. But after Tito died in the spring of 1980, tensions began once again to rise and age-old grudges were exhumed. The Serbs, who occupied the largest amount of land and who made up most of Tito's Yugoslav National Army, elected Slobodan Milosevic as their president in 1989. Milosevic was a rabid Serbian nationalist who had a long history of stirring up the Serbian population against Muslims by recounting the horrors that Serbs had experienced under Ottoman rule, recalling massacres that happened hundreds of years before.

As the Soviet Union fell apart, most observers felt that it was only a matter of time before civil war began in the former Yugoslavia. In the north, Slovenia and Croatia declared their independence on June 25, 1991. Milosevic sent the Yugoslavian army to try to bring them back into line, but their independence won international recognition, and the fighting in Slovenia lasted only ten days. However, the war in Croatia was a different matter. Bitter fighting erupted with both sides engaged in what came to be termed "ethnic cleansing" of Croatia's Catholic Croat and Orthodox Serb populations. After 10,000 deaths, the UN brokered a cease-fire in March 1992.

What was becoming known as The War of Yugoslavian Succession now entered its bloodiest phase: the Bosnian War. Croatian President Franjo Tudjman and Serbian President Milosevic made a secret deal to divide Bosnia between them, hoping to create a "Greater Croatia" and a "Greater Serbia." When Bosnia declared independence in August 1992, a vicious three-sided war began.

THE SERBIANS ADVANCE

The complexity of the ensuing war in Bosnia can be seen in the fact that, under Tito, the country had grown more religiously diverse. In a census taken in 1991, Muslims represented 44 percent of the population, Serbs 31 percent, and Croats 17 percent. So it was not simply a case of Croatia and Serbia cutting the country in half geographically, but linking up with those enclaves that were Croatian and Serbian, while at the same time destroying the Muslims.

In the meantime, an arms embargo imposed on all parties by the United States and United Nations heavily favored the Serbs, who had inherited the bulk of Tito's army and armaments. By the summer of 1992, they occupied 70 percent of Bosnia and were besieging the Bosnian capital city of Sarajevo. Snipers and artillery units in the hills around the city poured down fire onto the Muslim civilian population, killing thousands. Although sound militarily, the siege of Sarajevo was a bad move public-relations-wise for Milosevic and the Serbs. It was a city well known to the world, site of the 1984 Winter Olympics, and television footage broadcast around the globe showed the desperation and heroism of the city's inhabitants.

Reports also began to spread of mass murder of Muslims, especially in organized Serbian concentration camps. There were dozens of these, where Serbs abused, starved, and murdered Muslim men they herded together—places like Brcko, where 3,000 Muslims were executed in 1992, or Omarska, where hundreds died of starvation, beatings, shooting, and burning. "Rape camps" existed in eighty locations around Bosnia, where women age thirteen to sixty were held captive to be repeatedly raped by the soldiers of Serbian leader Radovan Karadzic and Serbian Army Commander General Ratko Mladic. In some cases, men were raped as well, and subjected to sexual atrocities—in one notorious instance, one prisoner was forced to bite off the penis and testicles of another.

All of this brought condemnation from the United Nations, which sent troops to the area. NATO began limited air strikes against Serbian troops, but the Serbians ignored these and pressed on with their attacks and ethnic cleansings against the Bosnian Muslims. Fighting had been particularly heavy around Srebrenica since the beginning of the war. The Serbian irregular troops, Bosnian Serbs armed by the Serbian army, and the Serbian National Army itself launched numerous attacks which, despite fierce defense from the poorly armed Bosnian Muslim army, gradually tightened a noose around the town. One by one, Muslim villages and enclaves were attacked and annihilated; those Muslims who weren't killed fled as refugees to Srebrenica where, by March 1993, there were more than 60,000 civilians packed into a tiny area. With the Serbs blocking UN relief shipments, the U.S. Air Force dropped in food by parachute. But the situation was rapidly becoming desperate.

"YOU ARE NOW UNDER THE PROTECTION OF THE UNITED NATIONS"

In April 1993, the UN commander in Bosnia, French General Philippe Morillon, visited Srebrenica and was moved by the plight of the thousands of Muslim women and children who surrounded him. Standing in the window of the town post office, he told the cheering crowd: "You are now under the protection of

the United Nations." On April 16, the UN declared Srebrenica and a 30-mile (48.3 km) area around it the UN's first "safe area." The UN proposed five such areas in Bosnia and wanted to send 34,000 peacekeepers to police them, but the United States, among other nations, did not want to send its troops into such a volatile situation, and so the task of guarding these safe areas was left to only 7,600 peacekeepers.

Under international pressure, the Serbs reluctantly accepted this situation, at least at first. Penned up in Srebrenica as well as civilians were Muslim fighters who were supposed to surrender their arms to the UN peacekeeping force with the understanding that the peacekeepers would protect them. Many Muslims did, but others hung on to their weapons and even used the safe area from which to stage attacks against the Serbs. The Serbs for their part began to stop shipments of food and water to Srebrenica; by May 1995, men and women within the safe area were once again in dire straits. By early July, eight children had starved to death in the town.

At the same time, Radovan Karadzic, the Serb politician who had declared himself president of Bosnia (which he had renamed Republika Srpksa) ordered the Bosnian Serb Army to attack Srebrenica once and for all, to cut it off and create for the Muslim population "an unbearable situation of total insecurity

IN A CONTROVERSIAL MOMENT, BOSNIAN SERB GENERAL RATKO MLADIC, LEFT, DRINKS WITH DUTCH UN MILITARY COMMANDER COLONEL THOMAS KARREMANS, CENTER, AFTER THE MUSLIM CITIZENS WERE EVACUATED FROM CAMP BRAVO. MANY FELT THAT KARREMANS DID NOT DO ENOUGH TO PROTECT THE MUSLIMS WHO HAD BEEN HARBORED BY THE DUTCH.

with no hope of further survival of life." On Thursday, July 6, Serbian forces led by General Ratko Mladic, attacked Srebrenica, which was defended by about 600 lightly armed UN Dutch peacekeepers led by Colonel Thomas Karremans. Seven Dutch soldiers were in an observation post on the southern outskirts of town when the Serbian forces began firing artillery at them. The Serbs swooped down on other observation posts and took thirty Dutch peacekeepers hostage. The Dutch withdrew from their forward observation posts, a move that so enraged local Muslim fighters that one of them threw a grenade at a Dutch armored personnel carrier, killing a Dutch soldier.

The Dutch commander Karremans begged for air support from NATO and at one point was told that he had submitted the request on the wrong forms. Finally, on July 11, two Dutch jets flew overhead and dropped two bombs. The Serbs replied by saying that they would kill the Dutch hostages if any more bombs were dropped. At this point, Karremans withdrew his forces from the town to his main base, Camp Bravo, three miles (4.8 km) away in the town of Potocari. With the town now completely exposed, refuges poured after the Dutch into their camp, frantically seeking protection; but after 5,000 had entered, Karremans declared that there was room for no more. Twenty thousand more hovered outside the gates, completely at the mercy of Mladic and his men.

"ALLAH CAN'T HELP YOU NOW"

Serbian television cameras caught General Mladic, a swaggering, chain-smoking, gray-haired man in his fifties, entering Srebrenica and shouting to an aide to tear a Muslim street sign down. He then turned directly to the camera and said: "Now it is time to get revenge for the Turks!" He was apparently referring to a Turkish massacre of Serbs that had happened in the early nineteenth century.

The same television cameras caught Mladic's Serb troops approaching the massive crowd of Muslim women and children huddled outside Camp Bravo. Separated only by blue police tape thrown up by the UN troops, the soldiers stared brazenly over the crowd, hunters seeking their prey. Mladic himself came up, but now he was reassuring. He told the Muslims that buses would be provided to take them and their families to Tuzla, in an area of central Bosnia controlled by the Bosnian Muslim army. Everything will be all right.

On camera, in his meetings with Colonel Karremans, Mladic said the same thing. But he added that men will be separated from women and children, so that they could be questioned about the activities of the Muslim army and so that their hands could be chemically tested for gunpowder residue, to see whether they had fired a weapon recently. Karremans objected, but Mladic overrode him, bullying him, telling him the Dutch must provide the diesel fuel for the buses or pay for the Serbs to provide it. He also told the representatives of the Muslims present that all Muslim soldiers must lay down their arms and surrender. If they do, they, along with the rest of the Muslims, would be given "food, water, and decent transportation" to Tuzla. Then he leaned over the table and said slowly: "Allah can't help you now. But Mladic can."

In the meantime, however, horrifying things began to happen. When a woman could not silence her crying child in a crowd outside the Dutch base, a Serbian soldier waded in and cut the infant's throat. One Dutch soldier saw two Serbs raping a woman, but felt helpless to do anything about it. And Serbs began entering the crowd and taking men and older boys away, seemingly at random. On the evening of July 11 one man was hustled off by the Serbs and not returned until the early hours of the morning on July 12. He claimed that he had been tortured and kept walking through the crowd saying that he was not going to go

AN ELDERLY WOMEN IS SHOWN IN JULY 1995 IN ONE OF THE REFUGEE CAMPS SET UP TO SHELTER MUSLIMS AFTER THEY FLED FROM SREBRENICA.

GETTY IMAGES

through such an ordeal again. In the morning, he was found to have hung himself, something that several other Muslim men and women did.

Finally, on July 12, the evacuation by bus of the Muslim women and children began. The Serbs sent the woman and children under thirteen onto the buses, but pushed the men off into separate groups, promising they would be on later buses. Dutch soldiers watched as five of these men were taken into a factory across the street from the UN base. They were accompanied by a Serb soldier with a pistol. UN soldiers heard five or six shots, then the Serb soldier returned alone.

"NOT A HAIR ON YOUR HEADS"

As the long line of buses full of women and children left Camp Bravo on July 12 and 13—it is estimated that about 23,000 Muslims were evacuated in thirty hours—the Serbs gathered the men they had taken into nearby warehouses and factories. After a time, many of these boarded buses themselves and were taken to outlying farms, soccer fields, school gymnasiums, and factories.

Hurem Suljic, a fifty-five-year-old carpenter, was separated from his family and placed with a group of 200 other men. After the buses of women and children left, the Serbs placed these men in an unfinished house not far from Camp Bravo. At about 6:00 p.m., General Mladic walked in and surveyed the group with a smile. He told them that he had 180 Serbs being held prisoner by the Muslims in Tuzla and that Suljic and his comrades would be traded in exchange for the Serbs. "Not a hair on your head will be touched," he said.

When dark fell on that hot summer evening, the Serbs put the Muslim men on buses and drove them away to the nearby town of Bratunac. They placed them in a warehouse formerly used to store cattle feed. Suljic noticed about two dozen soldiers wearing camouflage fatigues without insignia standing around with automatic weapons. The Muslims were crowded inside the warehouse, joined by groups of other men brought from other locations. They were packed so tightly they could barely breathe. Some of the men near the door heard an officer talking to the Serb soldiers: "You have been given an order to carry out the task assigned to you. Is that clear?"

"Clear, sir!" the soldiers shouted.

Shortly after, these men entered the warehouse with flashlights and pulled out a Muslim man sitting on the floor. When he was outside, those in the warehouse could hear blows, shouts, screams, and finally a blood-curdling gurgle. Then the Serbs came back in for another man, and the horror repeated itself. Some men wept and others prayed, as the flashlights played over them. As the dreadful night went on dozens of men were dragged out to be beaten to death.

Finally at dawn the killing stopped and the guards said the remaining men would be allowed to go to the toilet. They told them not to look to their left as they went outside. Suljic carefully kept his eyes down, but on the way back to the warehouse from the toilet, he saw the Serbs grab a Muslim, hit him in the head with a metal club, and then slam him in the back with an ax. Then his body was dragged around the corner of the building, where a huge pile of bodies lay.

More killing continued for the rest of the morning. The Serbs would come in and say: "We need ten volunteers for a special job." No one would volunteer and the Serbs were drag ten men out, never to be seen again. That afternoon, to the astonishment of the terrified Muslims who remained, General Ratko Mladic visited them again.

"Why are you torturing us?" cried one Muslim prisoner.

"No one is going to kill any more of you," Mladic reassured them in soothing tones, as if they were children he was protecting. He told them he was going to take them to the prisoner exchange. There were now about 300 prisoners left. That evening, buses lined up to take them away. Some of the prisoners had actually begun to think they might live.

"They've drawn their share of blood," one told Suljic. "Now they'll let us go."

But instead of heading for Muslim territory, the buses took a turn away, and the prisoners turned silent. They were taken instead to a small village and crammed into a school gymnasium in sweltering heat and kept there until noon on Saturday, July 15. They were given nothing to eat or drink and had nowhere to relieve themselves.

Once again, as if in a nightmare, General Mladic appeared. He told the miserable prisoners huddled in the gymnasium that the Muslims had refused to take them, but that he was making arrangements for them to be placed with a renegade Muslim leader who was now fighting with the Serbs; some of them would also be used as forced labor. He told them they would leave shortly and would be given water as they walked out the door of the gym. Many of the Muslims believed this, but others wept. Water was given to them as they left the school, but then, group by group, they were blindfolded, placed on trucks, and driven away.

When Suljic's turn came, he found that he could see easily out from under his blindfold if he tilted his head. His truck turned a corner and parked by a field where he could see the bodies of the Muslims who had been taken away earlier. They lay in rows in ditches, on their faces. Before he could take in what this meant, Suljic and the others in his truck were forced to jump out. Everything began to happen very quickly. Suljic and his comrades were told to face the ditch by the side of the road, the soldiers stood behind them, and opened fire with automatic weapons. The body of the man just behind Suljic hit him and toppled him into the ditch; Suljic lay there, uninjured, waiting while the Serbs examined each of the men to see whether he was dead.

Soon it grew dark and the Serbs began killing men in another part of the field, illuminating the murders with the headlights of a backhoe they apparently would use to bury the men. Unobserved, Suljic crawled to a nearby thicket. When the Serbs left he was joined by another Muslim who had survived the slaughter. Under the cover of a fierce summer rainstorm, they snuck away through the woods and, a few days later, managed to reach Muslim-held territory.

"EVERYTHING WILL BE ALL RIGHT"

In addition to the men who had been separated from their families and bused to the various killing grounds, there was another large group of men, perhaps as many as 15,000, who attempted to escape the Serbs by making their way through the extremely hilly, forested terrain to Tuzla, about thirty-five miles (56.3 km) away. Many of these men were Muslim soldiers trying to escape, although some were civilians. The Serbs had thrown a tight cordon around the Srebrenica safe area in an attempt to stop them. Most of the exhausted refugees had little food and water, and were not armed.

THE DUTCH AT SREBRENICA

After the Muslim civilians were taken away from Srebrenica, most of the men to be killed, the Dutch peacekeepers negotiated the release of the hostages held by General Ratko Mladic and then evacuated their base under the watchful eyes of the Serbs. Cameras captured Colonel Thomas Karremans drinking a toast with Mladic and accepting a parting gift from him.

Back in Belgrade, the Dutch soldiers celebrated their escape from such a tense situation, but in the Netherlands, celebrations were the last thing on anyone's minds. The Dutch public echoed the questions asked by the Muslim survivors of Srebrenica; that is, why did the Dutch do so little to save them? In some cases, Dutch peacekeepers even abetted the separating of Muslim men from their families. The Dutch government actually resigned in 2002 in a scandal over its role in Srebrenica, although it continued to refuse to apologize for its actions. An association of Srebrenica mothers has even sued the Dutch government for a billion dollars in damages for failing to protect their children.

There are numerous reasons the Dutch did not protect the Muslims at Srebrenica, the two chief ones being that they were outnumbered and outgunned and that their mission forbade direct intervention. The first reason has more validity than the second; Thomas Karremans did request air strikes that would probably have saved the Muslims, had the UN responded vigorously enough. But although the Dutch mission was not specifically to keep the Serbs from carting off Muslim civilians, it was apparent to everyone there what was happening and a different commander, one bolder and more resolute, might have made a stand against the bullying of Mladic.

In October 2007, twelve former Dutch peacekeepers revisited Srebrenica, many of them weeping as Muslim woman shouted at them: "Why did you betray our children under the UN flag?" One of the Dutch soldiers told a reporter: "I feel the same helplessness I felt in those days. Not being able to do anything is a horrible feeling which has haunted me for years."

The Serbs, some of whom wore the blue helmets of UN soldiers—stolen from Camp Bravo, where the Dutch peacekeeping army had been forced to evacuate—paced up and down the little asphalt roads of the countryside and shouted through megaphones up to the hills:

"Surrender. We will dress your wounds."

"Surrender and you will be able to go wherever you wish."

Thousands of Muslim men did surrender, coming down from the hills with their hands on their heads. Video shot by Serbian cameramen of these moments is full of dark menace. The Muslims are surrendering because they are at the end of their rope, wounded and starving. The Serbs finger their weapons and joke with each other.

The Serbs lined up some of the Muslims and shot them immediately. They cut the throats of others. Men watching these killings from the woods began to commit suicide. Other Muslims lured to surrender in this way were taken away to the same farmer's warehouse where Suljic had originally been placed. There, several Muslims overpowered a guard and killed him, at which point the Serbs threw grenades into the warehouse and killed those who came out firing machine guns. More than 200 died this way. Others were taken to a soccer field near the village of Nova Kasaba. They were forced to sit there for hours with their hands tied behind their backs. Here, too, General Mladic appeared: "Everything will be all right," he told them. But the Serbs took these men out, shot them, and dumped them in mass graves.

In the end, about 3,000 to 4,000 men managed to reach the Muslim lines at Tuzla, most of these soldiers who fought their way through ambushes, captured weapons from the Serbs, and managed to kill a few of their opponents. Another 2,000 or so wandered through the woods for months, evading the Serbs. Some of them were killed, some starved to death; others managed, at last, to reach safety.

For the most part, the women and children of Srebrenica reached safety in Tuzla, too, although the buses were stopped numerous times along the way at Serb checkpoints, where they were searched for men dressed in women's clothing. The Serbs raped some of the women.

In the killing fields, backhoes were used to dig mass graves. These mass graves—which were spotted by U.S. spy planes using infrared technology—along with the stories of the survivors who had begun trickling into Tuzla, gave the Serbs away. While the United States and the United Nations did nothing to stop the Serbs at Srebrenica, in many ways, the massacre was the last straw. Or almost the last straw.

On August 28, the Serb forces surrounding Sarajevo fired mortars into a crowded marketplace, killing thirty-seven civilians and injuring ninety. This wanton, very public attack on a target of no military value—an attack that took place before the eyes and cameras of the world, unlike the dark executions at Srebrenica—finally goaded the world powers into action. On August 30, the United States began a serious bombing campaign against the Serbian army, one that very quickly destroyed its infrastructure and fighting capabilities. By November 1995, they were willing to sign the Dayton Peace Agreement, which ended the war with a partitioned Bosnia, with the Serbs controlling 49 percent of the country.

WHY?

The massacres of more than 8,000 Muslim men in the Srebrenica safe area were obviously well-planned, methodical, and well-organized. Hurem Suljic's experience, although atypical in that he survived, is typical of what usually happened—men were taken to common holding points, such as warehouses or schools, held there, periodically brutalized, and then trucked at night to remote fields, where they were shot. And yet, these prisoners would have been a good deal more valuable to the Serbs alive than dead, as hostages, or to be used in prisoner exchanges. Some speculate that Mladic's strange visits to prisoners being

POLISH ANTHROPOLOGIST EVA KOSLOVSKI EXAMINES A MASS GRAVE CONTAINING THE BODIES OF MUSLIM MEN MURDERED BY THE SERBS NEAR SREBRENICA. MORE THAN ONE HUNDRED BODIES WERE EXHUMED FROM AN AREA THAT ONCE HELD A SEPTIC TANK.

THE FATES OF MLADIC AND KARADZIC

After the war ended, Ratko Mladic resigned as commander of the Bosnian Serb forces to live with his wife in a bungalow that was inside Serb Army headquarters, in a secure complex built by Tito in case of attack. Despite being charged with genocide, complicity in genocide, and crimes against humanity by the International Criminal Tribunal of the former Yugoslavia, he lived relatively openly, even raising a herd of goats named after the former UN commanders in Bosnia. He disappeared after former Yugoslav President Slobodan Milosevic was arrested in 2001 and put on trial at The Hague (Milosevic died in prison awaiting trial).

Radovan Karadzic, indicted for the same crimes, had gone underground even earlier, hiding in plain sight in Belgrade as a practitioner of alternative medicine named Dragan Dabic, growing a full white beard, giving lectures, and writing magazine articles. He called himself a "spiritual explorer" and claimed on his website to be a researcher "in the fields of psychology and bio-energy." He even frequented a local pub where his "Wanted" picture hung above the bar and would often play a musical instrument and sing songs for the assembled bar patrons.

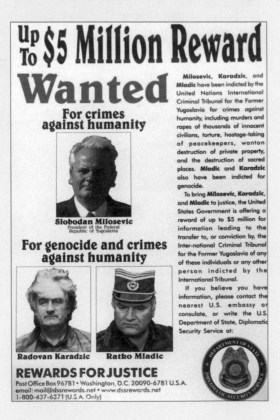

Karadzic was finally arrested in July 2008 and awaits trial. Ratko Mladic, however, remains underground. Supposedly protected by a phalanx of bodyguards, he is now sixty-seven years old and, rumor has it, in poor health. There is a good chance he will never be brought to justice.

A WANTED POSTER RELEASED BY THE U.S. STATE DEPARTMENT IN 2000 SHOWS THE TRIO OF WAR CRIMINALS WANTED FROM THE SERBIAN CONFLICT IN BOSNIA—YUGOSLAV PRESIDENT SLOBODAN MILOSEVIC AND SERBIAN COMMANDERS RATKO MLADIC AND RADOVAN KARADZIC.

AFP/GETTY IMAGES

held in warehouses and schools meant that he was struggling with the notion of whether or not to kill them, but Mladic never contacted any Muslim authorities to try to arrange prisoner exchanges.

Part of genocide is to kill people even when it is not to your advantage to do so—to kill Jewish scientists and doctors and Armenian teachers and businessmen—and ultimately Mladic and Karadzic were swayed not by practical considerations, but by racism. They wanted to avenge massacres by the Turks of hundreds of years before, or the pain the Serbs suffered in World War II (both Mladic's parents were killed by Croatian Nazis). And they acted as boldly as they did because the weak response of the UN deluded them into thinking they were more powerful than they really were. Although these two men have been indicted for war crimes (see "The Fates of Mladic and Karadzic," page 306) Srebrenica can never return to what it was.

There are only 4,000 Muslims in this now-predominately Serbian town and its surroundings, compared with the 25,000 or so who once lived in the area. Although websites for the region have now returned to talking about its pastoral beauty and its bubbling thermal springs, most of the Muslims who live there are women who lost husbands, children, and fathers, so it is a town peopled by the ghosts of the dead and the ghostly living.

BIBLIOGRAPHY

Balakian, Peter. *The Burning Tigris: The Armenian Genocide and America's Response*. New York: HarperCollins, 2001.

Brown, Dee. *Bury My Heart at Wounded Knee: An Indian History of the American West*. New York: Holt, Rinehart & Winston, 1970.

Chang, Iris. *The Rape of Nanking: The Forgotten Holocaust of World War II*. New York: Basic Books, 1997.

Chandler, David P. *The Tragedy of Cambodian History: Politics, War and Revolution Since 1945*. New Haven: Yale University Press, 1991.

Charney, Israel W., Parsons, William S., Totten, Samuel. *Century of Genocide: Eyewitness Accounts and Critical Views*. New York: Garland Publishing, 1997.

Cienciala, Anna M., Lebedeva, Natalia S., & Materski, Wojciech, editors. *Katyn: A Crime Without Punishment*. New Haven: Yale University Press, 2007.

Dalley, Jan. *The Black Hole: Money, Myth and Empire*. London: Penguin Books, 2007.

Denton, Sally. *American Massacre: The Tragedy at Mountain Meadows, September, 1857*. New York: Knopf, 2003

Diaz del Castillo, Bernal. *The Discovery and Conquest of Mexico*. New York: Farrar, Straus & Giroux, 1956.

Diefendorf, Barbara B. *The Saint Bartholomew's Day Massacre: A Brief History with Documents*. Boston: Boston University, 2009.

Foner, Eric. *Reconstruction: America's Unfinished Revolution, 1863-1871*. New York: Harper and Row, 1988.

Frankel, Philip. *An Ordinary Atrocity: Sharpeville and Its Massacre*. New Haven: Yale University Press, 2001.

Gilbert, Martin. *The Holocaust: A History of the Jews of Europe During the Second World War*. New York: Holt, Reinhart & Winston, 1985.

Gillette, William. *Retreat From Reconstruction, 1869-1879*. Baton Rouge: Louisiana State University Press, 1979

Goldsworthy, Adrian. *The Punic Wars*. London: Cassell & Co, 2000.

Gourevitch, Philip. *We Wish To Inform You That Tomorrow We Will Be Killed With Our Families: Stories from Rwanda*. New York: Farrar, Straus & Giroux, 1998.

Graber, G. S. *Caravans to Oblivion. The Armenian Genocide, 1915*. New York: John Wiley & Sons, 1996.

Hatzfeld, Jean. *Machete Season: The Killers in Rwanda Speak*. New York: Farrar, Straus, & Giroux, 2003.

Hersh, Seymour. *Cover-Up: The Army's Secret Investigation of the Massacre at My Lai 4*. New York: Random House, 1972.

Hoig, Stan. *The Sand Creek Massacre*. Norman, Oklahoma: University of Oklahoma Press, 1961.

Keane, Fergal. *Season of Blood: A Rwandan Journey*. New York: Viking, 1995.

Khader, Aicha, Slim, Hedi & Soren, David. *Carthage: Uncovering the Mysteries and Splendors of Ancient Tunisia*. New York: Simon & Schuster, 1990.

Kiernan, Ben. *The Pol Pot Regime: Race, Power and Genocide in Cambodia Under the Khmer Rouge, 1975-1979*. New Haven: Yale University Press, 1996.

Krakauer, Jon. *Under the Banner of Heaven: A Story of Violent Faith*. New York: Doubleday, 2003.

Kristoff, Nicholas and WuDunn, Sheryl. *China Wakes: Struggle for the Soul of a Rising Power*. New York: Times Books, 1994.

Lane, Charles. *The Day Freedom Died: The Colfax Massacre, The Supreme Court and the Betrayal of Reconstruction*. New York: Henry Holt & Company, 2008

Lemann, Nicholas. *Redemption: The Last Battle of the Civil War*. New York: Farrar, Straus and Giroux, 2007.

Leon-Portilla, Miguel. *The Broken Spears: The Aztec Account of the Conquest of Mexico*. Boston: Beacon Press, 1990.

Meredith, Martin. *In the Name of Apartheid: South Africa in the Postwar Era*. New York: Harper & Row, 1988.

Meredith, Martin and Rosenberg, Tina. *Coming to Terms: South Africa's Search for Truth*. New York: Public Affairs, 1999.

Miller, Donald F. and Miller, Lorna Touryan. *Survivors: An Oral History of the Armenian Genocide*. Berkeley: University of California Press, 1993.

Paul, Allen. *Katyn: Stalin's Massacre and the Seeds of Polish Resurrection*. Annapolis, Maryland: Naval Institute Press, 1991.

Rieff, David. *Slaughterhouse: Bosnia and the Failure of the West*. New York: Simon & Schuster, 1995.

Rohde, David. Endgame: *The Betrayal and Fall of Srebrenica, Europe's Worst Massacre Since World War II*. New York: Farrar, Straus & Giroux, 1997.

Salisbury, Harrison Evans. *Tianamen Diary: Thirteen Days in June*. Boston: Little, Brown, 1989.

St. George, George. *The Road to Babyi-Yar*. London: Neville Spearman, 1967.

Sudetic, Chuck. *Blood and Vengeance: One Family's Story of the War in Bosnia*. New York: W.W. Norton & Co., 1998.

Thomas, Hugh. *Conquest: Montezuma, Cortes and the Fall of Old Mexico*. New York: Simon & Schuster, 1993.

Toland, John. *Battle: The Story of the Bulge*. Lincoln, Nebraska: The University of Nebraska Press, 1999.

Warmington, B.H. *Carthage*. London: Robert Hale Ltd., 1960

Zobel, Hiller. *The Boston Massacre*. New York: W.W. Norton & Co., 1970.

INTERNET SOURCES:

Genocide and Crimes Against Humanity: http://www.enotes.com/genocide-encyclopedia/carthage

The Boston Massacre Historical Society: http://www.bostonmassacre.net/plot/index.htm

"A Sight Which Can Never Be Forgotten" http://www.archaeology.org/online/features/massacre/

"Reconstruction: The Second Civil War" The American Experience: http://www.pbs.org/wgbh/amex/reconstruction/kkk/ps_colby.html

The Nanking Atrocities: http://www.geocities.com/nankingatrocities/Tribunals/nanjing_02.htm

"Massacre at Malmedy" http://www.historynet.com/massacre-at-malmedy-during-the-battle-of-the-bulge.htm/2

Thirtieth Infantry Division official account: http://www.30thinfantry.org/malmedy.shtml

Malmedy Massacre Trial: http://www.scrapbookpages.com/dachauscrapbook/DachauTrials/MalmedyMassacre01.html

My Lai: PBS: The American Experience http://www.pbs.org/wgbh/amex/vietnam/trenches/my_lai.html

An Account of the My Lai Courts-Martial

http://www.law.umkc.edu/faculty/projects/ftrials/mylai/Myl_intro.html

NSA declassified security documents: Tianamen Square

http://www.gwu.edu/~nsarchiv/NSAEBB/NSAEBB16/documents/index.html

INDEX

ACKNOWLEDGMENTS

THANKS ONCE AGAIN GO TO Will Kiester, indefatigable publisher, to Cara Connors, judicious editor, and to Ellen Goldstein, incisive copyeditor. I would also like to thank my friend Diederik Lohman of Human Rights Watch, whose brain I picked about Responsibility to Protect and other issues relating to contemporary responses to genocide.

ABOUT THE AUTHOR

JOSEPH CUMMINS is the author of *War Chronicles: From Chariots to Flintlocks*, *War Chronicles: From Flintlocks to Machine Guns*, *History's Great Untold Stories*, *Great Rivals in History: When Politics Gets Personal*, *President Obama and a New Birth of Freedom*, and *Anything for a Vote: Dirty Tricks, Cheap Shots, and October Surprises in U.S. Presidential Campaigns*. He has also written a novel, *The Snow Train*. He lives in Maplewood, New Jersey.